Law, Political Thought, and the Ancient Constitution

A Case Study of George Saltern's
Of the Antient Lawes of great Britaine

The title page from John Speed's *Theatre of the Empire of Great Britaine* showing the major national characters of the ancient constitution narrative – the Briton, the Roman, the Saxon, the Dane, and the Norman.

LAW, POLITICAL THOUGHT, AND THE ANCIENT CONSTITUTION

A CASE STUDY OF GEORGE SALTERN'S *Of the Antient Lawes of great Britaine*

ERIN RAHNE KIDWELL

TALBOT
PUBLISHING
Clark, New Jersey

ISBN 978-1-61619-539-7

TALBOT PUBLISHING

AN IMPRINT OF

THE LAWBOOK EXCHANGE, LTD.

33 Terminal Avenue

Clark, New Jersey 07066-1321

Please see our website for a selection of our other publications and fine facsimile reprints of classic works of legal history:
www.lawbookexchange.com

Library of Congress Cataloging-in-Publication Data

Kidwell, Erin Rahne, author.
Title: Law, political thought, and the ancient constitution : George Saltern's "Of the antient lawes of Great Britaine" : a case study / by Erin Rahne Kidwell.
Description: Clark, NJ : Talbot Publishing, 2016. | Includes bibliographical references and index.
Identifiers: LCCN 2016014461 | ISBN 9781616195397 (hardcover : alk. paper)
Subjects: LCSH: Saltern, George. | Law--Great Britain--History. | Lawyers--Great Britain--Biography.
Classification: LCC KD532 .K53 2016 | DDC 349.4109--dc 3
LC record available at https://lccn.loc.gov/2016014461

Cover image: The History of the British Islands, in one Image, taken from the Chart of Universal History, published by T. Jefferys the Corner of St. Martin's Lane. … The great periods in the British history are, the invasion of the Romans, their expulsion by the Britons, the erection of the seven Anglo-Saxon kingdoms, their union under Egbert, the invasion of the Danes, and the Norman conquest. These are severally distinguished by colours, which mark out the time of each revolution as precisely, and impress it upon the memory more strongly than any chronological table. The Roman colour covers England, and part of Scotland from the year 44 to 445, when it is exchanged for the British colour. This is gradually driven into a corner of England, where it continues to denote an independent principality until the year 1254. The Saxon Red covers the rest of the island, till in 1017 it gives way to the Danish Green, which lasts only till 1042. From that time a deep red begins to encompass the British islands….

23 GENTLEMAN'S MAG. 403–404 (1753)

Printed in the United States of America on acid-free paper

Dedicated to my parents:

my Mom, Betsy Dimond,

— the teacher who gave me a lifelong love of learning;

my Dad, Dick Dimond,

— the lawyer who taught me to question the law

ACKNOWLEDGMENTS

Earlier versions of the introductory chapters were presented to seminars at the Folger Institute Center for the History of British Political Thought in 2002 and 2003, to the Renaissance Society of America in 2004, and to faculty workshops at Georgetown Law Center. I am indebted and grateful for comments and suggestions offered by the participants and colleagues, especially John Pocock, Gordon Schochet, Clare Carrol, Linda Levy Peck, Mark Tushnet, Robin West, Gerry Spann, Mike Seidman, Norman Birnbaum, James Oldham, Daniel Woolf, Paul Halliday, John Cairns, and David Seipp. Portions were also adapted from an ongoing book project, *The Once and Future Constitution: Exploring British-American Constitutionalism through Myth and History*, based upon my 2000 doctoral dissertation at Georgetown Law — *Arthur and the Ancient Constitution: History... Story... Literature... Myth... Law: the indivisible link between culture and constitution.* Thanks are also extended to Lesley Whitelaw, Archivist of the Middle Temple, and Robin Griffith-Jones, Master of the Temple Church, for providing invaluable additional information about the otherwise elusive life of George Saltern. This book would never have seen the light of day without Greg Talbot and Valerie Horowitz of Talbot Publishing. I am also grateful to Talbot for allowing me to use Bluebook style for the notes and Bibliography entries. I would also like to thank Georgetown Law Library for allowing me to facsimile our copy of Saltern's *Of the Antient Lawes*; my colleagues in Special Collections; and, lastly, but first in memory, the late Head of Special Collections and my dear departed friend, Laura Bédard.

TABLE OF CONTENTS

Preface

George Saltern's *Of the Antient Lawes of great Britaine* was the first (by its own standards now ancient) rare law book by an English lawyer I encountered references to King Arthur as a lawgiver in nearly 20 years ago when I was researching my doctoral dissertation at Georgetown Law — *Arthur and the Ancient Constitution: History... Story... Literature... Myth... Law: the indivisible link between culture and constitution.* I had been assured by several experienced historians of English law that I was engaged in a pointless quest trying to find any worthwhile connections between Arthurian literature and Anglo-American jurisprudence. That moment therefore stands large in my memory even though I subsequently began to find Arthur and other figures from the Arthurian stories cropping up in some very unexpected sources (at least unexpected based upon that advice), especially in the works of Sir Edward Coke. This work therefore began as a small piece of what was primarily a law and literature study with interdisciplinary forays into legal history, jurisprudential theory, and Pocockian 'new' British history. What follows is now primarily an inter-disciplinary work of legal history and the history of political thought with law and literature tangents. As a consequence there are aspects of the discussion that may be unfamiliar and perhaps disconcerting to specialists in each of those fields. Rather than disrupt the flow of discussion in the introductory chapters a preface seemed the proper place to provide some clarification of those elements for those readers who may find them of interest.

The use of *British*-American in this work's title, as well as throughout, rather than *Anglo*-American is perhaps the most obvious. While the constitutional and legal history of England did indeed influence and in many ways overshadow those of the Welsh, Scots and Irish, those English histories by no means per se tell the whole story of British constitutional history. Nor did the early modern English constitution extend beyond the territorial borders of England to encompass the entirety of the emerging British empire. There truly was an imperial *British* constitution that bound the disparate dominions of the British (especially post-1707) multiple monarchy, and through which the increasingly far-flung subjects of that imperial government were governed and (most notably in the case of the American colonists) demanded their rights under. Delineating all the ways in which that can be demonstrated is far beyond the scope of this present study. Should any reader wish to pursue the subject further, I would recommend starting with the initial essays by J.G.A. Pocock calling for a 'new' pedagogy for British history as well as the many works produced along the lines he called for over the four decades since, especially Norman Davies's excellent discussion of all the varied ways in which English and British (and their related terms) have been and continue to be conflated and confused with each other.[1] In this vein, the term *Britannic* is used herein to differentiate the earlier ancient constitutionalist narratives that focus on the ancient Britons as the origin point for Britain's immemorial common law and rule of law traditions from those later *Gothic* ancient constitutionalist variants that shift the origin point slightly forward to the Germanic Anglo-Saxons. Brittanic began to surface in the mid-

---

[1] *See e.g.*, J.G.A. Pocock, *British History: A Plea for a New Subject*, 8 N.Z. HIST. J. 3 (1974) and *The Limits and Divisions of British History: In Search of the Unknown Subject*, 87 AM. HIST. REV. 311 (1982) *and* NORMAN DAVIES. THE ISLES xxi–xlii (2000).

seventeenth century and became the term used in the royal style of the post-1707 Union British monarchy. This nearly contemporaneous term seems appropriate for the discussion of the significance of Saltern's work which claims to trace the developmental traces of "the ancient British constitutions."

The use of the term *juridical* may also cause some consternation and confusion. I use it throughout in place of the longer, inarguably cumbersome phrase *legal, political, and constitutional*. Juridical was once commonly used as a synonym for legal, especially in Scotland. It has long since fallen into what the Scots might call desuetude. The OED defines juridical as "Of, relating to, or connected with the administration of law or judicial proceedings; sometimes in more general sense = legal." It should be stressed, however, that the Latin word at the root of juridical is *jus*, which refers to law in its broadest most abstract sense, not to any particular system of substantive laws; juridical is used throughout in that broad, abstract sense. In that Parliament undeniably originally had and later asserted and maintained at least a quasi-administrative role as well as a quasi-judicial role, in the English and later British, legal and constitutional systems this seems to me to be an acceptable use of the word juridical. Every legislative assembly that subsequently developed from that origin point has similarly asserted and maintained at least the right to have a voice and influence in the administrative and judicial functions of government even after the rise of separation of powers principles in British-American constitutionalism. The executive is even more clearly involved in the administration of law, and is clearly as much a political office as it is a legal and constitutional one. The judiciary is undeniably not the only branch of governance concerned with the administration of the law.

Law, politics, and constitutionalism are inextricably intertwined rather than discrete and insular disciplines, especially when considered in the context of the history of political thought. The earliest uses of juridical noted in the OED date from the era of Saltern's text and the rise of explicit and coherent ancient constitutionalist narratives and rhetoric in British juridical discourse. As will be discussed more fully in the introductory chapters, the spheres of law, politics, political thought, and literary culture, as well as the emerging sphere of constitutionalism were undeniably then not discrete and insular disciplines as they are often asserted to be today. It is in that light that juridical is used throughout, as a not so subtle reminder that law, legal actors, and legalities are not the only relevant subjects being discussed. In my work as a curator of a rare book collection at a law library, juridical has also been a useful term in explaining the need to include works of political thought, political science and other works not specifically related to legal and constitutional subjects in our collection development priorities. My use of juridical as shorthand for legal, political, and constitutional throughout has been informed as well by similar uses by Foucault and other post-modern and post-structuralist literary theorists whose works I was first introduced to through the field of law and literature.[2]

Which brings me to my last points of clarification, the use of terminology from the literary fields of the history of English literature and of law and literature. The first is the use of the term *Galfridian history* to refer to the tradition of chronicle histories that grew out of the early

---

2 *Juridical*, OXFORD ENGLISH DICTIONARY, available online at www.oed.com. For the use of juridical by Foucault, see, e.g., MICHEL FOUCAULT, DISCIPLINE AND PUNISH: THE BIRTH OF THE PRISON 222 (1977) ("Historically, the process by which the bourgeoisie became in the course of the eighteenth century the politically dominant class was masked by the establishment of an explicit, coded, and formally egalitarian juridical framework, made possible by the organization of a parliamentary, representative regime.") Foucault also referred to "the juridical structures of society…." *Id.*

twelfth century *Historia Regum Britanniae* [*The History of the Kings of Britain*] of Geoffrey of Monmouth, who was also referred to himself as Galfridus Monumentis, hence *Galfridian* history. *The History of the Kings of Britain* inspired both admiration and criticism by later authors of British chronicle histories, many of whom freely used elements of Geoffrey's work. That influence was so profound that by the early modern period it had become common to refer to that entire genre of chronicle history as Galfridian history. The same collective body of work including the Arthurian stories themselves and the body of literature that developed around them has also often been referred to as the *Matter of Britain*, as in the literary and historical matter out of which the national identity of Britain was constituted. Both of these terms are used (hopefully judiciously) throughout the introductory chapters that follow. A summary chronological account of the principle (often allegedly historical) figures of Galfridian history can be found below in chapter one's discussion of the influential role played by the lawyers of the English Inns of Court on late Tudor and early Stuart courtly culture.[3]

In addition to my use of the term juridical, two other elements of the original law and literature study remain. First is the use of the model of the *literary lawyer* as embodying the best aspects of an effective legal practitioner and advocate together with the noble ideals of civic virtue extolled in eighteenth century political thought and espe-

---

[3] Readers interested in learning more about the origins and influence of the Galfridan chronical history traditions and the *Matter of Britain* may generally consult works such as A. L. MORTON, THE MATTER OF BRITAIN: ESSAYS IN A LIVING CULTURE (1966) *and* JOHN E. CURRAN, JR., ROMAN INVASIONS: THE BRITISH HISTORY, PROTESTANT ANTI-ROMANISM, AND THE HISTORICAL IMAGINATION IN ENGLAND, 1530–1660 (2002) *and* Francis Ingledew, *The Book of Troy and the Genealogical Construction of History: The Case of Geoffrey of Monmouth's Historia Regum Britanniae*, 69 SPECULUM 665 (1994).

cially that of the American Founding period. In her 1996 article, *The Literary Lawyer*, Robin West offered the model of the literary lawyer inculcated with legal and literary classics as a means to create a common agenda for the interdisciplinary movement known as law and literature studies. The literary lawyer model bridges the gap between calls for the development of "a conception of law and of the 'good lawyer' that is, generally, humanistic and literary, rather than *either* autonomously professional or tied to scientific or economic ideals," and those who assert that "the movement's 'point' . . . is almost exactly the opposite; [] to provide a humanistic basis for legal *criticism*, . . . a humanistic and literary basis from which to *criticize*, rather than bolster, law and legal authority." The hope of this agenda is that the more literary lawyers our system of legal education produces and supports as practitioners, the better able we will be as a culture to both create better laws and lawyers and effectively criticize and remedy harmful laws and bad attorneys.[4] In the discussion that follows it will be seen that the model of the literary lawyer is perfectly suited to the legal and literary world of the Jacobean Union Tracts.

Second, in light of the undeniable fact that the text of Saltern's Union Tract and much of the juridical historiography of the period freely made use of elements from Galfridian history that are now known without a doubt to be historically inaccurate (or at the very least highly suspect) it seems useful to have some other means of evaluating the constitutional fictions so thoroughly embedded in such texts. This is of importance to exploring the historiography of the Union Tracts and ancient constitutionalist texts, as well as to the current debate over the relationship between law and literature today. West, L.H.

---

[4] Robin West, *The Literary Lawyer*, 27 Pac. L. Rev. 1187, 1188–1190 (1996).

LaRue, and Winnifred Sullivan have all suggested examples of how constitutional fictions have been employed to convey aesthetic and moral truths. For example, the forensic histories American lawyers and judges routinely recount concerning the quest of the Mayflower Pilgrims for religious liberty and the origins of the First Amendment in modern American constitutional law convey both aesthetic and moral truths.[5] The evaluative standards suggested by West and LaRue are discussed in more detail in chapter one. Acknowledging the persuasive power of the aesthetic and moral truths conveyed by such constitutional fictions should by no means be construed as approving any and all uses of constitutional fictions. For example, Nazi propaganda derived much of its power and influence over Nazi Germany precisely because it conveyed what were aesthetic and moral truths within the cultural milieu of Nazism. Recognition of the persuasive power of constitutional fictions by no means requires one to conclude that Nazi propaganda was true in either the normative or scientific senses of the word. The tragic influence of the constitutional fictions of Nazi propaganda does, however, underscore the risks inherent in the many uses of constitutional fictions still routinely employed by lawyers, judges and politicians to this day.

What follows is an exploration of the extent to which, to borrow a phrase from Saltern, the secret footsteps of ancient constitutionalism can be discerned in the history of British-American constitutionalism from the late Tudor period when ancient constitutionalist rhetoric first fully crystallized into a coherent juridical tradition to the

---

[5] *See* Winnifred Fallers Sullivan, *Finding a True Story of American Religion*, 53 WASH. & LEE L. REV. 981 (1996) *and* L.H. LARUE, CONSTITUTIONAL LAW AS FICTION: NARRATIVE IN THE RHETORIC OF AUTHORITY (1995) *and* Robin West, *Constitutional Fictions and Meritocratic Success Stories*, 53 WASH. & LEE L. REV. 996 (1996).

present day. The discussion of the perdurance of that constitutional antiquarian tradition in the culture of British-American constitutionalism that is the subject of the concluding chapter are this (hopefully) literary lawyer's musings based upon pondering that very question ever since I first encountered Saltern's text. These concluding thoughts are not offered merely from the perspective of a scholar of legal history and the history of British-American political thought. They also flow from the perspective of an academic lawyer and curator of the heritage of British-American jurisprudence who quite frankly is both fascinated and mystified that those secret footsteps of ancient constitutionalism have not only survived the tides of time but have continued to adapt and influence our juridical culture to this day. The aesthetic and moral truths conveyed by constitutional fictions would appear to prevail over the standards of historical accuracy far more often than not.

INTRODUCTION

Restoring Britanniae

The Union Proposal of James VI and I

When James the VI and I addressed his first English Parliament in March of 1604, his intention to unify the two nations whose crowns were already united in his person into a single realm was at the forefront of his opening speech. Although his words implied that the union was a fait accompli "which God hath in my Person already established," there was in fact a great deal of work to be done to make the union of Scotland and England into one realm a constitutional reality.[6] Before the end of the year, parliamentary commissions would be appointed by both the Scots and English parliaments. Royal proclamations were ultimately issued to accomplish as much of the union as possible through the prerogative powers of the crown as it became apparent that the English parliament was not going to simply rubber-stamp the king's union plans. The first of the royal proclamations concerning the planned "union of the two Realmes" had actually been issued in May of 1603 and called for all "his Highnes Subjects to repute, hold, and esteeme bothe the two Realmes as presently united, and as one Realme and Kingdome, and the Subjects of both the Realmes as one people, brethren and members of

---

[6] *A Speach as it was delivered in the Upper House of Parliament to the Lords Spiritual and Temporall, and to the Knights, Citizens and Burgesses there assembled, On Monday the XIX. Day of March 1603 [sic]. Being The First Day of The First Parliament, in* THE POLITICAL WORKS OF JAMES I 269, 272 (London: Oxford 1918) (1616) [hereinafter *Speach of 1604*].

one body."[7] Although James did his utmost to inspire the English Parliament with hopes of peace and prosperity flowing from the proposed imperial union, he instead "found himself faced with ingrained suspicion and distrust, despite assurances that he would do nothing to undermine his subjects' liberties."[8]

In the months following his speech, James frustrations with the deliberative processes of his new parliament in England led to his proroguing the session in July and an increasing reliance on the prerogative power to push his plan forward.[9] The royal proclamation issued in October 1604, revealed the name of James' proposed imperial realm — "GREAT BRITTAINE," and changed the royal style accordingly. It was timed to coincide with the first joint meeting of the commissions appointed to consider the union proposals by the Scots and English parliaments. The text contained language asserting the antiquity of the two realms of Scotland and England and the compatibility of their ancient laws that would be echoed in many of the tracts and pamphlets produced in the debate over the union in the following years. It began by reminding all of how God had "bestow[ed] upon Us; Namely the blessed Union, or rather Reuniting of these two mightie, famous, and ancient Kingdomes of England and Scotland, under one Imperiall Crowne ...." After further extolling the blessed nature of this happy event, the proclamation continues by stating that the King has been advised by:

---

[7] *A Proclamation for the uniting of England and Scotland, in* 1 STUART ROYAL PROCLAMATIONS: ROYAL PROCLAMATIONS OF KING JAMES I 1603–1625 18, 19 James F. Larkin & Paul L Hughes eds., 1973) [hereinafter 1 STUART ROYAL PROCLAMATIONS].

[8] PAULINE CROFT, KING JAMES 60 (2003).

[9] *See id.*, at 62–63.

> those that be skillfull in the Lawes of this Land, That immediately upon our Succession, divers of the ancient Lawes of this Realme are Ipso Facto expired, As namely, that of Escuage, and of the Naturalization of the Subjects, And that there is a greater affinitie and concurrence betweene most of the ancient Lawes of both Kingdomes, then is to be found betweene those of any other two Nations, As namely, in states of Inheritance and Freehold, as Fee-Simple, Fee-taile, Tenant for life, by Courtesie, Dower, and such like, In cases of descents of Inheritance, In Tenures of Lands, as of Knights service, Socage, Frank Almoigne, Burgage, Villenage, and such like, In Writts and formes of Processe, In cases of Triall by Juries, Grand Juries; And lastly in Officers and Ministers of Justice, As Sheriffes, Coroners, and such like, which We leave to be further considered by the Commissioners of both Realmes.

As for whether the new name for the realm used in the royal style was a "new affected Name devised at Our pleasure," the proclamation defends its use as "out of undoubted knowledge . . . the true and ancient Name, which God and Time have imposed upon this Isle" and found "in Histories," maps and charts describing the Isle, official letters from "Forrain Princes," and further "warranted [] by Authenticall Charters, Exemplifications under Seales, and other Records of great Antiquitie ...."[10] The October proclamation was followed by a proclamation in November 1604 announcing the use of the new style on coins, and in December of 1606 a proclamation concerning the correct flags to be flown by "South and North

[10] *A Proclamation concerning the Kings Majesties Stile, of King of Great Britaine, &c., in* 1 STUART ROYAL PROCLAMATIONS, *supra* note 6 at 94–98 (partially quoted in BRIAN P. LEVACK, THE FORMATION OF THE BRITISH STATE: ENGLAND, SCOTLAND, AND THE UNION 1603–1707 76 (1986)).

Britaines … at Sea."[11] In 1607 the king made a final speech to both Houses, summoned to the Painted Chamber especially for his Majesty's plea for reason (his) to prevail, but the project was such that only the passage of much more time than four short years would be enough to bring it to full fruition. The immovable English parliament had met the irresistible monarch in virtual constitutional stalemate over the issue of the union of Scotland and England into an imperial realm of Great Britain. Stymied, James and his Council turned then to crafting a limited union through the prerogative power and the courts, thereby producing the landmark holdings of *Calvin's Case*.[12]

This collision of royal intent and parliamentary deliberation and inaction over the union proposals of James VI and I would result in the production of a body of literary and legal texts over the next few years by proponents and opponents of the proposed union; the length of some belying the appellation of Union Tracts given them by posterity. The blending of myth and legal history in this body of literature illustrates the seamless nature of the legal and literary canons at a pivotal formative moment in the history of British-American constitutionalism, as well as the potent and lasting influence of literary lawyers in the political institutions and traditions of early modern Britain, especially so in that workhorse of the late seven-

---

[11] *A Proclamation for Coynes, in* 1 STUART ROYAL PROCLAMATIONS, *supra* note 6 at 99; *A Proclamation declaring what Flaggs South and North Britaines shall beare at Sea, in* 1 STUART ROYAL PROCLAMATIONS, *id.* at 135.

[12] *Calvin's Case*,77 Eng. Rep. 377, 394; 7 Coke's Reports 1a, 14b–15a (1609) (holding that no British subjects could be considered aliens within any of the dominions of the Crown, and establishing the rules for the reception of the English common law in extra-territorial dominions). [hereinafter *Calvin's Case*] See discussion *infra* in Chapter Three.

teenth[th] century Whigs — the '*ancient constitution*'. The work facsimiled herein, George Saltern's 1605 *Of the Antient Lawes of great Britaine*, is a paradigmatic example of this discursive style of juridical rhetoric.[13]

Chapter One explores the cultural and historical context of the authors of the Jacobean union tracts within a discussion of recent works in law and literature that call for a renewal of the literary lawyer as a model for the education and training of today's attorneys. It will be seen that many of the authors of the union tracts were, like Saltern, lawyers who epitomized the best qualities of literary lawyers trained to create "law at its best [ ] continuous with culture at its best."[14] The first chapter then explores examples from various union tracts and contemporaneous works in British history in order to illustrate and evaluate the creative mix of mythical and historical elements present in the indispensable juridical trope of the ancient constitution. Chapter Two focuses on Saltern's *Of the Antient Lawes* in order to demonstrate that the emerging constitutional culture of Jacobean Britain was among the few "sophisticated enough to assert" that their "prescriptive [] immemorial tradition [was] merely one whose beginnings [were] not to be found in any single moment or moments," but were to be found instead in a recurring process spanning the centuries. Chapter Three undertakes a comparative examination of Saltern's tract within the context of late Tudor and early Stuart political thought, the Union Debates and *Calvin's Case* to better understand the origins of ancient constitutionalism as a coherent and explicit trope in seventeenth century British juridical discourse. The concluding chapter closes this

---

[13] For reasons more fully discussed in the Preface, the term *juridical* is used throughout in place of the longer, more cumbersome phrase — legal, political, and constitutional.

[14] West, *supra* note 4 at 1188–1190.

introductory essay by suggesting that we should view the variant tropes of ancient constitutionalism that subsequently developed in British-American juridical thought as an enduring cultural meme embracing what J.G.A. Pocock has aptly termed both "moments of creation" and "moments of transmission;" a canon of constitutional myth "so worn and domesticated with constant varying use that it may be described as belonging to [the] traditions" of British-American constitutionalism.[15]

---

[15] *Time, Institutions and Action: An Essay on Traditions and Their Understanding, in* J.G.A. POCOCK, POLITICS, LANGUAGE AND TIME: ESSAYS ON POLITICAL THOUGHT AND HISTORY 233, 243 (1973).

CHAPTER 1

The Matter of Britain and the Common Law in Jacobean Union Texts 1604–1607

The Elizabethan and Jacobean Literary Lawyer

The ruling political class of both Scotland and England in this period included many individuals who, like George Saltern, exemplify the paradigmatic literary lawyer whose absence from today's legal culture has more recently been lamented in the field of law and literature. The "lawyer-writer" of the 18th and 19th centuries schooled in the literary and legal classics of his day is the historical model for the literary lawyer.[16]

The literary lawyer is the very paradigm of a lawyer produced by the already well-established English Inns of Court. Although the literary lawyer doubtless has been in decline since the late nineteenth century, it is equally certain that he existed well before 1700. Indeed, the institutions and pedagogical culture of juridical education and practice in Britain had been producing such literary lawyers and courtiers from their earliest days in late thirteenth century England and fifteenth century Scotland.[17] There is much that still needs to be done in terms of detailed historical studies of the origins and early

---

16 West, *supra* note 4 at 1188, passim.

17 An even earlier ancestor of the literary lawyer may be found in the bardic lawyers and judges of medieval Wales and Ireland. *See generally e.g.*, ROBIN CHAPMAN STACEY, DARK SPEECH: THE PERFORMANCE OF LAW IN EARLY IRELAND (2007) *and* THOMAS GLYN WATKINS, THE LEGAL HISTORY OF WALES (2007).

development of the systems of legal education in England and Scotland. However, enough is known about what they had developed into by 1603 to support viewing the lawyer of the Jacobean period as embodying the very essence of a literary lawyer.

The Elizabethan and Jacobean Inns of Court were not institutions of merely practical legal education. Indeed, they had become so imbued with an equal, if not weightier, emphasis on the thriving literary and historical traditions of the late renaissance that Sir Edward Coke, Francis Bacon and others would soon be calling for a re-emphasis on providing a practical legal education in the substance and process of the law.[18] Masques and revels had been an integral part of the Inns since the early sixteenth century, and some of the first plays in several genres of English drama were produced for, and in no small degree by, the Inns, especially the Inns of the Inner and Middle Temples.[19] Due to the location of the Inns in the capital of the realm and the fact that students of the Inns "were usually of families of higher rank than were students at the universities," the Inns had a significantly close relationship to the leadership of the kingdom. As the principal "residence of the intellectual class of" London, the Inns "were often called upon to establish the criteria of taste even for the court." The responsibility of the legal profession of the Inns to provide entertainment for "the royal family and the nobility required them to display great dramatic diversity and ingenuity in providing such amusement." As a result of the close collaboration between the legal and literary professions this duty encouraged, the very first British history play,

---

[18] *See generally* WILFRID R, PREST, THE INNS OF COURT UNDER ELIZABETH I AND THE EARLY STUARTS: 1590–1640 (1972).
[19] *See generally* A. WIGFALL GREEN, THE INNS OF COURT AND EARLY ENGLISH DRAMA (1931).

Gorbuduc, and the first Arthurian play, *The Misfortunes of Arthur*, were produced by the Inns. *Gorbuduc* was first created for their 1561–1562 Christmas revels by the Inner Temple under the title *Ferrex and Porrex*, and subsequently performed at Whitehall for Queen Elizabeth the following January. It was co-authored by two lawyers from the Inner Temple, Thomas Sackville (later Lord Buckhurst and Earl of Dorset) and Thomas Norton (courtier to the Queen). *The Misfortunes of Arthur* was collaboratively produced by Gray's Inn in 1588. Among the members of that Inn who participated were Christopher Yelverton and Francis Bacon. Both plays used the chronicle histories that developed out of the twelfth century *Historia Regum Brittaniae* [*History of the Kings of Britain*] of Geoffrey of Monmouth for source material.[20]

Geoffrey of Monmouth's *Historia* had almost immediately fostered a highly influential genre of British chronicle history that became known as *Galfridian history* after the Latin versions of his name. The tragedy of Gorbuduc dividing the realm between his sons, Ferrex and Porrex, was a standard part of Galfridian British chronicle histories. The cultural significance of the stories of Arthur was such that the genre of Arthurian literature had become linked to the Galfridian chronicle history tradition under the collective term the *Matter of Britain.* Stated briefly as laid out in Galfridian chronicle history the Britannic myth asserted that Britain was first civilized by a group of refugees from the Fall of Troy led by Brutus, great-grandson of the Trojan prince Aenas. Brutus had allegedly established the seeds of the traditions of common law jurisprudence and rule of law constitutionalism in ancient Britain only to imperil its posterity by dividing Britain between his sons, Locrinus, Albanactus, and Camber upon his death. Nonetheless,

---

[20] *Id.* at 17–21, 142–146, 148–153.

this form of limited monarchic government was then faithfully restored and preserved over the centuries by a succession of wise and noble kings of Britain. Brutus was supposed to have settled in Britain circa 1100 BCE. Other figures who found their way into the literary traditions of the *Matter of Britain* include King Lear circa 750 BCE and Gorbuduc circa 700 BCE, both of whom had also imperiled the realm by dividing it upon their deaths. Figures believed to be significant lawgivers include Dunwallo Molmutius, promulgator of the Molmutian laws, circa 650 BCE, and good Queen Marcia (who was credited with first enacting the Marcian (or Mercian) laws circa 350 BCE. Most significant of these ancient British lawgivers was good King Lucius, who alleged converted the Britons to Christianity circa 150 AD and revised the British laws together with a conciliar assembly in accordance with guidelines contained in a letter from Pope Eleutherus written in reply to Lucius's request to be sent a copy of the Roman laws. The Lucian laws would then be preserved and improved upon by succeeding British kings, including, of course, the paragon of the myth, King Arthur circa 500 AD.[21] This ancient and immemorial tradition of preserving and improving upon the best laws and governmental institutions of prior generations of Britons was then continued by a succession of undeniably historic kings, like Alfred, Aethelstan, and Edward the Confessor. The historicity of the origin story of Brutus

---

[21] *See generally, e.g.,* GEOFFREY OF MONMOUTH, THE HISTORY OF THE KINGS OF BRITAIN (Lewis Thorpe, ed. 1966) (circa 1136) [hereinafter HISTORY OF THE KINGS OF BRITAIN] *and* CURRAN, supra note 3 *and* Ingledew, supra note 3. The chronological chart included by Thorpe in his translation of Geoffrey's work is invaluable in grasping the nearly 2,000 years of alleged British history at the heart of the Galfridian tradition of chronicle histories. The correspondence between the names of the three sons of Brutus and the realms of England, Scotland, and Wales was no doubt intentional.

and the more fantastic aspects of the Arthurian legends were called into question by the *Historia Anglorum* [*History of England*] written in the early sixteenth century by the Italian humanist scholar and naturalized emigrant to England, Polydore Vergil, who began working on the *Historia* at the suggestion of Henry VII. After it was printed in 1534 Vergil's work prompted a backlash of works by British authors occasionally reviling it and inevitably defending the native British sources and stories. That insular criticism of Vergil's *Historia* and his favorable treatment of the Roman sources and Rome's influences on British history understandably increased after Henry VIII's break with the Roman Catholic Church.[22] It is hardly surprising that the lawyers and students of the Inns of Court should have drawn inspiration from their culture's most cherished historical traditions of ancient and noble rulers and lawgivers.

In addition to their favored literary extra-curricular endeavors, "listening to sermons and political gossip" rounded out the non-academic part of an Inn member's professional education. The academic study of law was complemented by studies in the classics and the new humanist disciplines of the sciences, philosophy, and history; "students were frequently advised that humane studies were an indispensable basis and complement to legal learning." The pedagogical environment of the Elizabethan and Jacobean Inns was one where an almost seamless understanding of law, literature, and politics was inculcated in the mental habits of their members; a singular spectrum for examining the past in relation to the present. The Inns had in effect become "the third university of England, . . . in which revels and pageants had their part to play and where conversation might wander

---

[22] *See generally, e.g.*, DENYS HAY, POLYDORE VERGIL: RENAISSANCE HISTORIAN AND MAN OF LETTERS (1952).

away from the arid ground of writs and terms into the greener pastures of history and literature . . . ."[23]

Indeed, the era itself is a critical watershed moment in the development of a critical antiquarianism cap-able of discerning matters of fundamental meaning and import in the myth-histoire of chronicle histories and origin stories while nonetheless challenging them as historically accurate in significant details.[24] While these early antiquarians may not have been historians by twenty-first century standards, they were without doubt significant contributors to the early development of those very standards; the antiquarian's "preference for the original documents, his ingenuity in discovering forgeries, his skill in collecting and classifying the evidence and, above all, his unbounded love for learning are the antiquary's contributions to the 'ethics' of the historian."[25] In England this culture of critical antiquarianism was itself a product of the Inns. The membership of the Society of Antiquaries that was formed in 1586 and met in London until disbanded in 1614, at least in part due to James I having formed a suspicion that its members had dangerous political leanings, "was largely legal and centered on the Inns of Court."[26]

---

[23] PREST, *supra* note 18 at 158–160. DAVID IBBETSON, COMMON LAW AND *IUS COMMUNE* 21 (2001).

[24] *See generally,* DONALD R. KELLEY, HISTORY AND THE DISCIPLINES: THE RECLASSIFICATION OF KNOWLEDGE IN EARLY MODERN EUROPE (1997) *and* THE WRITING OF HISTORY OF AND THE STUDY OF LAW (1997); *and* DANIEL R. WOOLF, THE IDEA OF HISTORY IN EARLY STUART ENGLAND: ERUDITION, IDEOLOGY, AND THE 'LIGHT OF TRUTH' FROM THE ACCESSION OF JAMES I TO THE CIVIL WAR (1990) *and* READING HISTORY IN EARLY MODERN ENGLAND (2000).

[25] Arnaldo Momigliano, *Ancient History and the Antiquarian,* in CONTRIBUTO ALLA STORIA DEGLI STUDI CLASSICI 67, 102 (1979).

[26] STUART PIGGOT, ANCIENT BRITONS AND THE ANTIQUARIAN IMAGINATION: IDEAS FROM THE RENAISSANCE TO THE REGENCY 14 (1989).

Less is known about the extra-curricular literary aspects of the legal education of the Scots lawyer. In part this is due to the absence of a centralized academy of legal learning and professional training analogous to the English Inns of Court. Many Scots lawyers still received their education in law at universities on the continent in addition to those who matriculated with a degree in law from universities in Scotland or those of Oxford and Cambridge in England. In all of these institutions the *ius commune* of the civil law and canon law was the subject of study, rather than the substantive law of Scotland which they would spend their careers practising. The legal education delivered to Scots lawyers had been supplemented with studies in history, philosophy, and the arts and sciences from the very founding of St. Andrews in 1412 until the decline of university based legal education in Scotland in the late sixteenth century led to its final demise at St Andrews about 1600. It is reasonable to postulate that the Scots lawyer received almost as much education in non-legal disciplines in the four years it took to receive a degree in canon law or the six years required to attain a degree in the civil law as did their English counterparts. Furthermore, the fact that Scots lawyers were trained in law they would not actually apply as practitioners in a legal system still primarily based upon the common laws and statutes of Scotland rather than civil or canon law suggests that learning to 'think like a lawyer' was the most important part of the education. It is at the least highly unlikely that the Scottish legal profession would have viewed studies in the humanities as being less important to imbuing the proper mindset for a lawyer than did English lawyers.[27]

---

[27] *See* DAVID M. WALKER, 2 A LEGAL HISTORY OF SCOTLAND: THE LATER MIDDLE AGES 277–285 (1990) *and* John W. Cairns, *Historical Introducion, in* 1 A HISTORY OF PRIVATE LAW IN SCOTLAND 86–

George Saltern (also spelled Salterne or Salteren) was very much part of this culture of literary lawyers. Although Saltern's birth date is unknown, the Middle Temple Records state that he was the "son and heir of William Salterne of Bristol," who was one of the Sheriffs for Bristol in 1574[28] At age fourteen, Saltern left his birthplace of Bristol for Oxford where he "matriculated from Christ Church on 23 March 1581/2," subsequently attending the Inns of Court where he became a "barrister-at-law of the Middle Temple" on November 20, 1590.[29] From the Middle Temple Records it would appear that he was either mentored by or became an associate of a noted lawyer from Bristol, Sir George Snigge, who had been Mayor of Bristol when Saltern's father was Sheriff; it was Snigge who called Saltern to the Bar in 1590.[30] At

---

91 (Kenneth Reid & Reinhard Zimmerman eds., 2000). At the time of the Union of the Crowns the substantive law was still very much one of common law and statutes, with civil law being used in a gap filling fashion by Scots lawyers and judges,. The development of the more thoroughly mixed civil/common law system of modern Scotland began later in the seventeenth century. *See* Cairns 100–101 *and* DAVID M. WALKER, 4 A LEGAL HISTORY OF SCOTLAND: THE SEVENTEENTH CENTURY 341–347 (1996).

[28] 1 MIDDLE TEMPLE RECORDS 270 (Charles Henry Hopwood ed., 1904); WILLIAM ADAMS, CHRONICLE OF BRISTOL 114 (Francis F. Fox ed., 1910) (ca. 1623–1648).

[29] M. A. Rogers, *"Sacrae Heptades"* (*1625*), 20 NOTES & QUERIES 164 (May 1973) (citing J. FOSTER, 4 ALUMNI OXONIENSIS 1303 (Oxford & London, 1891–1892)). 1 MIDDLE TEMPLE RECORDS, *supra* note 27 at 316–317. *See also* JANELLE GREENBERG, THE RADICAL FACE OF THE ANCIENT CONSTITUTION: ST. EDWARD'S "LAWS:" IN EARLY MODERN POLITICAL THOUGHT 128 (2001) (discussing Saltern's connection to Bristol and the Middle Temple).

[30] ADAMS, *supra* note 28 at 114. 1 MIDDLE TEMPLE RECORDS, *supra* note 28 at 317. Sir George Snigge was a credit to the Middle Temple, serving as a Bencher, Reader and Treasurer. He had been a Sheriff of Bristol in 1556, Recorder of Bristol from 1593 to 1603, and was then raised to the rank of Serjeant at Law in 1603, becoming Baron of Exchequer in 1604. Snigge ended his legal career as Chief Justice of the Glamorgan and Brecknock Circuit. *See* ADAMS, *supra* note 28 at

the time he wrote *Of the Antient Lawes of great Britaine* Saltern was well established professionally with chambers in the Middle Temple. Saltern had a fairly average career as a lawyer, rising no higher than Cupboard man assisting the Reader on February 7, 1611/12. He apparently chose to forgo becoming a Reader himself, instead paying a fine. This meant that he ended his career as an *Ancient* (the term for barristers who chose not to rise further than the Cupboard) of the Middle Temple, which seems quite appropriate given the title and subject of his sole surviving Union Tract. Saltern kept his chambers in the Middle Temple until December of 1624.[31] In addition to *Of the Antient Lawes of great Britaine* and its now no longer extant companion tract from 1603, *De Union Britanniae seu de Regnorum Angliae et Scotiae omniumque adiacentium Insularum Brittanicarum in unam Monarchiam Consolidatione Deque multiplici eius unionis utilitate* [On the union of Britain, or on the consolidation of the Kingdoms of England and Scotland and of all islands adjacent to Britain into one Monarchy, and on the multiple benefits of the union], Saltern has been further

---

104, 143, 150, 178; *and* 1–2 MIDDLE TEMPLE RECORDS, *supra* note 27 at 160, 176, 181, 206, 265, 292, 295, 297, 298, 300, 303, 306, 308, 310, 314, 317, 332–333, 358, 363, 365, 380–381, 388, 391–392, 394–395, 400–401, 408, 413, 416, 422–424, 430; 439–440, 445, 477, 513, 569, 571, 573, 597; *and* EDWARD FOSS, 6 THE JUDGES OF ENGLAND: WITH SKETCHES OF THEIR LIVES, AND MISCELLANEOUS NOTICES CONNECTED WITH THE COURTS AT WESTMINSTER, FROM THE TIME OF THE CONQUEST 13, 21, 23, 26, 29 (London, 1857); *and* ARTHUR ROBERT INGPEN, THE MIDDLE TEMPLE BENCH BOOK: BEING A REGISTER OF BENCHERS OF THE MIDDLE TEMPLE FROM THE EARLIEST RECORDS TO THE PRESENT TIME, WITH HISTORICAL INTRODUCTION 86 (J. Bruce Williamson ed., 2nd ed. 1937); *and* HISTORY OF PARLIAMENT ONLINE, at http://www.historyofparliamentonline.org/volume/1558-1603/member/snigge-george-1545-1618.

[31] For the complete records of Saltern's career in the Middle Temple, *see* 1–2 MIDDLE TEMPLE RECORDS, *supra* note 28 at 270, 317, 323, 328, 400–401, 405–406, 420; 473, 539, 546, 550, 552–553, 570, 610, 669, 677, 697.

credited with the "Latin verses prefixed to William Est, *The Right Rule of Religious Life*" published in 1616, and a 1625 work, *Sacrae Heptades, or Seaven Problems concerning Antichrist. 1. Of his Place. 2. Of his State. 3. Of his Names. 4. Of his Rising. 5. Of his Raigne. 6. Of his words and actions. 7. Of his times. Necessarie to be read and knowne of all men, who professe Christ Iesus, and hope to be saved by no other Name*."[32] *Sacrae Heptades* is an extensive and virulently anti-Catholic work that reviles the Roman Church as the very source of Anti-Christian beliefs and the Pope as the Beast and Antichrist. It clearly places Saltern in the mainstream of rabidly anti-Catholic English Protestantism thought that arose in the aftermath of the 1605 Gunpowder Plot of Guy Fawkes and his followers. The anti-Roman Catholic sentiments of *Sacrae Heptades* make the anti-Roman aspects of *Of the Antient Lawes* seem mild by comparison; perhaps a sign that by 1625 Saltern was no longer quite the royalist supporter he had been when he wrote his two Union Tracts. The content of a further tract published posthumously in 1641 also places Saltern firmly within the Puritan leaning factions of English Protestantism — *A Treatise against Images and Pictures in Churches. And an Answer to those who object that the times are changed. Written by George Saltern, Esquire*." Saltern had also been credited

---

[32] Id. The 1604 Union Tract by Saltern is no longer extant, but was likely "that volume entered to 'Master Byshop' (George Bishop) on 22 March 1603/04: Entred for his copie Aswell in Lattyn as in English a book Called in Lattyn *De Vnion Britanni[a]e seu de Regnorum Angli[a]e et Scoti[a]e omniumque adiacentium Insularum Brittanicarum in vnam Monarchiam Consolidatione Deque multiplici eius vnionis vtilitate.*" Id. It should not be confused with the dialogue published in Edinburgh in 1604 by the Scottish clergyman and lawyer, Robert Pont, which has the exact same title other than the final words "dialogus, per R.P." Pont's work is entirely in Latin, while Saltern's now lost tract was entered into the Stationers' Register as being in both Latin and English.

by Edmund Howes, who edited the continuation of *Stow's Chronicle*, as one of the individuals "to whom he has beene particularly beholding in the furtherance of his general worke,...."[33] Finally, in 1883 Saltern was listed as an alternate potential author of a 1606 work titled "HISTORIE (the) of Great Britannie declaring the successe of times and affaires in that iland, from the Romans first entrance, vntill the raigne of Egbert, the West-Saxon Prince; who reduced the severall principalities of the Saxons and English, into a monarchie, and changed the name of Britannie into England" which had until then been ascribed to John Clapham.[34] George Saltern was clearly an exemplary product of the Inns.

Juridical Historiography in the Union Tracts

A survey of the Jacobean Union Tracts illustrates the blending of literary, philosophical, legal and historical discourse that resulted from such training. Both myth and history are called upon to ground and augment the legal and political arguments being made for and against the Union proposals. The constitutional historiography produced shows the marks of literary lawyers working to create "law at its best [ ] continuous with culture at its best."[35] Before proceeding further, however, and at the risk of belaboring the point, it will be helpful to stop for a moment and disengage from twenty-first century notions of the stark difference between fact and fiction, history

---

33 EDMUND HOWES, ANNALES, OR, A GENERALL CHRONICLE OF ENGLAND. BEGUN BY IOHN STOW: CONTINUED AND AUGMENTED WITH MATTERS FORRAIGNE AND DOMESTIQUE, ANCIENT AND MODERNE, VNTO THE END OF THIS PRESENT YEERE, 1631 1087 (London, 1632).

34 SAMUEL HALKLETT, A DICTIONARY OF THE ANONYMOUS AND PSEUDONYMOUS LITERATURE OF GREAT BRITAIN 1124 (London, 1883).

35 West, *supra* note 4 at 1189.

and myth. An argument based explicitly and equally in myth as well as history today would likely elicit cries and accusations of falsehood and error. History and fact are thought to be what actually happened; they are concrete and valid. Myth and fiction, on the other hand, are considered intrinsically unreliable and more often than not demonstrably false. They are to be avoided at all costs in serious scholarship and debate. Seen through this contemporary lens of perception, the literature of the Union Tracts is riddled with error and almost laughably primitive and specious. In marked contrast, the early seventeenth century culture of critical antiquarianism still found and treasured matters of significant and persuasive import in the chronicle histories and mythic texts they were interrogating with increasingly objective, yet highly fluid, standards of historical accuracy.

This moment in the development of the critical standards of historical research and writing is so fluid that Daniel Woolf has noted in discussing several examples of contemporary criticism from this era: "Here, not for the last time, was new history identified with romance, myth, and imagination, old chronicle with truth and the hard facts of reality."[36] This period was therefore very much a watershed moment in the history of British historiography capable of flipping modern historical standards on their head in the very name of historical accuracy. Within such a culture the stark twenty-first century distinction between works of myth as essentially fictional and works of history as per se factual inevitably fails as a critical standard of evaluation. In order to understand that they are instead the products of a sophisticated and self-aware culture willing to acknowledge that they do not know the exact origins of their system of law and government and willing to reach into the world of myth, story, and allegory to fill in the

---

[36] READING HISTORY IN EARLY MODERN ENGLAND, *supra* note 24 at 23.

gaps it will be helpful to first look outside of the tracts themselves.

The works of William Camden and John Selden are both praised as early examples of genuine historical scholarship marked by the humanist preference for verifiable sources over the pseudo-mythical chronicle histories that characterized the works of earlier chronicle writers. They are considered among the first, if not the first, genuine British historians. Yet, each shows great respect for myth as a valuable source of knowledge and belief about the ancient past. Both are critical of the work of Polydore Vergil (whose English history is so often pointed to as having debunked the Galfridian myth of Brutus as the eponymous founder of Britain's *dominium politicum et regale*) for asserting that none of the existing institutions of English law and government pre-dated the Norman conquest. Both show reverence for the myth of Brutus, while openly discussing its flaws as accurate history. Camden opens his *Britanniae* by discussing existing beliefs about the origins of the name Britain as a prelude to examining who the first inhabitants were. He pauses shortly after beginning an extensive discussion and critique of the myth of Brutus as told by Geoffrey of Monmouth to tell the reader "it is not my intent, I assure you, to discredit and confute that story which goes of him … [f]or that were to struggle against an opinion commonly and long since received." He then proceeds to share the by then well-known proofs of the falsity of the Brutus myth by characterizing them as ones related to him as "so often I stand in defence thereof," by those who "come upon me fiercely with these and such like arguments." This detailed discussion of the historical flaws of the Brutus myth is brought to a close with the following:

> As for these observations and judgements of other men, which I have recited, I beseech you, let no man commence action against mee, a plaine meaning man,

> and an ingenuous student of the truth, as though I impeached the narration of Brutus; forasmuch as it hath alwaies (I hope) been lawfull for every man in such like matters, both to thinke what he will, and also to relate what others have thought. For mine owne part, let Brutus be taken for the father, and founder of the British nation; I will not be of contrary mind. Let the Britaines resolve still of their originall, to have proceeded from the Trojans (into which stocke, as I will hereafter prove, they may truly ingrasse themselves) I will not gain-stand it. I wot full well, that Nations in old time for their originall, had recourse unto Hercules, & in later ages, to the Trojans. Let Antiquites herin be pardoned, if by entermingling falsities and truthes, humane matters and divine together, it make the first beginnings of nations and cities more noble, sacred, and of greater majestie: seeing that, as Pliny writeth, *Even falsely to claime and challenge descents from famous personages, implieth in some sort a love of virtue*. As for myselfe, I willingly acknowledge with Varro, the best learned of all Romans, such originals as these, fetched from the gods, *to be profitable; that valorous men may believe, although untruly, that they are descended from the gods, and thereby the mind of man assuredly perswaded of some divine race, may presume to enterprize great matters more boldly, act the same more resolutely, and upon the very securities thereof, performe all more happily.*[37]

These are Camden's original italics for emphasis; done to emphasize why the use of myth is justified when consti-

---

[37] WILLIAM CAMDEN, BRITAIN, OR A CHOROGRAPHICALL DESCRIPTION OF THE MOST FLOURISHING KINGDOMES, ENGLAND, SCOTLAND, AND IRELAND, AND THE ISLANDS ADJOYNING, OUT OF THE DEPTHS OF ANTIQUITIE 4–8 (Philemon Holland trans., London, 1637). Perhaps the most straightforward assertion of the correctness of this view of constitutional truth is to be found a century later in Roger Acherly's *Brittanic Constitution*. See discussion *infra* at 144.

tuting a narrative of national origins. It is hardly insignificant to the study of juridical literature written to debate the creation of an actual realm of Great Britain that the most respected native British historian for the next century was willing to endorse a mythical British origin as constitutionally true although factually inaccurate.

But, how *can* a story be constitutionally true though historically inaccurate? Two possible ways of measuring the truth of constitutional myths have been suggested by scholars in the field of law and literature. The first is an aesthetic theory of truth, which holds that "a historically inaccurate story can nevertheless be true if it meets two conditions: first, if it is 'more or less' true, and second, if it illuminates something 'strange and wonderful' about some relevant aspect of our history ...."[38] This resonates nicely with the passage from Camden quoted above, as it also does with several ways in which historical fiction can legitimately be used to convey moral truth. The first is the sort of symbolic truth told in a fable, wherein a moral truth is symbolized to such a degree that the story told can be highly inaccurate or completely fictional without impairing the moral truth.[39] Second, historical fiction might be offered as a concrete example of the moral truth in action. When used in this evidentiary fashion it does matter whether the events of the story happened at all or varied widely from the story told. If the story told never happened or happened very differently, a sort of literary perjury has taken place that greatly diminishes or negates the weight of the moral truth being conveyed.[40] Finally, where the historical fiction is meant

---

[38] Robin West, *Constitutional Fictions and Meritocratic Success Stories,* 53 WASH. & LEE L. REV. 996 (1996) (quoting L.H. LARUE, CONSTITUTIONAL LAW AS FICTION: NARRATIVE IN THE RHETORIC OF AUTHORITY 150–153 (1995)).

[39] *Id.*, at 1001–1002.

[40] *Id.*, at 1002–1003.

to be "constitutive of the moral truth that the story is designed to convey," the degree of historical accuracy matters a great deal.[41] Historical fiction "'constitutes' a moral truth to whatever degree the bare fact that we have lived this way in the past in some way implies that we should live this way in the future," and, for that matter, the present as well.[42] This constitutive sense of fictional truth lies at the very heart of the juridical trope of the ancient constitution.

Aesthetic truth, symbolic moral truth, and constitutive moral truth are the most likely ways that the myths of antiquity can be said to be true in the work of Camden, Selden, and the Union Tract writers, yet there are clear indications that ancient myths were also used as concrete examples in the juridical literature of this period as well. This is especially true of stories that involve ruin ensuing upon the division of the ancient realm of Britain among the heirs of significant legendary kings such as Brutus and Gorbuduc. Although a single story comprised of constitutional fable may be open to a charge of literary perjury, when there is a well-established literary tradition of such stories the cumulative weight of analogy ringing true with an author's contemporary situation ameliorates the charge of perjury to a great degree, if not negating the charge entirely. Such academic charges of 'perjury' abound in the scholarship surrounding the ancient constitution. They are especially pointed when aimed at famous lawyers:

> Such was the authority, the personality, and the historical importance of Lord Coke that his Reports, his Institutes, and his other writings formed the core of what the later legal profession 'remembered' about medieval

---

[41] *Id.*, at 1003–1004.
[42] *Id.*, at 1003.

> common law. The unfortunate part was that Coke made things up....
>
> ....
>
> And he repeated fanciful stories of ancient British history as solemn fact."[43]

That lawyers 'make things up' is a fairly common charge even for lawyers of the present day. Yet, one should be cautious drawing such a conclusion regarding the multifaceted presence of the ancient constitution trope in medieval and early modern juridical works. As Woolf has quite aptly stated in this regard:

> [a] particularly unfortunate (and unintended) implication of Pocock's [*Ancient Constitution and the Feudal Law*], exacerbated by its very persuasiveness, has been the frequently expressed view that somehow the writings of Spelman, which recognized the impact of the [Norman] Conquest, are 'historical' while those of Coke, because they are 'insular' and argue that the law dated from time immemorial, are 'fantastic.' Such language is not very helpful in coming to terms with the historical thought of earlier periods.[44]

The mythic historiography of the ancient constitution undeniably needs to be read within its historical context rather than of several centuries later.

---

[43] David J. Seipp, *The Law's Many Bodies, and the Manuscript Tradition in English Legal History*, 25 J. LEG. HIST. 74, 78 (2004) (reviewing J. H. BAKER, THE LAW'S TWO BODIES: SOME EVIDENTIAL PROBLEMS IN ENGLISH LEGAL HISTORY (2001)).

[44] WOOLF, THE IDEA OF HISTORY IN EARLY STUART ENGLAND, *supra* note 24 at 26 (discussing the influence of J.G.A. POCOCK, THE ANCIENT CONSTITUTION AND THE FEUDAL LAW: A STUDY OF ENGLISH HISTORICAL THOUGHT IN THE SEVENTEENTH CENTURY (rev. ed. 1987) (1957) [hereinafter POCOCK, THE ANCIENT CONSTITUTION])).

The early works of John Selden exemplify the style of juridical historiography so common in late Tudor and early Stuart Britain. In his *England's Epinomis* and *Jani Anglorum Facies Altera (The Reverse or Back-Face of the English Janus)* (subtitled *To-wit, All that is met with in Story Concerning the Common and Statute-Law of English Brittany, From the first Memoirs of the two Nations, to the Decease of King Henry II. set down and tackt together succinctly by way of Narrative*), both written prior to the latter's publication in 1610, Selden weaves a chronicle account of the origins of Britain's ancient constitutions that begins in unabashed myth and ends by discussing the most accurate history then available to scholars.[45] His use of historical fiction in these accounts matches up well with a progression from conveying strictly aesthetic and moral truth with the clearly mythical accounts of antiquity to conveying concrete and constitutive truth as well once he begins to deal with more reliable recent sources and periods of history.

In both works he begins by placing the mythic origins of "English-Brittish Law" in "SAMOTHES (the very same who is ycleped *Dis*) the Founder of the Celtick Colonies" who established law and government in the ancient world of Northern Europe, and whose descendants settled in Gaul and Britain under the laws of the ancient druids and the rule of chieftains in a world where the "DEIS MATRIBUS" found in ancient British inscriptions were worshipped as goddesses of justice. After alluding to the culture of bards and druids "talked of in *Cæsar*, *Pliny* and others" Selden recounts how "*Brutus* … being happily arrived by Shipping, … and coming to land at *Totnes* in *Devonshire*, the *Britans* salute and own him

---

[45] *See generally* Paul Christianson, *Young John Selden and the Ancient Constitution*, 128 PROC. AM. PHIL. SOC'Y 271, 274–283 (1984). [hereinafter Christianson, *Young John Selden*].

King." Brutus then goes on to build "*New Troy* (that is *London*) gave Laws to his Citizens and Subjects; those such as the *Trojans* had, or a Copy of theirs." Six centuries later, Selden continues, "*Dunvallo Molmutius* being King ordained" the Molmutian laws and is later buried in London "near the Temple of Concord (by which Temple, there are not wanting those who understand that Illustrious Colledge on the Bank of *Thames*, consecrated to the study of our Common Law, now called the Temple and) 'which he himself had built for the confirmation of his Laws.'"[46]

At this point in the lengthier discussion of the *Jani Anglorum* and the more summary account of the *Epinomis* Selden pauses to explain and justify the stories recounted so far, especially those of Brutus, as stories "patched up out of Bards Songs and Poetick Fictions taken upon trust, like *Talmudical* Traditions, on purpose to raise the *British* name out of the *Trojan* ashes." In this, he notes, the British are no different than many other nations of antiquity in tying their origins to the mythic Trojans.[47] He closes his discussion of myth in each with a similar sentiment before moving on to discuss the more reliable histories of Caesar and Tacitus, among others, concerning the ancient Britons:

---

[46] *JANI ANGLORUM FACIES ALTERA*, RENDERED INTO ENGLISH, WITH LARGE NOTES THEREUPON, BY REDMAN WESTCOT, GENT., *in* TRACTS WRITTEN BY JOHN SELDEN OF THE INNER-TEMPLE, ESQUIRE 1–12 (London, 1673) (1610) [hereinafter JANI ANGLORUM]. *See also* ENGLAND'S EPINOMIS., *in* TRACTS WRITTEN BY JOHN SELDEN OF THE INNER-TEMPLE, ESQUIRE 1–3 (London, 1673) [hereinafter ENGLAND'S EPINOMIS]. Selden's *Jani Anglorum* would later be cited as good authority by Sir Mathew Hale in his *History and Analysis of the Common Law of England*. SIR MATHEW HALE, HISTORY AND ANALYSIS OF THE COMMON LAW OF ENGLAND 5 (London, 1713).

[47] JANI ANGLORUM, *supra* note 46 at 9. *Compare* CAMDEN, *supra* note 36 at 9.

> I could wish for a sight of *Jupiter*'s *Dipthere*, or an Oracle from *Apollo*, that so, resolution might be had touching the certainty of these reports, whether fabulous, or sealed with the stamp of a true History. The main Authors are that *Chaldee* Priest and the *Arthurian Jeoffrey*; both exceedingly suspected, but especially the first, by the penetrating Judgements of most learned men. But admitting them, as your Mercurial Spirit shall move you, you have a fair passage from these Mythick reports, selected out of Bardish Hymns, unto most allowed truths of authentick Historians.[48]

In other words, our British stories concerning the origins of our systems of law and governance and are worth recounting even if they might be mythic fables because they connect the world of the present and its constitutional issues and concerns with a noble and inspiring past.

The works of Camden and Selden bracket the production of Saltern's *Of the Antient Lawes* and the other Union Tracts in time, and not surprisingly we find the same literary mix of myth and history used in many of them as well.[49] Even in those that do not share this characteristic there is often a denial of the Brutus myth in terms that make it clear that it was an element of the juridical culture that could not simply be ignored. There are also references to other British kings like Gorbuduc, Lucius, and Arthur potentially "patched up out of Bards Songs and Poetick Fictions" into myth mixed in with historical rulers such as Cunobelinus, Cassibellan, and Cadwallader. In tracts written by Scots, the supposed founder of Scotland, Fergus

---

[48] ENGLAND'S EPINOMIS, *supra* note 46 at 3. *Compare* JANI ANGLORUM, *supra* note 46 at 12.

[49] Camden in fact prepared a new edition of *Brittania* for publication in 1607 as public interest in the debates began to peak and the last of the Union Tracts were being published.

mac Erc, is mixed in with historical Scots rulers in a similar ancient constitutionalist literary style.

The most significant of the Scottish tracts was Thomas Craig's *De Unione Regnorum Britanniae Tractatus* from 1605. Craig was a member of Scotland's Commission on the Union, so it is safe to grant his work with at least a modicum of official status and influence. After beginning with a short ode to the blessings of Britain's current state under a single monarch, Craig asserts "that to all the evils which Britain has undergone, the plurality of her kings and kingdoms has opened the door" and states his intention to "display the shifting history of Britain from its origins, … [f]or though the recollection of them be sad, the warnings of the past are of value as guidance for the future." He follows this immediately with an unequivocal statement that "[u]ntil our own days Britain has never been under one king or governor." The obscure nature of early British history is such that "no record throws light upon it." A situation shared by that most noble of ancient realms Greece, whose early history prior to the advent of "Theseus … was shrouded in darkness."[50]

This parallel with ancient Greek history "relieves [him] of the charge of belittling the early history of Britain." At this point, only three paragraphs into a manuscript that ran to 264 folios in length Craig first mentions the myth of Brutus. "Haply," he states, "there are those who accept the story of Brutus. I shall not challenge them, provided they hold with me that his asserted division of Britain among his three sons, to the eldest of whom, Locrin, he gave superiority, was an error of judgment; for it is a woeful tale of disasters and civil wars that resulted from that step." Of course, Craig "hold[s] the asserted political division of

---

[50] THOMAS CRAIG, DE UNIONE REGNORUM BRITANNIÆ TRACTATUS [A TREATISE ON THE UNION OF THE BRITISH REALMS] 207–208 (C. Sanford Terry trans., Edinburgh 1909) (1605).

Britain by Brutus to be exceedingly improbable" in light of the fact that the earliest recorded mention of Brutus and his sons is "nearly two thousand years after Brutus lived." It is at this point that he then turns to "consider the actual state of Britain from the earliest times, so far as it can be deciphered in written records," immediately noting that "Britain was ruled by more than one king is clearly stated by the Dictator Caesar … ."[51]

Note how this opening discussion is composed. It follows the same basic pattern as that found in Camden and Selden of defending the fables of the mythical history of British antiquity as something to be expected in the origin stories of any ancient and noble realm, and finding some discursive value in grounding the practice of calling the entire isle Britain and its ancient inhabitants Britons in the tale of Brutus. For Craig this value lies in emphasizing the dangers of dividing the Isle of Britain into separate realms; for "warnings of the past are of value as guidance for the future," a paradigmatic example of using myth to convey both aesthetic and moral truth. Significantly for our viewing Craig as a Jacobean literary lawyer, his recounting of Brutus' "error of judgment" is not the finish of Craig's use of literary myth to bolster his arguments in support of the Union. Before he is through he will allude to or recount, among other potentially fantastic tales, the tragedy of "Ferrex and Pollex [sic], kings of Britain," from the story of Gorbuduc; a story apparently as popular with the Scots Bar as it was with the English lawyers of the Inns of Court., Like Brutus, Gorbuduc was believed to have ruled Britain as sole monarch in an age when, as Craig has already asserted, there were no kings who ruled Britain as a single realm. Like Brutus, Gorbuduc foolishly divided his unified Britain between his two sons with the result that the younger, Porrex, murders the eldest and is in turn slain by

---

[51] *Id.* at 208–209.

his mother who then kills herself. This tale is referred to as one of several from antiquity illustrating the harms that ensue when the "quarrelsome" siblings "sprung from the womb of the same mother, Britain" obstinately "refuse to be reconciled ...."[52]

This metaphor of Britain as distraught and tragic mother is immediately followed by likening "Britain as it were a corporation such as lawyers describe a corporate body to be." The dangers illustrated by this discussion flow from the members' refusal to cooperate to sustain the whole. Among the fables told to illustrate these dangers of refusing the union proposals, Craig recounts as a recent and well-known fact the birth and life of a "two-headed monster with a single body which was born on the confines of England and Scotland at the time of James IV.'s marriage to Margaret, daughter of that most Sapient prince Henry VII." In anticipation that someone "should suppose that the creature is fictitious, though in fact it was actually seen by many persons, including my own father ... [and] George Buchanan, who saw it with his own eyes, and also expounded its significance to me." The translator's note to this passage points out that when Buchanan included the story in his *History of Scotland* he did not claim to have seen it personally, but like Craig, insisted that many others had. To this, Craig adds a two-headed woman born in the time of Edward the Confessor, and another such 'monster' in the time of Augustine. As with his use of the Brutus story at the outset of his tract, these 'fictions' are followed closely and merge with discussions of examples from history of kingdoms divided into ruin and catastrophe.[53]

There are in fact too many instances of this literary palette of myth and history in Craig's *De Unione* to cata-

---

[52] *Id.* at 232–233.
[53] *Id.* at 233–241.

log within the frame of this introduction. But, two more merit mention before proceeding to Saltern's *Of the Antient Lawes*. The first is Craig's explication of how James VI and I is "the legal heir to the throne of Britain" as a matrilineal descendant of the line of Aurelius Ambrosius.

> Aurelius Ambrosius had two sisters, Anna and Ada, who were taken to wife by the kings of the Picts and Scots. On them and their issue, therefore, the rightful succession to Britain devolved upon the extinction of the male-issue of Aurelius and his brother Uther Pendragon. ...When that contingency occurred, the throne of Britain passed through to the issue of Anna and Ada, the sisters of Aurelius, and through them to the Picts and Scots.

And just who might the issue of Anna be but "Modred, king of the Picts, the son of Anna and nephew to Aurelius," who had been spurned by the Britons as their rightful king in favor of Uther's son, Arthur. In response Modred "made a league with his kinsman the king of the Scots, and sought by might of arms to maintain his right" in "so fierce a war ... that the leaders on both sides and more than 30,000 men were slain." As a result of the unnamed battle (of Camlann) neither the Britons or the Picts and Scots can resist the Saxons when they usurp the estate of the ancient Britons. This story is introduced by recounting how God "has united in the person of our most gracious king the right and title of each of the races that have dwelt in Britain since it was a Roman province; any flaw in the title of any of the past dynasties being amply made good in him." The title flowed to the Picts and Scots both through the law of abandoned property (that of the Romans), "since by *Jus Naturale* abandoned property is the prize of the finder, as though it had been placed in his hands by its former owner," and through the failure of the line of the surviving Britons in Aurelius,

Uther, and Arthur. As was true of many Scots chronicle histories, Craig pointedly omits any mention of the usurper Arthur from his discussion.[54]

Later in the tract after a lengthy discussion explaining why the union would be restitution rather than an innovation, Craig reiterates his version of James' right to inherit the ancient British kingdom as the heir of Modred.[55] The union can be seen as restitution because:

> The king's recent succession to the two kingdoms is rather the resumption of a condition previously existing, the healing of a division, than the institution of something new. And it is a resumption which carries an augmentation of power and honour to both sides. For, *as the lawyers say, cause and character pass with the thing itself.* Thus, if the antiquity of the Scottish kingdom be added to the resources and renown of England, each of them, auspiciously merged under the *original name Britain*, will gain in honour and lustre among the nations.[56]

How can we take Craig's work seriously without viewing it as the work of a literary lawyer willing to use fictions as well as facts to convey constitutional truth? His tract began with an assertion that Britain had never been united prior to the accession of James VI and I, an assertion diligently supported with historical sources. The only way a unified kingdom of Great Britain can be defended as restitution is if the myths were as persuasive and binding a source of authority for Craig as history is; a paradigmatic example of how the literary, legal, and historical canons

---

[54] *Id.* at 264–266. For another example of such negative treatment of Arthur, see William Stewart, *The Buik of the Chronicles of Scotland, in* KING ARTHUR IN LEGEND AND HISTORY 134–40 (Richard White ed., 1997).

[55] *Id.* at 444.

[56] *Id.* at 403 [emphasis added].

were seamlessly intertwined in the constitutional culture and juridical discourse of Jacobean Britain.

There are signs of this mingling of canonical tropes in other Union Tracts as well, some of which "also took the opportunity to recite precedents for 'Britain' itself" as an example of unions by lawful descent rather than conquest "including Brutus, Roman Britannia, and the use of '*Rex Britanniae*' by Anglo-Saxon kings like Athelstan."[57] In the anonymous *A Treatise about the Union of England and Scotland*, believed to be written by a Scot, the author asserts that "conquest or usurpation can no wayes be called a new erected kingdome" as well because "then should England have been erected in a new kingdome so often as it hath been conquered by Albion, Brutus, the Saxons, Dannes and Normans."[58] The *Historicall Collections* of Sir Henry Saville, in discussing "whether this title, King of Britany, be a meer innovation or but a renovation," first cites to "Jeffery of Monmouth," in whose work "we have kings of Britany enough from Brutus to Cadwallader, but leaving him with his Welsh fables," he moves on to discuss the absence from the Roman period of any mention of a "*Rex Britanniae* [except] Beda calleth Lucius *Brittanorum Rex*," which Saville states he just cannot understand since the Romans had already made their conquest.[59] Once the Romans abandon Britain, Saville cites to William of Malmesbury for "Voltigerne called *Rex Britaniae* and Guartimer his son; and lastly Ambrosius is termed by him *Monarcha Regni Britonum*."

---

[57] *Introduction* to THE JACOBEAN UNION: SIX TRACTS OF 1604 xxxi (Bruce R. Galloway and Brian P. Levack eds., 1985). [hereinafter THE JACOBEAN UNION: SIX TRACTS OF 1604]

[58] [Anonymous], *A Treatise about the Union of England and Scotland, in* THE JACOBEAN UNION: SIX TRACTS OF 1604, *supra* note 57 at 39, 65–66.

[59] The significance of Bede's testimony regarding King Lucius is discussed *infra* at 174–175.

After which the title "King of Britany" is not found until "King Edgar … stileth himself *totius Albionis basileus*, king of all Albion."[60]

Sir Edward Coke and the Juridical Trope of the Ancient Constitution

The literary discourse concerning the Union proposals contributed to the crafting of an enduring juridical trope; in short, the deliberate maintaining, if not the original production, of a multi-variant British constitutional mythology — that of the ancient constitution. Late Tudor and early Stuart writers of political and legal tracts and treatises built upon the foundations laid by earlier sources in order to more fully formulate the variants of this body of myth-histoire that would exert an indelible influence on constitutional discourse in the seventeenth century and well into the age of enlightenment in the eighteenth century. As has already been noted, the systems of legal, literary and political patronage at the heart of Tudor and Stuart governance were coextensive and interdependent to such a degree that the practices of law, literature and politics operated virtually in tandem. In the world of "the Renaissance courtier, history, poetry, and government administration were not separate and distinct practices as they tend to be" today; this world of patronage produced and was sustained by individuals like Edmund Spenser, the author of both *The Faery Queene* and *A View of the Present State of Ireland* in the 1590s, who in addition to being "a poet and antiquarian … was also a minor government

[60] Sir Henry Savile, *Historicall Collections, in* THE JACOBEAN UNION: SIX TRACTS OF 1604, *supra* note 57 at 184, 210–211.

official . . . secretary to the governor of Ireland ..."[61] It also undeniably produced literary lawyers, and foremost among them at the end of the Tudor era was Sir Edward Coke. Like Saltern, Coke's legal learning was acquired in the Elizabethan Inns of Court, where he became a member of the Inner Temple. By the end of the century he was Elizabeth's attorney-general and his knowledge of law widely respected.

His authority on law was so widely respected that his reports of cases, known afterward simply as *The Reports*, displaced all others so that 'during the nineteen years that Coke's reports were being published, no others appeared, 'as it became all the rest of the lawyers to be silent whilst their oracle was speaking.'"[62] The first eleven volumes of *The Reports* were published from 1600–1616, during which time Coke became successively Chief Justice of Common Pleas, Chief Justice of King's Bench, and finally a member of the Privy Council. *The Reports* are a blend of commentary and case reporter. They "were conceived as instructional law books built around actual cases."[63] A law school casebook is the best modern analogue, rather than a set of case reports. Like a modern casebook, *The Reports* combines essays on history, law, culture and politics with excerpted cases embellished with legal commentary. The essays are to be found in the prefaces to the eleven vol-

---

[61] Laurie A. Finke, *Spenser for Hire: Arthurian History as Cultural Capital in 'The Faerie Queen,' in* CULTURE AND THE KING: THE SOCIAL IMPLICATIONS OF THE ARTHURIAN LEGEND 212, 213–215 (Martin B. Schichtman & James P Carley eds., 1994).

[62] HASTINGS LYON & HERMAN BLOCK, EDWARD COKE: ORACLE OF LAW 352 (1929) (quoting without citation WILLIAM NELSON, THE PREFACE, 5 MOD. REP. v, viii (1711)). *See also* J.H. BAKER, AN INTRODUCTION TO ENGLISH HISTORY 210 (3d ed. 1990) (discussing Coke's Reports) *and* WILLIAM HOLDSWORTH, 5 A HISTORY OF ENGLISH LAW 235, 456–490 (1982) (1903–1936) (discussing Coke's writings).

[63] BAKER, *supra* note 62.

umes published during Coke's judicial tenure. Although Coke did not originate the myth of the ancient constitution, he "did more than any other man to summarize it and make it authoritative."[64] His early work in this respect is found in the prefaces to *The Reports* and shows the same blend of literary, legal, historical and antiquarian elements found in the Union Tracts.

In the preface to the *Second Reports,* Coke explains that his reason for publishing the reports is to contribute to the noblest of learning "for prince and subject," that of the "common laws of England," which protected the realm from the tyranny and despotism that typified the realms of civil law. He then offers an example of the supremacy of law in England:

> Queen Elizabeth, whose continual charge to her justices, agreeable with her ancient laws, is, that for no commandment under the great or privy seal, writs or letters, common right be disturbed or delayed. And if any such commandment (upon untrue surmises) should come, that the justices of her laws should not therefore cease to do right in any point. And this agreeth with the ancient Law of England, declared by the great Charter, and spoken in the person of the King; Nulli vendemus, nulli negabimus, aut differemus Justiciam ven Rectum.

This is followed by an explanation, paraphrasing but not citing chapter 17 of Fortescue's *De Laudibus Legum Angliae*, that:

> If the ancient laws of this noble island had not excelled all others, it could not be but some of the several conquerors and governors thereof, that is to say, the Romans, Saxons, Danes or Normans, and specially the

---

[64] POCOCK, THE ANCIENT CONSTITUTION, *supra* note 44 at 38.

> Romans, who (as they justly may) do boast of their civil laws, would (as every of them might) have altered or changed the same.[65]

That Coke did not cite Fortescue in this passage strongly suggests that being taught to believe in the ancient nobility of the native British laws was by his time an unexceptional element of the legal education provided in the Inns, and perhaps of the broader English culture itself. It was also not unreasonable at the time to believe that those ancient British laws and customs had been preserved even through multiple conquests of Britain:

> [d]espite a wide spectrum of opinion on the antiquity of the law and its relationship to the successive conquests not just of the Normans, but of Romans, Anglo-Saxons, and Danes, neither proved to be the occasion of an early Stuart historical controversy, either among prose historians or lawyers....
>
> In other words, there existed by about 1600 an identifiable 'corridor' or safe zone of correct opinion about the past, which was flexible enough to allow for some deviation and nuance....[66]

Such beliefs and rhetoric linked the rule of law and the current Tudor monarch with the ancient British past and setting the notion of a native and immemorial common law tradition that had always included the rule of law as the cornerstone of the proper study of law.

---

[65] SIR EDWARD COKE, 2 THE REPORTS, PART II v–viii (Jos. Butterworth & Sons, London, 1826) (ca.1600) (citing to the English judicial oath enacted in 2 E.3 c.8, 20 E.3 c.1–2, Magna Carta c.29 [of the 1225 and 1297 issues], and paraphrasing chapter 17 of SIR JOHN FORTESCUE, DE LAUDIBUS LEGUM ANGLIAE (S.B. Chrimes ed. and trans., 1942) (ca. 1470)).

[66] WOOLF, THE IDEA OF HISTORY IN EARLY STUART ENGLAND, *supra* note 24 at 29, 32.

The details of this cornerstone would appear in the preface to the *Third Reports,* in which Coke advises a student how to engage in the study of law. Coke first summarized the many authorities available ranging in descending order of authority as comprising reports of cases, royal judicial records, and the various learned treatises of Glanville, Bracton, Littleton, and others. He then cautions the prospective student of law to "beware of chronicle law reported in our Annales" that suggest the error of believing that the familiar institutions of English law were established after the Norman conquest and offers several examples of legal proofs that the laws of England predate the Normans. After this lengthy warning Coke states what the student should believe in the chronicle histories he endorses. Coke tells the student:

> if you will give any faith to them, let it be to those things they have published concerning the antiquity and honour of the common laws: first, they say that Brutus the first King of this land, ...for the safe and peaceable government of his people, wrote a book in the Greek tongue, calling it the Laws of the Britons, ... that the laws of the ancient Britons, their contracts and other instruments, and the records and judicial proceedings of their Judges, were wrote in the Greek tongue, it is plain and evident by proofs luculent and uncontrollable ....

These proofs are to be found in "the commentaries of Julius Caesar," the writings of Pliny the Elder and Strabo, as well as the works of "Gildas, . . . Galfr. [(Geoffrey)] of Monmouth, Will.[iam] of Malmesbury, ..., Polydore Vergil, ...,Caxton, Fabian, ..., and others ...."[67]

---

[67] SIR EDWARD COKE, 2 THE REPORTS, PART III iii–xx, viii, xiv, xv, xx (Jos. Butterworth & Sons, London, 1826) (c.1601). The 'Caxton' referred to is likely the Galfridian chronicle history variant Caxton

Coke then noted that Caesar, Pliny and Strabo all agree that the Celtic Druids of Gaul and Britain were capable of using the Greek language. Caesar further recorded that the Druidic judges and lawyers used Greek "for the dispatching and deciding of causes, as well public as private, … to the end that their discipline might not be made common among the vulgar." Having asserted that the ancient Britons wrote their laws in Greek, Coke proceeds to give three examples drawn from Geoffrey of Monmouth of pre-Christian era British legal texts — Dunvallo's *Stat. Municipalia* and *Leges Judiciare* from 441 B.C., and the laws of Queen Mercia, the *Merchenleg*, from 356 B.C. He follows this with his list of historical sources stating that "it appeareth by them that before the Conquest there were, amongst others, seven volumes or books" of British laws written.[68]

This pre-Norman history is followed by a recounting of the failed attempts by the first Normans and their successors to displace the ancient British laws of England. At which point Coke counseled that to "the grave and learned writers of histories, [his] advice is, that they meddle not with any point or secret of any art or science, especially with the laws of this realm, before they confer with some learned in that profession." It should be remembered that Coke does not base his belief in the law's antiquity on these histories. That was already proven legally in the preface to the *Second Reports* and at the outset of this preface. Rather, he was "using them to illustrate a proof that the law was immemorial which he drew

---

printed in 1480 known as the *Chronicles of England*. *See generally* WILLIAM CAXTON, CHRONICLES OF ENGLAND (Westminster, 1480).

[68] *Id.*, at xv–xx. *See* HISTORY OF THE KINGS OF BRITAIN, *supra* note 21 at 89, 101 (chronicling the law-making of Dunwallo Molumutis and Queen Marcia).

from the thought of the law courts ....”[69] The remainder of the preface to the *Third Reports* is concerned with further “sound advice as to the study of law, the degrees in law and how they are attained, and a brief history of the Inns of Court.”[70] To recap, at this point in the first preface essays to *The Reports*, Coke has affirmed the sovereign supremacy of the ancient law of England, and established the law’s antiquity and its British origins through legal reasoning and historical illustration. He further asserts that an appreciation and understanding of these two things — the sovereign supremacy of the law and its antiquity — are the first thing a student of the law, whether “prince or subject” should possess. Thus, Coke gives authoritative voice to the emerging myth of the ancient constitution of Britain.

In the preface to *Ninth Reports*, Coke would detail the institutional structure of government under the ancient constitution of Britain. He had already asserted the existence of a handful of legal institutions, such as “the Sheriffs,” ”the writ of assise, and other original writs,” and, therefore, “the King’s Courts,” that pre-existed the Norman Conquest in the preface to *Third Reports*.[71] He had been forced to rely upon non-legal sources for historical illustrations of the common law’s antiquity in the earlier preface. In the preface to *Ninth Reports*, Coke in-

---

[69] POCOCK, THE ANCIENT CONSTITUTION, *supra* note 44 at 41. *See id.*, at 38–41 (discussing Coke’s construction of the ‘ancient constitution’ in the Prefaces to *The Reports*).

[70] LYON & BLOCK, *supra* note 62 at 353. *See* SIR EDWARD COKE, 2 THE REPORTS, PART III xxiv–xliii (Jos. Butterworth & Sons, London, 1826) (c.1601).

[71] SIR EDWARD COKE, 2 THE REPORTS, PART III viii–x (Jos. Butterworth & Sons, London, 1826) (c.1601). *See* POCOCK, THE ANCIENT CONSTITUTION, *supra* note 44 at 38–41(discussing and quoting Preface to *Third Reports* ix–xiixiv–xx, xxiii and Preface to *Ninth Reports* xi, xxi–xxiii).

troduced a legal source as authority for historical illustrations of the 'ancient constitution'. At some point in the decade after the publication of *Third Reports* Coke discovered the *Mirror of Justices*, a thirteenth century legal treatise from the reign of Edward I, who had demanded and received the crown of Arthur from the Welsh.[72] The *Mirror of Justices* was purportedly compiled by Andrew Horne around the same time that Edward I was laying the foundation for the establishing of the Inns of Court. Horne was a lawyer and fish merchant in London. He "served as a judge in the Guildhall court," and was the Chamberlain of London from 1320 until his death in 1328. During this time he "carefully compiled a large collection of statutes and London charters, and composed a chronicle of London history and a report of the London eyre of 1321." The *Mirror* itself apparently predates Horne's compilation and its precise origin is unknown. Horne "possessed the only extant copy of the text and ... included it in his large collection of legal materials ...." Horne's revision of the original *Mirror* should be considered "the first of the thirteenth-century updates and abridgements of [ ] *Bracton* [ ], followed by *Fleta* and *Britton* ...." A comparison of it to these better known treatises reveals that "the *Mirror* fits the profile of reputable legal treatises from the same period" in every respect.[73]

Manuscript codices of the *Mirror* had resurfaced in Coke's day, and it was first printed in 1642 around the same time as the second volume of Coke's *Institutes*. It has been republished ten times since, at least twice each century. Doubts about its veracity surfaced in the early

---

[72] *See* R. R. DAVIES, CONQUEST, COEXISTENCE, AND CHANGE—WALES, 1063–1415 355–356 (1987) (discussing the seizure of the Welsh regalia by Edward I).

[73] David J. Seipp, *The Mirror of Justices,* in LEARNING THE LAW: TEACHING AND THE TRANSMISSION OF LAW IN ENGLAND 1150–1900 89–91 (Jonathan A. Bush & Alain Wijffels eds., 1999).

eighteenth century, yet Blackstone included it in his Viner lectures with only minor reservations. It remained a cited legal authority through the early twentieth century in spite of the growing debate over its authenticity until it came to the attention of William Maitland in the late nineteenth century. Maitland already considered Coke and the 'ancient constitution' myth a blight on the study of legal history and the 'true' positivist nature of law, and the continued viability of the *Mirror* could not be allowed.[74] It is primarily due to Maitland's diligent maligning of the *Mirror* that it subsequently became known as "nonsensical fiction," "wholly unworthy of credit," "in which insolence joins hands with romance" — "a curious legal romance." Terming the *Mirror* a "legal romance" is perhaps the most accurate of these many diatribes based upon Maitland's utter disdain. The *Mirror* fits in perfectly with the Plantagenet era of Arthurian romances and chronicles that produced Horne's compilation. Far from detracting from its "standing as an authority for the thirteenth century" state of belief about the state of the law, such a characterization accurately places the *Mirror* in its cultural context. David Seipp's more recent study of the *Mirror* details Maitland's maligning of the *Mirror* and Andrew Horne, and concludes that the *Mirror* "is a reformist textbook on law, it states general propositions with remarkable clarity and insight, and it should be given all the attention it so richly merits."[75]

---

[74] *Id.*, at 107–111. *Compare also* WILLIAM HOLDSWORTH, 2 A HISTORY OF ENGLISH LAW 327–333 (1982) (1903–1936) (agreeing with Maitland's opinion) *and* William C. Robinson, *Introduction* to ANDREW HORNE, THE MIRROR OF JUSTICES xi, xvi–xix (Legal Classic Series ed., 1903) (c.1290) (discussing the critics and supporters of the *Mirror* and questioning Maitland's judgment).

[75] Seipp, *supra* note 73 at 85–88 (quoting from the works of Frederick Pollock, William Holdsworth, and E.S. Turner, among others, all

Coke would subsequently use the *Mirror of Justices* as a legal authority and historical illustration of the ancient constitution of Britain in order to place virtually every aspect of the legal and constitutional institutions of his own day in the pre-Norman era.[76] To Coke the *Mirror* must have seemed the Holy Grail of legal history, for it claimed to be a "summary of the law of persons, or the law of the folk, in five chapters ..., according [to] the virtues and the substances sanctioned by bulls and by holy usages which have obtained since the time of King Arthur in accordance with the rules aforesaid."[77] At the very outset of the preface to the *Ninth Reports* Coke quotes this passage from the *Mirror* together with one to the effect that:

> [t]he law whereof this [*Mirror*] is made, is of ancient usages, warranted by holy scripture; and because it is generally given to all, it is therefore called Common. And for that there is no other law but this alone of antiquities, it is by general Councils or Parliaments permitted to be used by holy usages, &c.

Following which, he states that:

> In this book in effect appeareth the whole frame of the ancient common laws of this realm, as by a few particulars shall appear: as the diversity and distinction of the Courts of Justice (which are officinae legis). And first of the High Court of Parliament, which Court is

in reliance upon Maitland). *id.*, at 112. David Seipp's refreshingly contextual approach to evaluating a historical source should serve as a model to future scholars of the texts of ancient constitutionalism.

[76] POCOCK, THE ANCIENT CONSTITUTION, *supra* note 44 at 41. *See also* Seipp, *supra* note 73 at 85, 108 (discussing Coke's use of the *Mirror* "to support his argument that the institutions of the common law predated the Norman Conquest").

[77] ANDREW HORNE, THE MIRROR OF JUSTICES 3 (Selden ed. 1895) (c.1290).

> mentioned before by the name of Council General of Parliament, ...

From this point on Coke begins to "quote[ ] extensively from the *Mirror* to support his argument that the institutions of the common law predated the Norman Conquest."[78]

Coke used the *Mirror* to craft a comprehensive legal argument placing everything from the Courts of Chancery, King's Bench, Common Pleas, Exchequer, and the circuit-riding Justices in Eyre to the local Frankpledge, baronial and county courts and on through Serjeants-at-law, attorneys, Coroners, Bailiffs, among others in the reign of King Alfred in the ninth century. Also in force in the time of Alfred were various aspects of the common law, from that governing succession of estates to "crimes and their divisions ... [s]o as in this Mirror you may perfectly and truly discern the whole body of the common law of England." Having used the *Mirror* to place the ancient constitution in the reign of Alfred, Coke then pauses his summary, "for this grave and learned author will shew us in this Mirror the great antiquity of the said courts of the common law, and particularly of the High Court of Parliament since the time of King Arthur, who reigned about the year ... 516."[79] Coke conceded that the *Mirror* did not place the origins of Parliament in Arthur's reign, it merely recorded "the laws and usages of this realm continued since the reign of that king." But, the implication is clear that the ancient constitution that Coke had earlier placed in the reign of Brutus flowed faithfully through Arthur as well. Coke painstakingly traces Parliamentary history up to his day before proceeding to

---

[78] SIR EDWARD COKE, 5 THE REPORTS, PART IX iii–iv (Jos. Butterworth & Sons, London, 1826) (1612). Seipp, *supra* note 73 at 108.
[79] SIR EDWARD COKE, 5 THE REPORTS, PART IX iv–x, x, xi (Jos. Butterworth & Sons, London, 1826) (1612).

point out that "[i]n this ancient mirror you may discern as far as the reign of the often named King Arthur, the great antiquity of the officers and ministers of the common law, and of their inferior courts." He then proceeds to painstakingly trace these institutions up to his day before closing — "thus much by way of addition to my former Preface shall suffice."[80] Coke would later use the *Mirror* to trace institutions of the common law into the ancient past of Alfred and Arthur in his *Institutes*.[81] He cites to the *Mirror* in his discussions concerning "Of Kights [sic] Service," "Frank-almoigne," "Of Villenage," "Of Rents," "Of Parceners," "Of Estates upon Condition," "Of Quo Warranto," "The Court of Chancery," "The Court of Exchequer," "The Court of the Justices of the Assize, and Nisi Prius," "The Courts of Wards and Liveries," and, "The Courts in the City of London," for a total of thirty-four citations to the *Mirror* in what was to become the most influential legal treatise of the next two centuries.[82] Coke's use of the *Mirror* to refer to the reign of Arthur in explaining the ancient origins of Quo Warranto process at the Justice-Eyres in the *Second Institutes* provides a useful example of another aspect of the common law mind that is essential to take into account when evaluating ancient constitutionalist claims of the continuity of legal

---

[80] *Id.*, at xi, xi–xxix, xxx, xxx–xxxv, xxxv *See also* POCOCK, THE ANCIENT CONSTITUTION, *supra* note 44 at 39, 41 *and* Seipp, *supra* note 73 at 108.

[81] Seipp, *supra* note 73 at 108 (citing to thirteen different pages in the *Institutes*).

[82] SIR EDWARD COKE, 1 INSTITUTES OF THE LAWES OF ENGLAND 79, 94, 135–138, 140, 142, 154–155, 157–159; 2 INSTITUTES OF THE LAWES OF ENGLAND 498; 3 INSTITUTES OF THE LAWES OF ENGLAND 165, 169, 201; 4 INSTITUTES OF THE LAWES OF ENGLAND 78, 103, 158, 192, 251 (Garland ed. 1979) (1628–1644).

institutions and procedures since time immemorial — the routine use of analogical reasoning.[83]

When authors like Coke and Saltern asserted that there were Quo Warranto proceedings, courts, sheriffs, Parliaments, and so on in the ancient Britain of King Arthur or King Lucius, it is just as likely that they are drawing an analogous relation between the laws, legal officers and juridical institutions of their own day rather than asserting a literal correspondence and unbroken continuity. In his discussion of Selden's use of history in *Titles of Honor*, Woolf nicely characterizes the rationale underlying this analogic form of analysis of available historical sources in the early seventeenth century:

> Institutions, titles, and customs constantly changed in name and form, and it was foolish to assume that the absence in the records of the past of a specific word denoting and officer or rank meant that the thing itself did not exist under another name. The Saxon *ealdormen*, for instance, performed essentially the same role as the post-Norman sheriffs.[84]

Colin Kidd has made a similar observation regarding the common assertions of the pre-Norman antiquity of Parliament, noting that although "Saltern's claim that King Arthur presided over an ancient British Parliament might not stand up to scholarly scrutiny, circumstantial evidence did support the likely existence of an ancient British *concilium*...."[85] Legal writers like Coke, Selden and Saltern were trained to discern and formulate ana-

---

[83] COKE, 3 INSTITUTES, *supra* note 82 at 498.

[84] WOOLF, THE IDEA OF HISTORY IN EARLY STUART ENGLAND, *supra* note 24 at 215.

[85] COLIN KIDD, BRITISH IDENTITIES BEFORE NATIONALISM: ETHNICITY AND NATIONHOOD IN THE ATLANTIC WORLD, 1600–1800 84 (1999).

logical connections like these, as are lawyers in common law jurisdictions to this day. Evaluating such statements as if they asserted, and therefore required, literal historical correspondences in every detail of substance and form in order to be considered valid imposes an inappropriate standard of accuracy the statements are guaranteed to fail to meet.

It is also important to bear in mind that while it is now commonly thought that Polydore Vergil debunked the Arthurian cycle as pure myth, he in fact recounted the basic elements of the *Matter of Britain* as part of Britain's history. Vergil even stated that Arthur "was indeed such a man that, had he lived longer, he would have finally restored the British state, which was all but ruined." It is only after that statement that Vergil then notes that it was precisely because Arthur was such an extraordinary ruler that later generations invented fabulous tales about him so that "even now the common folk praise Arthur to the skies...."[86] Vergil had even recounted the story of King Lucius and his correspondence with Eleutherus, as well as the story of Gorbuduc, Ferrex and Porrex.[87] This continuing belief in both Arthur and Lucius as significant British historical figures is, as has already been noted, utterly common in this period. Selden's mention of Arthur in *Titles of Honor* is paradigmatic of this perception — "[neither can any question be of his raigne, although much is and justly, of his absurd victories.]"[88] Rather than being indications of ignorance, the inclusion of the basic elements of the *Matter of Britain* by Coke, Selden, Craig, Saltern and so many other legal writers in this pe-

---

[86] POLYDORE VERGIL, ANGLICA HISTORIA Bk.3 Par.13 (Basel: 1555), hypertext edition with English translation by Dana F. Sutton, http://www.philological.bham.ac.uk/polverg.
[87] *Id.* at Bk.1 Par. 22, Bk.2 Par. 11.
[88] JOHN SELDEN, TITLES OF HONOR 160 (London, 1614).

riod is indeed utterly unremarkable. What would be truly remarkable would be for any writer in this period to have not believed it was a significant part of British history. Even a scholar now widely credited as being the leading critic and skeptic of the ancient constitution in this period was sufficiently proud of this *British* heritage that he styled himself as "Henrici Spelmanni Equit. Anglo-Brit" in the first edition of his dictionary of ancient words, *Glossarium Archaiologicum*, more fully spelled out by the publisher of the 1687 third edition as "authore Henrico Spelmanno, equite, Anglo-Britanno."[89]

In tracing the origins of the institutions of law and government of his day through the court of Arthur, Coke's works illustrate a common and shared theme of national origins. Such themes of Arthurian origins had permeated the literature of the *Matter of Britain* ever since similar assertions had been deliberately placed therein by Geoffrey of Monmouth in his early twelfth century *Historia Regum Brittaniae* as well as by the un-

---

[89] HENRICI SPELMANNI EQUIT. ANGLO-BRIT. ARCHAEOLOGUS IN MODUM GLOSSARII AD REM ANTIQUAM POSTERIOREM: CONTINENTIS. LATINO-BARBARA, PEREGRINA, OBSOLETA, ET NOUATAE SIGNIFICATIONIS VOCABULA, QUAE POST LABEFACTATAS À GOTHIS VANDALISQ[UE] RES EUROPAEAS, IN ECCLESIASTICIS PROFANISQ[UE] SCRIPTORIBUS; VARIARUM ITEM GENTIUM LEGIBUS ANTIQUIS, CHARTIS ET FORMULIS OCCURRUNT. SCHOLIIS ET COMMENTARIIS ILLUSTRATA, IN QUIBUS PRISCI RITUS QUÁM PLURIMI, MAGISTRATUS, DIGNITATES, MUNERA, OFFICIA, MORES, LEGES, ET CONSUETUDINES ENRRANTUR [SIC] (London, 1626) *and* GLOSSARIUM ARCHAIOLOGICUM. CONTINENS LATINO-BARBARA, PEREGRINA, OBSOLETA, & NOVATAE SIGNIFICATIONIS VOCABULA. QUAE POST LABEFACTATAS A GOTHIS, VANDALISQUE RES EUROPAEAS, IN ECCLESIASTICIS, PROFANISQUE SCRIPTORIBUS, VARIARUM ITEM GENTIUM LEGIBUS ANTIQUIS MUNICIPALIBUS, CHARTIS, & FORMULIS OCCURRUNT. SCHOLIIS & COMMENTARIIS ILLUSTRATA. IN QUIBUS PRISCI RITUS QUAM-PLURIMI, MAGISTRATUS, DIGNITATES, MUNERA, OFFICIA, MORES, LEGES IPSAE, & CONSUETUDINES ENARRANTUR. AUTHORE HENRICO SPELMANNO, EQUITE, ANGLO-BRITANNO (London, 3rd ed., 1687).

known compiler of the early thirteenth century legal text known as the *Leges Anglorum* (ca. 1200). Bruce O'Brien has identified the *Leges Anglorum* as the first instance of such a use of Arthur as a lawgiver. He also notes that "[b]y the time of the Angevins, the [Galfridian] *History* had erased the legal differences not only between the Normans and English, but also between Angevins, Normans, Bretons, Manceaux, Poitevins, Scots, Irish, Welsh, and English").[90] The enduring popularity and influence of such Arthurian origin stories was in large part due to their ability to obscure and transcend the otherwise insurmountable legal and cultural differences between the various peoples, or nations, of the British Isles and continental domains the Norman, Angevin, and Plantagenet dynasties claimed suzerainty over. This persuasively binding Britannic myth had also recently been used by the Tudors to similar effect. The *Matter of Britain* had been employed most recently within the work of John Dee commissioned by Queen Elizabeth in order to support English claims to territories in the New World — *The Limits of the British Empire*. Dee had combined Roman law principles of territorial acquisition requiring both discovery and occupation to acquire full legal title together with assertions of pre-Columbian British discoveries and conquests in what would eventually be termed North America in order to "serve the practical purpose of offering legal justifications for empire." This juridical rhetoric was subsequently employed by the court of

---

[90] Bruce R. O'Brien, *Forgers of Law and Their Readers: The Crafting of English Political Identities between the Norman Conquest and the Magna Carta*, 43 POL. SCI. & POL. 467, 470–472 (2010). O'Brien further suggests that the anonymous author of the *Leges Anglorum* likely included Arthur to increase the likelihood that King John, who wore the sword supposedly carried by Sir Tristan and whose brother Richard had similarly worn a sword reputed to be Excalibur, might heed the lessons of good kingship contained therein. *Id.*

James VI and I in order to expand and secure the English presence in the New World. The Arthurian origins of Britain's trans-Atlantic territorial claims could also be found in legal literature in the section of William Lambarde's 1568 *Archaionomia* that recounts the laws of Arthur titled – *De jure & appendicitis coronae Brytanniae* –within the Laws of Edward the Confessor.[91]

The mental world of ancient constitutionalism stands in stark contrast to the current post-Enlightenment and Darwinian view of the ancient and pre-historic past as per se more primitive and barbaric than the present. In a very real sense, the pre-Enlightenment mental world lacked any concept of a pre-historic past as all of history had been revealed to humanity through the sacred (and therefore incontrovertible) history of Scripture. This point about the now utterly commonplace concept of prehistoric is so crucial that Stuart Piggot began his study of early modern antiquarianism by noting that "the word [prehistoric] was only coined to express a then novel concept in 1851..., and came into general use ... in

---

[91] KEN MACMILLAN, SOVEREIGNTY AND POSSESSION IN THE ENGLISH NEW WORLD: THE LEGAL FOUNDATIONS OF EMPIRE, 1576–1640 61, *passim* (2006). *See also* JOHN DEE, THE LIMITS OF THE BRITISH EMPIRE (Ken MacMillan ed., 2004). *See* WILLIAM LAMBARDE, APXAIONOMIA [ARCHAIONOMIA]: SIVE DE PRISCIS ANGLORUM LEGIBUS LIBRI, SERMONE ANGLICO, VETUSTATE ANTIQUISSIMO, ALIQUOT AB HINC SECULIS CONSCRIPTI, NUNC DEMUM, MAGNO JURISPERITORUM, & AMANTIUM ANTIQUITATIS OMNIUM COMMODO, ÈTENEBRIS IN LUCEM VOCATI. GULIELMO LAMBARDO INTERPRETE. SEXCENTIS I LOCIS À LIBRO IPSIUS CASTIGATA, QUO PRO EXEMPLARI UTIMUR; CUM MULTIS ALIIS ADDITIONIBUS. ACCESSERE IN HAC NOSTRA ULTIMA EDITIONE LEGES HENRICI PRIMI NUNC PRIMÙM EDITÆ, EX MANUSCRIPTO IN FISCO REGIS HABITO: UNÀ CUM GLOSSARIO EARUM ANTIQUO EX MANUSCRIPTO CODICE OLIM S. AUGUSTINI DOROBORNIENSIS. REGU QUI HAS LEGES SCRIPSERUNT NOMENCLATIONEM, & QUID PRÆTEREA TUM PRIMÙM AB ILLO, & NUNC DENUO À NOBIS ACCESSERIT, SUBSEQUENS MONSTRABIT PAGINA 148-49 (Cambridge & London, 1644) (1568).

1865." Furthermore, "for the antiquaries, and indeed the whole literate public over the period with which we shall be concerned, the word would be meaningless, for the Universe was entirely historical from its Creation, documented in an infallible text by an unimpeachable author…."[92]

The standard story of the origins of law told by that sacred history was one of long lost Edenic and Patriarchal Golden Ages of law, governance, and culture from which human societies had progressively fallen away from over the long centuries since the dawn of Creation. This also means that the very concept of *ancient* itself must be corrected from twenty-first century historical standards. Today, the word *ancient* is taken to refer to a time thousands of years ago at the very least, if not even older. Yet for the Tudor and Stuart writers of ancient constitutionalist works, *ancient* most likely meant merely beyond the time of *living* memory; roughly somewhere between one to two hundred years ago rather than thousands of years ago. This much shorter duration of time defining *ancient* lasted well into the nineteenth century, even making occasional appearances in American legal works.[93] Somewhat counterintuitively, the English legal writers of the works reviewed in this study also had another longer view of ancient than the time of living memory. Legal memory had been set by

---

[92] *See generally* PIGGOT, *supra* note 26 at 7.

[93] For example, the first chapter of the first volume of Hening's 1823 Virginia *Statutes at Large* is titled "Ancient Charters, relating to the first settlement of Virginia" and contains, under a matching "Ancient Charters" running title, the 1606, 1609, 1611/12, and 1621 royal charters; materials that hardly seem worthy of the appellation *ancient* as of 1823. WILLIAM WALLER HENING, 1 THE STATUTES AT LARGE : BEING A COLLECTION OF ALL THE LAWS OF VIRGINIA, FROM THE FIRST SESSION OF THE LEGISLATURE, IN THE YEAR 1619 : PUBLISHED PURSUANT TO AN ACT OF THE GENERAL ASSEMBLY OF VIRGINIA, PASSED ON THE FIFTH DAY OF FEBRUARY ONE THOUSAND EIGHT HUNDRED AND EIGHT 57–120 (New York, 1823).

Parliament in the reign of Edward I by the *Statute of Quo Warranto* itself at "before the Time of King Richard our Cousin, or in all his time," which had by the late sixteenth century been simplified through case law to the year 1189. This point further underscores the prior discussion of common law analogical reasoning in that Coke doubtless knew of this statutory origin of *Quo Warranto* proceedings when he linked those origins to the reigns of King Alfred and King Arthur.[94]

Yet another meaning of the word *ancient* is also relevant to more fully deciphering the meaning of the ancient constitution trope. Saltern's status as an *Ancient* of the Middle Temple is a paradigmatic example of this now obscure variant usage of the word ancient to denote a status of venerable dignity and acquired wisdom; or, put another way, a status of reverence; so, *revered constitution* or *cherished constitution* are good variants to keep in mind when considering the meaning and significance of the rhetorical phrase — ancient constitution. The Oxford English Dictionary includes the following historical usage example within this obscure definition of *ancient*: "1792 T. Jefferson *Writings* (1859) III. 347 'Congress would take it off your hands, in compliance with an ancient vote of that body.'" It is doubtful that Jefferson was using the word in its more ordinary sense of denoting great age at a time when Congress had only existed for, at most, 18 years; and, that figure even includes the Continental Congress. A

---

[94] 18 Edw.1 Stat.2 (1290). *See also* GREENBERG, *supra* note 29 at 214: "[s]ince statutes of Edward III and Richard II referred to the lower house as 'ever' present and enjoying a customary right to be summoned, and since all Englishmen knew that 'no custom can begin since Richard I,' then 'it must of necessity follow' that the Commons was summoned before 1189." *Id.* (quoting ROGER TWYSDEN, CERTAINE CON-SIDERATIONS UPON THE GOVERNMENT OF ENGLAND (John Mitchell Kimbell ed., London, 1849) (ca. 1642–1644)).

similar use by Jefferson is in a 1797 letter to James Madison referring to his friendship with John Adams: "I am glad of the first information, because though I saw that our ancient friendship was affected by a little leaven, produced partly by his constitution, partly by the contrivance of others, yet I never felt a diminution of confidence in his integrity, and retained a solid affection for him."[95]

Clearly, the use of *ancient* to mean *revered* rather than merely incredibly old still had some notable adherents almost two centuries after the works of Coke and Saltern. This matches up quite well with "the attitude of early Stuart Englishmen to their law as a form of reverential conservatism."[96] It is also useful to keep in mind the word *antique*, the root of *antiquarian*. In a very real sense the supposed ancient laws and constitutions of Britain were revered and cherished cultural antiques. These late medieval and early modern ways of perceiving the past, and of using the word *ancient*, must be fully and non-judgmentally acknowledged and embraced in order to best understand and appreciate the lasting rhetorical and juridical force of ancient constitutionalism.

---

[95] *Ancient*, OXFORD ENGLISH DICTIONARY, available online at www.oed.com. (quoting Thomas Jefferson, Letter to the Commissioners of Washington (April 9, 1792), *in* 3 THE WRITINGS OF THOMAS JEFFERSON 346 (Washington, D.C.: 1853)). Thomas Jefferson, Letter to Madison, (Jan. 22, 1797), *in* 3 MEMOIR, CORRESPONDENCE, AND MISCELLANIES, FROM THE PAPERS OF THOMAS JEFFERSON 346 (Thomas Jefferson Randolph ed., Boston 2nd ed. 1830).

[96] BRUCE GALLOWAY, THE UNION OF ENGLAND AND SCOTLAND, 1603–1608 38 (1986).

CHAPTER 2

De Antiquis Britanniae Legibus

George Saltern's 'Of the Antient Lawes of great Britaine'

Servato Ius, metue Mortalis Deum
[Preserve the law, mortal, fear God][97]

In addition to concerns that the union would in various other ways destroy or diminish the existing realms of England and Scotland, there were also strenuous objections raised that the union would damage the existing laws and liberties of each, if not requiring an entirely new British legal system. The fear was that adding anything of the laws of Scotland to those of England would create havoc and confusion in the immemorial English common law and destroy the fundamental liberties of English subjects; or, for the Scots, that the English law would totally displace the laws of Scotland and destroy the fundamental liberties of Scottish subjects. Among the many tracts that dealt with this objection, Saltern's *Of the Antient Lawes of great Britaine* is unique in its singular focus on demonstrating the existence of a British common law tradition from the mists of antiquity to his own day in order to assuage the fears of this objection to the union. Pub-

---

[97] The maxim chosen by Saltern for the title page; it also closes the very first paragraph of the work. In light of the multitude of contemporaneous and often inconsistent variant spellings found throughout Saltern's text (i.e. — v for u, j for i, the tilde ~ used above vowels to denote missing consonants, and so on) has been corrected throughout this chapter for ease of reading. The original uncorrected text is reproduced in facsimile in Appendix II.

lished in London in 1605 after Saltern had first "presented the king with a manuscript of his treatise," Saltern's central theme was a call to preserve the common juridical heritage fortuitously blessing both nations at that moment in their shared histories thanks to divine providence; a preservation only the proposed Union could secure.[98] In style, Saltern's work is a kind of juridical sermon delivered as an appeal to the good Christian lawyers of England and Scotland to see "[h]ow Godly and just a thing it is to establish a perfect Unity in these Kingdoms, for the confirmation of an everlasting peace between them," through the work of one who has already demonstrated the Union's benefits "for the increase and propagation of Gods truth . . . in a former treatise," and now "take[s] in hand to speak of our ancient Laws, and God is the beginning and end of my work."[99]

Such a work:

> is no less fit and necessary for this time to be known, then obscure and difficult to expound. For whether we consider our Statutes enacted since the *Norman*, we shall find them grounded upon most just and prudent intentions: or the remnants of our Acts made by the *Saxons*, we shall see them full of Godly & devout ad-

---

[98] WOOLF, THE IDEA OF HISTORY IN EARLY STUART ENGLAND, *supra* note 16 at 61. *See also* JANELLE GREENBERG, *supra* note 29 at 128 (2001) (describing Saltern's work as "a blatantly ancient constitutionalist defence of the union which James himself probably saw and approved."). *But see* GALLOWAY, THE UNION OF ENGLAND AND SCOTLAND, *supra* note 96 at 40 (1986) ("Saltern's work does not, however, appear to have had much influence on popular beliefs, or royal policy!").

[99] This earlier Union Tract by Saltern — *De Vnion Britanni[a]e seu de Regnorum Angli[a]e et Scoti[a]e omniumque adiacentium Insularum Brittanicarum in vnam Monarchiam Consolidatione Deque multiplici eius vnionis vtilitate* — referred to here is regrettably no longer extant. *See* Rogers, *supra* note 29 at 165.

> monitions, or the secret footsteps of the ancient British constitutions, appearing yet in the body of our common Laws, the principles thereof will appear to be the very Laws of the eternal God, written in the two immortal tables of nature & Scripture.[100]

Saltern had opened Chapter One by stating that: "[i]n all actions, in every election, in every counsel and deliberation, it is to be held for a certain and undoubted principle, that, Only things Godly, just, & necessary are to be done, & that with due invocation of Divine assistance, without the which nothing can be done." In all such moments of lasting import "the first consideration ought to be of the end, the second of the means, the third of the effectual working power...." That power is "the spirit of God all sufficient." Based upon this understanding Saltern asserts a foundational principle, "namely that in all innovations there ought to be urgent necessity, or evident uitility." Noting that this principle "was first proposed by a *Pagan* [(Ulpianus)], "[he] would say that it were altogether unperfect & defective...." However, "seeing the same is now taken and pressed by Christians," Saltern proposes a "Christian exposition... that Religion, Piety, Justice, do carry the weight of necessity and utility, and whatsoever is Godly and just, the same is necessary & profitable...." To the contrary, "whatsoever is not Godly & just, the same is not to be done whatsoever necessity or utility may seem to be in it...." He closes this opening paragraph by restating the motto used on the title page in the original wording of Ulpianus — "*Seruato ius et metue mortalis Deum*" [(Preserve justice, mortal, and fear God)] — in order to further emphasize that this foundational

---

[100] GEORGE SALTERN, OF THE ANTIENT LAWES OF GREAT BRITAINE [4] (London 1605) [hereinafter OF THE ANTIENT LAWES].

principle "is much more perfect & absolute" when applied by godly Christians like his British readers.[101]

Drawing on both myth and history Saltern writes like a juridical evangelist in order to reassure his primarily English audience that "England's safety lay . . . in the fact that Scottish and English laws were equally ancient, which meant that neither country need fear the other . . . [by] trac[ing] both legal systems back to the Britons and not[ing] their similarities across the centuries." Saltern credits the apocryphal King Lucius with a central role in preserving, if not in fact "creating the ancient laws," and finds evidence of parliaments in the time of "King Arthur and King Alfred" and "complete with the Commons, as early as Ine's reign." Praises of Lucius — that "Lucid starre of Britaine," and the apocryphal letter from Eleutherus, the Bishop of Rome, extolling the existing British laws as better suited for the British people than those of Rome — provide a running narrative of juridical continuity and wise preservation in Saltern's work. As Saltern notes, the story of how Lucius, supposed King of London circa 150CE, wrote to Eleutherus to request a copy of the laws of Rome so that his newly converted Christian kingdom could receive the blessings of them was to be found in the revered Laws of St. Edward the Confessor as well as in the canonical fifteenth century treatise of English law by Fortescue. Lucius was purportedly told that the existing laws of Britain were by providence already based upon the divine laws of nature and scripture and that he, Lucius, should by no means replace them with Roman laws. For good measure Saltern also cites to Bracton for the basic theme of the king's role as the vicar of God in crafting laws for his kingdom. In Eleutherus's reply to Lucius, he advised Lucius to that "you have there in your kingdom both Testaments [(na-

---

[101] *Id.* at [3]–[4].

ture and scripture)]; out of them, by God's grace and the advice of your realm, take a law, and thereby patiently govern your kingdom."[102] Saltern returns to this story throughout his exploration of the laws and juridical institutions of ancient Britain that follows in order to emphasize his conclusion that "our ancient common laws were begun in the times of the first *Britons*, grounded upon the laws of God, printed in Nature and Scripture, continued by the *Saxons* in their judgement books, & transmitted to us by Saint Edward and the Conqueror." Saltern is not here asserting that the common origin point for both the ancient laws of Scotland and England "was the laws of God, allegedly adopted entire by the 'British' King Lucius…."[103] Saltern is in fact making a more nuanced argument of foundational and inspirational influence, not rote reception of God's laws in their entirety. Before proceeding to that antiquarian exploration of Britain's juridical history, Saltern briefly discusses the Roman laws and law in general in Chapters Two and Three.

Saltern's Chapter Two on Roman law is his shortest, barely covering a page and a half of text. He claims to be discussing Roman law so "that it may appear that neither the reverend Eleutherus was deceived in his judgement, nor the Godly *Lucius* in his choice, nor the learned *Fortescue* in his testimony: but that said ancient Laws were, indeed, as well as by the *Romans* own confession (in that they did not change them) better than their own." Yet, rather than actually compare substantive examples

---

[102] GREENBERG, *supra* note 29 at 128-29. OF THE ANTIENT LAWES at [5]-[7], [31]-[33], [54]. Translated text of Elutherius' letter from: *Glastonbury Abbey, Past and Present. The Rise and Influence of English Monachism*, 66 DUBLIN U. MAG. 631, 640 (Dublin: 1865). See Appendix I, *infra*, for full translated text.

[103] OF THE ANTIENT LAWES at [6]–[7], [80]. GALLOWAY, THE UNION OF ENGLAND AND SCOTLAND, *supra* note 96 at 40.

from both British and Roman laws, Saltern merely refers "the reader that is desirous to know" to consult St. Augustine's *City of God*, the *Twelve Tables*, Justinian's *Institutes*, and various other Roman sources — "a work worthy the vacation of a learned man." A possible explanation for this tacit dismissal of any need to substantively discuss the laws of Rome is to be found later in Saltern's tract wherein he repeatedly defends the native British histories and sources from what he and other native authors considered to be biased accounts of Caesar, Polydore Vergil, and other "Italians."[104] A further reason for so cursorily 'examining' the Roman laws is, of course, the well-known insular reaction against the laws of Rome among the common lawyers of early modern England; a cultural bias to which Saltern would have been fully exposed through his legal education in the Middle Temple.

Saltern opens Chapter Three's jurisprudential discussion of law in general by combining Aristotle's definition of law as "a covenant of the society of men" with Tully's as "the reason and mind of God discerning just and unjust." Thus rendering law into a "covenant made by God with the society of men, according to his own reason, discerning just & unjust," which "agrees with the words of *Moses*" and is therefore "a perfect definition." The purpose of law is to assure God's "blessings of this life, and the life to come." He then states the standard jurisprudential distinction drawn from Roman law of laws being either "Divine or Human," as either "those which god immediately made, first written in nature, secondly described in the ten commandments, & the Scriptures" or those drawn by application of the general principles of divine laws for the benefit of "the principal parties *viz.* to God, to the

---

[104] OF THE ANTIENT LAWES at [8]–[9], [61–[62]. *Compare* SELDEN, JANI ANGLORUM, *supra* note 46 at 41 ("Away then with *Polydore Virgil*, who fetches *Sheriffs* from the *Norman* Conqueror.").

common estate, and to private men according to the twelve Tables: secondly to particular circumstances of Persons, things, actions, times, places, Penalties and such like, as the Institutes are divided."[105] In that Saltern passed over any detailed discussion of the *Twelve Tables* or the *Institutes*, one might imagine a contemporary reader puzzling over exactly what Saltern is referring to here. However, this can also be interpreted as an indication that Saltern is confident his intended audience of lawyers is already sufficiently familiar with these, to his trained mind, basic and therefore obvious juridical classifications.

Saltern next notes, again crediting Tully, that any human law contrary to the divine law is "not to be called a Law, (although all the world in a joint Parliament confirm it[])]." Such a law would not be properly derived from the divine law, constituting "not a covenant of God, but a confederacy against God." In that Saltern will repeatedly assert that the British common laws are properly derived from divine law, this may be a subtle hint to his readers that opposition to the proposed Union would also be "a confederacy against God." Having made this point, he then states that law should have three properties and effects: "first to make a distinction of just from unjust, secondly to command and forbid, thirdly to punish and reward." Divine law accomplishes these ends "originally and generally," while humane law does so "secondarily and particularly." In order to be a "[t]rue Law" a law should be "honest, just, possible, agreeable to nature and custom, to time and place, necessary or profitable and manifest…." The binding power of law should be focused on "knowledge, obedience, & punishment: no man may break it, no man may be ignorant of it;" and, once made, no single person is allowed to judge the law's fitness for themselves. Law's performance "is called

---

[105] OF THE ANTIENT LAWES at [10].

Justice," whereas its moderation "is called equity." Standing in contrast to law "are injury, injustice, iniquity, wrong, force, fraud, & such like." Happiness is the ultimate end of both divine and humane law. For the latter this "consists chiefly in the conservation of Religion, Peace, and Justice."[106]

Having established this basic juridical template, Saltern proceeds to summarily discuss and identify the current institutions and offices within Britain whereby these general and particular attributes of law are administered and enforced. He will return to specific examples in later chapters to assert and praise instances of wise preservation of and continuity with the ancient British common laws, as well as to note and condemn examples of failure to do so. Before proceeding to laws of the ancient Britons, though, Saltern states the necessity of examining the origins of those original "Inhabitants of this Land."[107] In asserting at the outset of Chapter Four his view that the "Nations of Britain [were] descended of *Gomer* the Son of *Japhet*, whose children, after the division of tongues, at *Babel*, spread throughout all *Europe*, & so replenished this Island," Saltern places the ancient origins of the British nations within the nobler branches of humanity's tree of descent as recounted in that second source of divine law, Scripture.[108] The sacred history of the Bible was considered the most authoritative source possible in this era. Recall as well Camden's defense of constitutional myth-making: "Let Antiquities her[e]in be pardoned, if by entermingling falsities and truths, humane matters and divine together, it make the first beginnings of nations and cities more noble and sacred, and of greater majestie: seeing that, as Pliny writeth, Even to

---

[106] *Id.* at [10]–[12].
[107] *Id.* at [14].
[108] *Id.* at [14]–[17]

falsely claime and challenge descents from famous personages, implieth in some sort a love of virtue."[109]

By claiming descent for the Britons from one of the two blessed sons of Noah, Sem and Japhet, rather than the one fated by God to be their servant, Cham, Saltern is fixing the origins of the ancient Britons in as noble a family tree as he credibly can. He then strengthens this claim by noting that the sons of Japhet's son, Gomer, are known to "learned men" as "the ancient *Kimbri* or *Gomeri*,... and the ancient Britons do yet call their country Cimbri" — drawing a connection to the Welsh referring to themselves as *Cymry* and Wales as *Cymru*. Furthermore, the other nations that later came to Britain are also descended from the sons of Japhet: "the *Saxons* and *Danes* of *Ashkenaz*, and the Scots, [o]f *Iberi* of *Tuball*, and all of *Japhet*." Even the claimed Gaelic and Trojan origins of the ancient Britons and Scots trace back into the blessed sons of Noah, "the *Trojans* themselves from *Ashkenaz*" and the Gaels ("*Getae*") "from *Gether*, the Son of *Sem*...." In identifying "the Inhabitants of this Isle" as "a most ancient nation of the posterity of *Japhet*," Saltern is justified "with reason, & with the best warrant of authority, to think they were governed by such Laws, and institutions derived from the Principles of the first age, that is from the Law of God written in nature...." This is the central tenet, or perhaps conceit, of ancient constitutionalism — that the more ancient a law, principle, or governmental institution is, the better it is due to its proximity to that sacred origin point when God first instructed humanity in law and government.[110]

Chapter Five finds Saltern returning to the Epistle of Eleutherus in order "to speak somewhat in general of the Laws instituted by our Christian King *Lucius* upon re-

---

[109] CAMDEN, *supra* note 37 at 8–9.
[110] OF THE ANTIENT LAWES at [17]–[18].

ceipt of *Eleutherus* Letters, meaning to descend in to particularities, by easy paces and degrees." It is in this chapter that Saltern sets a template for "every prudent, sober, & Christian Politician" to distinguish good and noble British kings, like *Lucius*, from those unjust and ignoble. It is also where he first decries the loss of verifiable indigenous historical sources "through the rage of the *Romans* and other savage idolaters, the scourges of this kingdom, in her godly infancy…," thereby establishing a viable mitigating defense against variant non-British sources "by *Polydore* and other Italians," such as the English history written in the reign of Henry VII by Polydore Vergil. Saltern reminds his reader that Lucius demanded "to have the Laws of *Rome* and *Caesar*," only to be instructed that "[w]e may … always reprove the Laws of *Rome* & *Caesar*," followed by "an exhortatio[n], to take a Law for his Kingdome, out of the Law of God" instead. The rationale for this as contained in the Epistle and subsequently confirmed by Edward the Confessor and Bracton is that as a king Lucius is "Gods Vicar, therefore you must rule by Gods Law & not by *Caesars*." Furthermore, it was God who "anointed [Lucius] to be King," not Caesar. This discussion is bracketed by Saltern rhetorically asking his readers, "what then would you do, being a godly Christian, upon the reading of such a Letter?" Saltern's answer is that "there is no man but will say that King *Lucius* did accordingly: that according to the contents and directions received, he did call a Counsel or Parliament, a thing used in those times, as I will show hereafter…." Saltern accomplishes two things here; first, he put the onus on skeptical readers to explain why they would have failed to follow the advice of Eleutherus, and second, foreshadows his later discussion of the antiquity of British parliamentary governance.[111]

---

[111] *Id.* at [19]–[22], [61]. The English history so roundly derided

Having set the stage to his rhetorical advantage, Saltern proceeds to assert that Lucius and his counselors "did survey the State and Laws of his Kingdom; that which was agreeable to God's holy word he did confirm, and that which wanted he did newly enact." The success of this ancient restatement project is evident in that "he ruled the *Britons* long time after in flourishing peace and tranquility." Lucius even had the "consent of his Nobles or people, seeing all, or the most part, yea the *Druids* and *Flamines* embraced Christian religion together with him, as our Histories testify…." Saltern then extols the manifest benefit of the process of the common law in remedying the "many times the importunity of men brings to pass, while they seek to cure one evil, they shake and weaken the public estate." For Saltern, "that nothing ought to be in the Law against reason [] is the universal Maxim, the main foundation, and as I may call it, the abridgement of all our common Law, which here you see to be the rule of those ancient fathers… [t]his is it whereby all our questions, and controversies, all our arguments and judgments, all our Statutes and customs, are ruled and overruled, enlarged and corrected." Not only do various (still to be stated) substantive parts of the common law originate in the ancient British past, the very method of common law jurisprudence does as well. Saltern closes chapter five by praising not only Lucius for keeping the best of the then ancient (and pagan) British laws, but also King Alfred for having also followed the advice of Eleutherus when he translated the best of the British laws "into *Saxon*; and so continued them to posterity." This common law process of preserving, adapting and augmenting the best of the past to meet the needs of the present is the noble pattern Saltern finds among not only the pagan British kings that preceded noble Lucius, but also in each and every period of British history up to

---

throughout by Saltern is, of course, Vergil's *Historia Anglorum*.

his day. Throughout Saltern's text one can discern that the ancient constitution so loftily and reverently praised by early modern British jurists is less one of precise substantive details than it is of general common law institutions and procedures; a guiding tradition of rule of law constitutionalism rather than an unchanging constitution of specific rules and provisions. Saltern's opening use of the plural *ancient British Constitutions* usefully illuminates this crucial distinction. Having identified this godly pattern in the reigns of Lucius and Alfred, Saltern turns to an exploration of "the remnants of the Laws of nature" to be seen in Britain's pre-Lucian pagan forms of governance.[112]

Saltern begins Chapter Six by observing that the most common form of ancient governance know from the available histories is that of "Kings or Princes, their Priests, their Elders or Senators, and their Dukes or Captains." This, then, is the most readily discernible remnant of "the Law of God & Nature" to be found in the ancient world. Citing Caesar, Saltern notes that ancient Britain had its "*Reges, Druidae, Principes, et Nobiles Duces*." He further clarifies that although some of the British *Reges* identified by Caesar were in fact sub-kings or mere princes, "such as we now call Earls or Dukes," nonetheless Caesar and other sources definitively show that "*Cassibellan*," "*Belinus* and *Brennus*, *Mulmutius*" and others genuinely "were Kings of this Island." Among these "ancient Kings as likewise of their Elders or Nobles," Saltern identifies two basic types — the paternal and the tyrannical — carrying through the distinction between good and noble kings in the pattern of Lucius and unjust and ignoble ones he established in chapter five. The former "ha[d] and maintain[ed] the authority of the first age," whereas the latter "obtained their authority by

---

[112] *Id.* at [5], [22]–[27].

war, violence or Rebellion." Both, he admits, are to be found in Britain's history. At this point in the text, Saltern's narrative takes a rather curious turn. Instead of continuing on with a comparative recounting of the forms of governance associated with each of these two ancient constitutional archetypes, Saltern engages in a muddled etymological discussion in order to allege British origins for the terms Thane, Ealdorman, and Senator; all of which he states to be synonymous with the "Elders or Nobles" of ancient Britain.

This narrative divergence reveals two aspects of Saltern's work. First, that it is not the cautiously researched and patiently crafted work of a professional historian. Second, the discussion Saltern proceeds with is instead clearly the product of a lawyer trained in the analogical reasoning methodology of common law jurisprudence. Sober students of history are not his audience, his fellow common lawyers are. Seen in this light, Saltern's apparent detour into etymology arguably does support his contention that ancient Britain had both paternal and tyrannical systems of governance. Saltern may also be forgiven this now clearly error-ridden discussion in that the professional disciplines of historians and etymologists of today were still at least two centuries away from his time. His contention of British origins for the Danish Thane and the Irish Tane in that "only the *Britons* use the word *Heane*, or *Hane*, to signify an Elder; which answers to the word *Thane*, as I said both in letter, signification & use" would have been reasonably sensible to his audience. So would his assertion that the Saxons abandoned their word "*Graves* or *Greves*, signifying a governor" in favor of the British "name of Elder," slightly modifying it to "Earls or eldermen." His contesting any claim that "that the *Britons* used the name of *Senator*, or borrowed this name of the *Romans*" on the grounds that "they lived in perpetual hatred and hostility with [the Romans], as they showed upon all occasions, & followed not their laws, nor institutions in any thing: but by constraint, seeing them to be Pagans, Idolaters, oppressors of their liberty, and persecutors of their Religion" is also an understandable error influenced by both the fervent opposition to all things Roman or Papist in post-Reformation Britain and the lack of any comprehensive and accurate knowledge of the juridical fusions of Roman and British culture that took place in Roman Brittania. Saltern's conclusion "that the *Britons* took this name & other institutions, not of [the Romans], but either of the ancient statutes of nature, or of the latter restitution by the Gospel" is of a piece with Saltern's overarching theme of the legacy of good King Lucius.[113]

Chapter Six is brought to a close with a discussion of how "[t]hese Nobles therefore together with the Priests & other selected commons, made the common Counsel of this Island whereof *Caesar* speaks, and which at this day is called Parliament, and in most of our Histories called *consilium Sapientum*." This parliamentary precursor is also to be found, according to Saltern, "[i]n the Laws of *Edward* before the conquest…." Furthermore, "in the Laws of King *Ine* made about the year 720… there is mention of this Parliament consisting of these degrees of men." Saltern then traces the origins of these parliamentary councils to "*Bertha*, the Christian Queen of *Kent*" a century earlier, and then a "hundred years before that again in the time of *Arthur* the warrior…." The laws of King Alfred are then cited to in support of the assertion that these common councils originated in "the time of King *Lucius*… after [whose] death, this Kingdom con-

---

[113] *Id.* at [27]–[31]. That such an incorporation of elements of Roman law did in fact occur in post-Roman Britain has recently been made clear. *See generally* chapters 2 through 4 of WATKINS, *supra* note 17 (discussing in detail the influence of Roman law on the ancient laws of Wales, which are the most complete surviving texts of the ancient British laws).

tinually labored with intestive wars, in which" according to Alfred "it was almost impossible to gather counsels, and to establish Laws and government," making the accomplishments of these named rulers highly praiseworthy. Finally, without citation or support, Saltern claims "as it was in the south part of *Britain*, so it was in the north, as appears by their Chronicles." Scotland too "had Kings, Priests, Nobles, and Parliaments, agreeable to the form of government of the most ancient Kingdoms, and to the laws of God written in Nature & Scripture: and in this form consists the estate of both the Kingdoms of great *Britain* even to this day." Having discussed "thus much concerning the principal persons, whereof the body of our state did and does consist," Saltern states that "the next thing to be considered is of things according to the proceedings of" these institutions. However, "because nothing can be without a place, and we shall have better occasion to speak of the division, property and dominion of things hereafter," Saltern proposes to first discuss "the ancient division of this Island, the common place & subject of our discourse, and of the judgements therein anciently used." The former is the subject of Saltern's seventh chapter and the latter of his eighth chapter.[114]

The central assertion of Chapter Seven is that the ancient Britons were a civilized rather than a barbarous

---

[114] OF THE ANTIENT LAWES at [31]–[33]. The "intestive wars" referred to by Saltern were a common feature of ancient Britain and early medieval Wales owing to the system of partible inheritance found in the indigenous laws of the Celtic cultures. The history of Medieval Wales is a paradigmatic example. See e.g., WATKINS, *supra* note 16 at 57–61. Terming these "intestive," however, likely stems from the more recent practice established by the Tudors of leaving the Crown through Wills, rather than allowing the common laws of inheritance and succession to dictate successors; hence "intestive wars" could be paraphrased as wars of intestacy. These "civil wars" are referred to throughout by Saltern as examples of periods of tyrannical governance in ancient Britain.

people, as illustrated by their divisions of land in principalities, cities and towns. "It is thought by some," Saltern states, "that this Island before the coming of the *Romans*, was rude and barbarous: & by other, that King *Alfred* was the divider of this Island into such Shires and portions (for so the word imports) as at this day we see." To "these two opini[on]s," Saltern, however, "cannot yield; for if [he] understands our stories, it will easily appear that this land was anciently long, before *Alfreds* time, divided almost into as many parts, & in like manner by the several families or nations of ancient *Britons*…." Saltern then quotes the list of ancient British nations from Hooker's *Description of England*, noting that "of these some (as Mr. Camden plainly shows) possessed one, others two or three of these Shires which are now known." Furthermore, the identities of these pre-Roman British nations are confirmed by none other than two of the chief proponents of the barbarous view, Caesar and Polydore Vergil, as well as by Camden. Therefore, "King *Alfreds* division seems not altogether new, but rather a reviving and more exact description of the old," which was not incidentally a claimed restorative goal of James VI and I's union proposal as well.[115]

Not only were the basic territorial divisions the same among the ancient Britons, they also had "diverse great Cities" and "Towns and Castles innumerable." This, for Saltern, is definitive proof of a civilized people, "[f]or if civility take his name of a City, or Citizen; & Cities, & Citizens cannot be ruled without good laws, the Britons were civil, and ruled with good Laws…." He underscores his point by stressing the inconsistency of "Caesar and other *Romanists*" calling "the Britons barbarous, and yet confess that they had many good Cities, Kings, Nobles, Governors, discipline of war, and peace, commerce, and

---

[115] *Id.* at [33]–[34].

traffic with foreign Nations, and all other parts of civility." That recent denouncers of Britain's noble past, like Polydore Vergil, make much of the lack of any references to the English names of "Canterbury, Bath, Garled, and Leicester" in the older Roman sources is, Saltern, drily notes, "somewhat ridiculous" in the face of the many Roman references to well-known British cities by their Latin names such as "*Londinium, Louentium & Maridunum*," and Vergil's own observation "that it was a Law among the *Britons*, that the inner parts of the Island should not be discovered to strangers." To this Saltern adds the comment that even those "barbarous touches" that did undeniably exist among the ancient Britons themselves are more properly seen as evidence of a prior history of civilized society, "the wild fruits of long continued civil wars that raged amongst them." In that "*Italy, France* and other Countries" suffered similar periods in their histories without being judged utterly barbarous and primitive, so too were these aspects of pre-Roman Britain the exceptions rather than the rule. Overall "the *Britons* maintained the manners of the ancients, so in that ancient division of this Land into several Nations and families, the most antique manner of great nations was observed." No less than "the *Hebrewes, … Persians, Athenians, Romans*," the ancient Britons had "good and Politic constitutions." These forms of governance were "agreeable to reason and nature, and … most consonant to the word of God."[116]

In Chapter Eight Saltern expounds upon the extent to which the ancient Britons used laws of real property, personal property, and outlawry derived from the divine law of nature as further proof they were a civilized society long before the Romans arrived to allegedly bestow the blessings of civilization on a barbarous and backwards

---

[116] *Id.* at [35]–[38].

people. "As in the distribution of persons, and of land, the *Britons* were politic and civil[,]" he begins, "so in their proceedings of Law, in their judgements, and in their Sciences, it appears that they were not so barbarous as has been taken…." For those who may doubt the veracity of this broad range of civilized attributes among the ancient Britons, Saltern suggests they consult the *Historia Britanniae Defensio* [*A Defence of the British History*] of Sir John Prise written for the court of Edward VI. Noting the strong inference that "any Nation given to the studies of all excellent learning, must needs be polished with good laws," Saltern's discussion turns to specific examples. Whether the ancient Britons understood the "distinction of properties" real and personal, or merely held all things in common in a pre-legal state of nature is the first issue addressed. In contrast to "the opinion conceived by *Gratian* that all things by the Law of nature, were common," Saltern asserts that "the distinction of properties was enacted by Almighty God in the beginning" citing Genesis 1:28–29: "Bear rule over the earth: which gave to man both dominion and property of all things." Even Cain and Abel possessed separate fields and properties, "and Cities inhabited," rather than holding all in a familial commons. After them, the Patriarchs added commerce and civil order to the expanding societies of the first peoples; the histories of those generations "mention … buying and selling, and [] diverse offences punished by Law."

Given this is, for the mental world of Saltern's day, the very beginnings of mankind, it begs the question — "by what Law, if not by the Law of nature?" In what is becoming a common turn in Saltern's text, he turns his Roman source against itself. In that the law of nature is acknowledged by Gratian to be "the same which is contained in the Law & the Gospel" and that he asserts that "the ten commandments be an abridgement or exposition of the Law of nature," it follows then that the consistent prohibitions against coveting "other men's goods" throughout those sacred sources is good proof that property, both real and personal, is an inherent and original part of the laws of nature — "for where there is no *Law*, there is no transgression says *St. Iohn*, & other law there is not to condemn a Pagan."[117]

As it unfolds, Saltern's discussion in Chapter Eight provides a vital clue to understanding the juridical trope of ancient constitutionalism. The legal continuity over time is not one of precise substantive provisions; it is one of reasonably similar forms and procedures preserved and adapted by different generations and iterations of British peoples — the very spirit of common law jurisprudence. At its simplest the trope of ancient constitutionalism is nothing more or less than a juridical truism — fidelity to the best of the past promises stability and prosperity for the present and the future. Saltern's purpose is not to prove that there were no differences whatsoever between the laws of the pre-Roman ancient Britons, the Romano-Britons, the post-Roman Britons, the Anglo-Saxons, Scots, Danes, Welsh, Normans and their descendants up to his time. Rather, Saltern emphasizes that all these sometimes disparate peoples of British history possessed and valued good laws and stable governance. Saltern's basic point here is that the ancient Britons had any law and civil government at all, rather than being the rabble of painted barbarians the *Roman* detractors of the *Matter of Britain* deride them as having been.[118]

---

[117] *Id.* at [38]–[40]. The work by Sir John Prise that Saltern refers to was written specifically to refute Vergil's criticism of Galfridian chronicle history in the *Historia Anglorum*. An edited translation has recently been published. JOHN PRISE. HISTORIAE BRITTANICAE DEFENSIO / A DEFENCE OF THE BRITISH HISTORY: STUDIES AND TEXTS (Ceri Davies ed. and trans. 2015).

[118] This assertion that the pre-Roman Briton's were a civilized people has been confirmed by more recent scholarship. *See, e.g.*, WATKINS, *supra* note 17 at 1–7 (discussing the "highly developed and sophisti-

It is the inspirational influence of the divine law of nature, "that law which is everywhere the same (howsoever some authorities have swayed to the contrary)...[,]" that provides the continuity discussed in his eighth chapter not the vagaries and specifics of each land's and people's substantive law. This becomes clear as Saltern continues:

> ... we find partly by the words of *Caesar & Dio*, that this Island had her own laws concerning the division of grounds, inheritances, Judges, & the distinction of properties, that there were certain courses of proceedings, and that there were punishments for contempts and offences.

Saltern arrives at this conclusion from Diodorus' statement "that 20 years after the coming hither of *Caesar*; *Brittania suis Legibus usa est*; Britain used her own Laws..." together with Caesar's well-known description of the jurisdiction of the Druids, who "judge for the most part of all public and private controversies." The matters under their jurisdiction included "any offence or Homicide..." and controversies "for bounds or inheritance...." Should any parties "stand not to their decree, they forbid them their sacrifices." Every aspect of a complete legal system is inferred from Caesar's words:

> under the names of offences and Homicides, he comprehends all criminal causes; under controversies of lands or inheritance are contained all civil actions; by the words of controversy, judgement, determination and decree, he shows that they had a certain form of

---

cated oral tradition[s]" and material, constitutional and legal cultures of pre-Roman British society) *and* T. M. CHARLES-EDWARDS, WALES AND THE BRITONS 350–1064 221 (2013) ("In AD 40, the British rulers of southern Britain had a coinage, were part of a trading system that revolved around the Empire, and had the ability to organize the building of great hill forts.").

> proceedings: by punishments and rewards, he shows that their sentence was compulsive.

This meets the basic elements of a legal system as defined by no less than Justinian in Saltern's view.[119]

Saltern acknowledges at this point that he is relying on inferential reasoning and offers a defense of his validity in doing so — "it must needs be inferred upon *Caesar's* words, that they had a certain form of conveyance and course of inheritance in their lands; For else how could controversies of inheritance and Lands arise to be decided in judgement?" Determining what those ancient British forms of property law may have been therefore requires a course of further inferential speculation based upon the survival of "relics of the fatherly age, wherein the Law of nature was with great wisdom observed," a course which Saltern readily embarks upon. Ranging from "our ancient form of conveyance by Feoffment and Liverie" to the grants of land and inheritance from Noah to Sem, Abraham to Isaac, and Isaac to Jacob, Saltern can "find no beginning unless [he] bring[s] it to those ancient times." In all of these instances there is the same need for "preciseness of words: I give you…[,]" an accurate description of the things to be granted, and the necessity of witnesses. For Saltern, even the basic principles of primogeniture and degrees of inheritance in the absence of a male heir are to be discerned in those ancient sacred sources. The similar forms and even some words, such as "heirs" are "either taken from the same law of nature, and example of the Patriarchs…: Or else it was instituted by King *Lucius* after the example of God himself."[120]

---

[119] OF THE ANTIENT LAWES at [40]–[42].
[120] *Id.* at [42]–[43].

Saltern brings his examples up to the present "manner of our succession by inheritance, & how one heir is to take after another, as they are in degrees of proximity" with a citation to *Ratcliffes Case* from Coke's Third Reports together with a pertinent quote from Coke's report of that case to the effect that "the common law is founded upon the Word of God." Then, perhaps caught up in the spirit of indigenous insularity inculcated by the Inns of Court into the English common lawyer, Saltern oversteps himself by sermonizing that "this our manner of conveyance, and limitation of inheritance, I have not read of in any other nation, neither can find any other beginning for it." Having laid the foundation for merely proving the existence of legal institutions and forms among the ancient Britons, he undercuts his position by claiming a degree of precise continuity his thesis does not actually require. Yet, like a revivalist preacher who has successfully stoked the enthusiasm of his intended audience, Saltern forges ahead with examples of the survival of those ancient requirements of precise granting and descriptive language, and presence of witnesses drawn from medieval English land patents. In doing so, he takes care to point out the references in those patents to even earlier ones, such as "a patent of King *Arthur* the worthy" contained in one of Henry II to the "Monastery of *Glastonbury*...." The final patent Saltern discusses is one "to the Abby of Croyland" from "King *Edred*" which not only granted the land but also "many ancient Customs and new liberties; by which may be understood the use of the Common law then and long before." The combination of "ancient Customs and new liberties" illustrates the preserving and adaptive qualities at the heart of common law jurisprudence.[121]

---

[121] *Id.* at [43]–[44]. Ratcliffe's Case, 76 ENG. REP. 713, 725–726; 3 COKE'S REP. 37a, 40a–40b (1592). The Glastonbury patent is, of

Saltern proceeds by asserting that the very "Manner of suits in Law, & taking distresses or pledges, & that the defendant should find sureties or mainpernors" in the "laws of King *Ine*" and the Book of Job. The taking of pledges, distresses and sureties is "a thing very ancient,... & yet continuing amongst us...." In addition to the prohibition against distraining millstones, Saltern then cites further to the sacred history of the Old Testament as to link "[o]ur ancient kinds of punishments, as by imprisonments, Fetters, Stocks. &c..." and "Capital executions to the divine law of nature. Saltern closes Chapter Eight with a lengthy discussion of the antiquity of the law of outlawry: "[l]astly our punishment by outlawry seems to be most ancient, & of the same beginning; for take *Bractons* description of outlawry, and compare it with the words of *Caesar*, and both with some passages of Scripture: and you shall find them agree very near together." In all these times, cultures and places the law of nature was given force through each legal system so that the outlaw "forfeited his Country and his possessions, the profits of his labour, & of his ground, his friends and his peace." Throughout all these societies and across the centuries can be seen the signs of civilized jurisprudence — "the ancient visible footsteps, of the law of nature."[122]

Saltern expands upon this established foundation of ancient British legal traditions in Chapter Nine by exploring specific examples "of the ordinances instituted by our ancient *Briton* Kings, agreeable to the word of God, and to this day remaining." It is here where we first meet Brutus in Saltern's tract, only after he has discussed in lengthy detail the same history elsewhere recounted by Camden

---

course, the very land patent that Henry II arranged in order to tie his court to the legacy of King Arthur. Saltern's use of it places him in a long line of British authors seeking to link their own narratives to the *Matter of Britain*, including Prise's *Historiae Brittanicae Defensio* which Saltern here cites to. PRISE, *supra* note 117 at 195–205.

[122] OF THE ANTIENT LAWES at [44]–[47].

and Selden of the ancient Britons and their laws from the Celtic Druids described by Julius Caesar and the various kings of the Celtic tribes, such as Cassibellan and Cingetorix, whom he describes as descending from the same heritage as "the famous *Brennus* that overran *Italy*, [who] was King of *Britain*." As he did in Chapter Four where he excused Camden's speculative history of the origins of the ancient Britons by stating, "neither will I prejudice any man's opinion, (though to [him] somewhat improbable) in deriving us from the *Trojans* ...," Saltern continues to follow this path of non-judgmental treatment of the Trojan origin myth of Brutus found in the works of Camden, Craig, and Selden. Yet he doesn't actually adopt this Trojan origin himself, and at this point pauses to note that:

> [a]lthough concerning the History of *Brutus*, there may be some reasons to doubt which learned men have gathered, yet, why there should not be one *Brit* or *Brute* King of this Land, whose Pedegree Sir John Prise out of an ancient Chronicle derived from *Japhet*: And if there were no such *Brit*, yet why the whole History of Briton Princes should for the fabulous interposition of one or two men be rejected, as some have done?

Stating that he "see[s] no reason seeing the concurrent testimonies of divers British monuments of great credit" for such a blanket rejection, Saltern then goes on to recount the myth of Dunwallo Mulmutius as the first great lawgiver of ancient Britain before King Lucius. Saltern's treatment of the origin myth of Brutus is worthy of notice in that belief in the Brutus story as history was in fact quite high in the early seventeenth century.[123] His cau-

---

[123] *Id.* at [48]. *See* GALLOWAY, *supra* note 96 at 51 ("[B]elief in the Brutus myth, the least credible part of the English case, remained high in the early seventeenth century.").

tionary use of the Brutus myth should in fact serve to counter erroneous perceptions of his having made ignorant use of history in favor of mythical fancy.

He introduces Mulmutius by challenging those who call into question "not only the History of Brit, but of his successors" to account for the fact that so many of the writers of Britain's history were no doubt familiar with "the writings of *Gildas* the wise Priest, and *Alfred* the excellent Prince," both of whom credited Mulmutius with instituting the laws "which were afterward called *Mulmutinae*, which *Gildas* translated into Latin, as he confessed himself, (say they) and afterwards King *Alfred* turned them into English." Based upon these (for Saltern) unimpeachable witnesses, he concludes that Mulmutius in fact existed, as did his laws. Furthermore, these laws had to be "very just" or else the Christian Gildas and Alfred "would not have translated and preserved them." Saltern's final introductory point in chapter nine is that the Mulmutian laws were still part of "our common Laws, although hardly to be discerned which they be: for the same writers testify that they being mingled amongst the laws of *Alfred*, were by *St. Edward* reduced to one common Law, which the Norman yielded unto, and himself and all his successors are sworn to observe them." After noting that this ancient common law is still known in his own day as "the Laws of Edward," Saltern concludes the introductory paragraphs of this chapter with the bold statement: [b]ehold therefore the Fathers, yea and the very name of our common Law." Saltern then quotes liberally from Book 1, para. 25 of Vergil's *Anglica Historia* to the effect that Dunwallo Mulmutius: "made laws for Sanctuaries, for weights, for measures: against theft, robbery, and other offences: for high ways & Nuisances, and for tillage and Husbandry…[;]" all of which laws, for Saltern, "are now, either continuing in the common Law, or revived by Statutes…." He then recounts, again following Vergil, how Mulmutius first divided the realm into counties, noting that the ancient rulers "*Brecus* and *Fergusius*, likewise in Scotland, near about the same time" similarly divided that realm into constituent units and established similar laws.[124]

Chapter Nine concludes with a discussion of how these ancient laws show that "Churches, Plows, Cities and High-ways, should enjoy a Privilege or liberty," relying upon Ranulf Higden's fourteenth century *Polychronicon*, "the best-known late medieval chronicle...."[125] Saltern notes Higden's characterization of this "Privilege or liberty" as a "kind of Sanctuary, ..., which interpretation cannot be made but only of the Church...." A mischaracterization Saltern encourages his readers to "let pass, as made by a Monk ignorant of Law."[126] This is a sort of lawyer's aside similar to Coke's cautionary note to law students in the preface to the second part of *The Reports* that they should "beware of chronicle law reported in our Annales" because they could be led astray. Saltern and Coke both exhibit a lawyer's desire to "enforce a distinction between documents with the status of official records and those that had not, a point often over-

---

[124] OF THE ANTIENT LAWES at [49]–[52]. It is worth noting that while no one has yet to definitively confirm the historical existence of Dunwallo Mulmutius, or Dyfnwal Moelmud, he is still credited with this role as an early lawgiver in the most recent comprehensive history of Welsh law. *See* WATKINS, *supra* note 17 at 35–40.

[125] OF THE ANTIENT LAWES at [52]. WOOLF, READING HISTORY IN EARLY MODERN ENGLAND, *supra* note 16 at 13. Higden's *Polychronicon*, "the first truly 'universal' history written in England," was printed in 6 different editions and translations between 1480 and 1691. *Id.* at 13, 52. Saltern had earlier cited to the *Polychronicon* at for the divisions of land by the ancient Britons and Gildas' references to the laws of Dunwallo Mulmutius and of King Lucius. OF THE ANTIENT LAWES at [25], [35], [49].

[126] OF THE ANTIENT LAWES at [52].

looked by non-lawyers."[127] Saltern immediately follows up this cautionary note by discussing at length how "our common Law gives a sound and very consonant exposition" of the liberties of "Churches, Plows, Cities and High-ways" recorded by Higden. For Saltern it is clear "that these four should be free from distress[;] [f]or no man ought to be distrained by the beasts of his Plow, nor in high ways, nor in Markets or Churches."[128] Not content to merely trace the well-known laws of distress back into the ancient past, Saltern further expounds that "[t]he four ways have a peace, which is, that all Nuisances in them shall be amended (note the antiquity of our Laws, of Nuisance)." He then finishes Chapter Nine's exposition of the Mulmutian laws by asserting that "the use of distresses by secondary conclusions and deductions of reason, followed many Laws amongst us, yet in common practise; as of Attornments, Replevies, Avowries, Tenures Services … & such like…," thereby tying the laws of Britain's first ancient lawgiver to significant portions of the common laws of his own day.[129]

Chapter Ten finds Saltern "[b]y many steps and degrees" finally arriving at "the Lucid star of Britain, well deserving that name, for that in his time, religion, Justice, & government began to shine more brightly in this kingdom," namely, King Lucius and his laws. Saltern prefaces the discussion in this chapter by noting three observations his readers should be guided by. The first is "that this Nation above all Nations of the earth (except the Hebrews) hath had the most virtuous, religious and Godly Princes." Second, in that "our ancient laws were most righteous, being derived from the laws of God writ-

---

[127] WOOLF, READING HISTORY IN EARLY MODERN ENGLAND, *supra* note 24 at 24.
[128] OF THE ANTIENT LAWES at [52].
[129] *Id.* at [52]–[54].

ten in nature," King Lucius and the British kings who succeeded him "established only such good and just Laws" that were compatible with the teachings of Christianity and its sacred texts. Finally, that every disaster that ever befell Britain could be traced back to "public & notorious crimes against God, his servants, our good Princes, and against religion and religious laws." These observations provide the foundation for Saltern to then claim that "King Alfred, a witness far above all exception," incorporated the ancient British laws into his own because the British laws had been compiled immediately "[u]pon the propagation of the Gospel" in Britain by "certaine Synods, of Bishops & Noble & wise men...." Those synods "must needs be mean[t] of Parliaments, as [Saltern] showed before." This period directly after "the propagation of the Gospel" must refer to the time of King Lucius as "it cannot be [u]nderstood of the Christian *Saxons*, for of them [Alfred] spoke by name afterwards, saying that he [u]sed choice and judgement in refusing some of their laws, and taking others...." Therefore, Alfred must be referring to "the first Christian *Britons*" of Lucius' reign because their laws "were more sincere & agreeable to Godliness then the *Saxon*." All of which leads Saltern to conclude that the Laws of Alfred "are some of the ancient common Laws... that he translated in *Saxon* the same which *Gildas* turned into Latin," which were in turn "gathered into our common law by *St. Edward* and called Saint *Edwards* laws," reiterating the very same conclusion Saltern had come to concerning the laws of Dunwallo Mulmutius in Chapter Nine. In order to support his claim that these ancient British laws could not have been made by later rulers, "but only by *Lucius*," Saltern deftly relies upon none other than Polydore Vergil, who had stated that Lucius left his kingdom in an advanced state with "the best institutions or Laws" inspired by Christian principles, "so that without question it is that he made some of our Laws."[130]

Saltern then leads off his more in-depth discussion of the Laws of Lucius by acknowledging, as he has consistently done throughout his text, that "particularly which of these laws or institutions now extant were enacted by *Lucius*, it is hard to say…." It is only "[Saltern's] opinion" that "first our Laws of fines and amercements was established in his time." Saltern bases his opinion upon King Alfred having stated "that those first Christian Parliaments … being taught by the mercifulness of Christ, did appoint for everie first offender a pecuniary pain, where you see not only the thing, but almost the very name of *Misericordia*[;]" which term was consistently used "in the Saxon and Norman Laws," and "is used to this day in amercements…." Even more significant for Saltern is that Alfred "took the precedent of their Law against Treason, from the examples of Christ and God… that the Traitor should forfeit, life, Lands, and goods." As examples of this godly punishment for traitors, Saltern refers to Judas and "*Elfredus* [] being convicted of treason in the days of King *Athelstane* as appears by the said Kings Charter, recited by Mr. Fox…." Saltern's citation to Foxe's *Book of Martyrs*, the most influential account of Protestant martyrdom in Reformation England, is perhaps included to more effectively connect this discussion

---

130 *Id.,* at [54]–[57]. *See* VERGIL, *supra* note 86 at Bk. 2 Par. 11. Saltern's first observation: "that this Nation aboue all Nations of the earth (except the Hebrewes) hath had the most virtuous, religious and Godly Princes," comes close to foreshadowing the Holy Commonwealth variant of the ancient constitution trope that viewed Britain as the New Israel and would emerge fully by the 1650s. *See generally, e.g.* REID BARBOUR, JOHN SELDEN: MEASURES OF THE HOLY COMMONWEALTH IN SEVENTEENTH-CENTURY ENGLAND (2003).

of the ancient British laws to the godliness all good English Protestants of his day were expected to aspire to.[131]

From this small set of examples Saltern proceeds to opine that the form of common law trials was also established by Lucius, even going so far as to place the origins of trial by juries of twelve in the reign of Lucius. He rhetorically asks whether "Lucius and those first Christians would imitate God and Christ in severity of punishment, and not much more study to imitate him in the Justice & sincerity of their Trials." Saltern "[t]herefore [] think[s] that the same *Lucius* ordained our Trials by twelve, ... [f]or, that is in agreement to the Scriptures, the learned Sir *John Fortescue* has fully proved." After further explication of these Scriptural foundations – "as our Savior Christ ordained, & chose twelve to bear witness of his resurrection" — for placing trial by jury in the days of the first Christian king of Britain, Saltern directly confronts "those that lean too much to the opinion of *Polydore* and other Italians, ... add[ing] more reasons & authorities to the same point." These au-

---

[131] OF THE ANTIENT LAWES at [57]–[58]. This is the second of only two cites to John Foxe's 1583 work, *Actes and monuments of these latter and perillous dayes touching matters of the Church, wherein ar comprehended and decribed the great persecutions [and] horrible troubles, that haue bene wrought and practised by the Romishe prelates, speciallye in this realme of England and Scotlande, from the yeare of our Lorde a thousande, vnto the tyme nowe present. Gathered and collected according to the true copies [and] wrytinges certificatorie, as wel of the parties them selues that suffered, as also out of the bishops registers, which wer the doers therof*, popularly known thereafter simply as *Foxe's Book of Martyrs*. Saltern's first cite to Foxe's work was one among many for the text of the Letter of Eleutherus to Lucius. For the significance of Foxe's work, *see generally, e.g.* ELIZABETH EVENDEN AND THOMAS S. FREEMAN, RELIGION AND THE BOOK IN EARLY MODERN ENGLAND: THE MAKING OF FOXE'S BOOK OF MARTYRS (2010) *and* JOHN FOXE AND THE ENGLISH REFORMATION (David Loades ed., 1997).

thorities are Fortescue, Camden, and Coke, three *British* sources that all refute Polydore Vergil's assertion that jury trials originated after the Norman Conquest. Saltern does not stop with simple citation of these landmarks of British constitutional history in his day. He continues into a discussion of a case from the reign of Edward III where he:

> find[s] *Mr. Belknap* a reverend Judge, concurring in opinion with these before named. The Law (said he) was founded in this, that every Inquest should be taken *Per duodecidum liberos et legales homines et non per pauciores*. If it were a foundation of the common law, then without question it was one of the first Laws; and we must needs confess that no Law can be without trials, and it cannot be proved that ever any other trial was used, besides this in pleas of land or inheritance in this kingdom.

This case is from the Yearbooks of 41 Edward III, where Serjeant Thorpe, rather than Belknap, who is actually another Serjeant-at-Law making arguments in the same case, does indeed state that trials have always been by twelve freemen and not by fewer in a manner that implies ancient usage.[132]

Saltern then continues by noting the many authorities from Caesar and Tacitus to "*Gildas Galfridus &c.*" who all agree that London was "a most ancient City, a place of government, & ruled by a governor, not a fastness of the

---

[132] OF THE ANTIENT LAWES at [59]–[62]. 41 Edw.3 pl.36 [p.31], *in* LES REPORTS DEL CASES EN LEY : QUE FURENT ARGUES À QUADRAGESIMO AD QUINQUAGESIMUM ANNUM DE TRES HAUT & PUISSANT PRINCE ROY EDWARD LE TIERCE (London: 1679). "Mr. Belknap" is likely Sir Robert Bealknap, who was subsequently Chief Justice of Common Pleas under both Edward III and Richard II. *See* John L. Leland, *'Bealknap, Sir Robert (d. 1401)', in* OXFORD DICTIONARY OF NATIONAL BIOGRAPHY 528 (2004).

woods as some have imagined upon the general and uncertain words of authors, which never saw it." He asks the reader to imagine "the form of such a City: and tell me how you can imagine it to stand without a Court of Justice, the bond of commerce, for the deciding of controversies? Or how can you imagine that such a Court should be without a due form of Trials." He further supports his assertion of this ancient origin of trial by jury with the story of Cassibellan summoning "*Cuelinus*, Nephew to *Androgeus* Governor … of London, [by] a commandment to Androgeus to bring *Cuelinus* to the King's Court, there to receive Justice." The reply of Androgeus to this request is that in "*Trinobantum* … he has his Court, wherein ought to be determined whatsoever any man laid to the charge of his men, & that right ought to be done unto them in the City of London according to the ancient custom." On the chance that "Mr. *Polydore* will not give us leave to think that London had this jurisdiction in *Caesars* time," Saltern then proceeds to further connect this vision of the ancient practice of trial by juries of twelve in London to the post-Norman period by discussing in detail a "*quo Warranto in Itinere in Turri London*" from "14.*E*.2." At this *Quo Warranto* proceeding the citizens of London were required to submit in writing all the privileges and liberties they claimed by either prescription or charter. Among those ancient liberties asserted as prescriptive are trials "*per duodecim Iuratores patrie secundum Legem communem vel per magnam Legem Civitatis, viz. per triginta sex legales homines civitatis. &c.*" According to Saltern "[n]othing can be more plainly proved, then the point in question is by this record: viz that the trial by twelve was used both by the common Law, and by the most ancient custom of London …." An examination of the record of this *Quo*

Warranto shows that Saltern is once again accurately quoting and conveying the text and substance of his sources.[133] Saltern was by no means alone in asserting that trials by twelve originated in the mists of British antiquity long before the Norman Conquest. In John Selden's illustrative notes to Michael Drayton's *Poly-Olbion*, for example, Selden states that "Trials by XII. Shrives, ... Parliaments, and other like" as among the facts of British history that Polydore Vergil and his followers are completely in error about when they insist that they did not exist until recent centuries after the Norman Conquest.[134]

The crucial detail that "those that lean too much to the opinion of *Polydore* and other Italians" ignore in Saltern's view is that the British origins of trial by jury were "by prescription, the beginning of which cannot be proved by any record, writing, or lawful testimony, & such a prescription is here to be understood."[135] That this potentially undercuts the very argument Saltern has constructed using legal precedents and chronicle histories seems to have escaped his notice. Or, perhaps this is better understood as a clear sign that Saltern is making an explicitly faith-based argument for belief in the ancient constitution; a sermon to the lawyers of Britain to maintain their juridical faith in the traditional British origin

---

[133] OF THE ANTIENT LAWES at [62]–[66]. 2 MUNIMENTA GILDHALLAE LONDONIENSIS: LIBER ALBUS, LIBER CUSTOMARUM ET LIBER HORN 321 (Henry Thomas Riley ed., London 1860).

[134] John Selden, *Introduction to the Illustrations* to MICHAEL DRAYTON, 1 POLY-OLBION ix (London 1612). The origins of jury trials in Britain was an enduring subject of early modern speculative history. For an eighteenth century example *see generally* JOHN PETTINGAL, AN INQUIRY INTO THE USE AND PRACTICE OF JURIES AMONG THE GREEKS AND ROMANS, FROM WHENCE THE ORIGIN OF THE ENGLISH JURY MAY PROBABLY BE DEDUCED (London: 1769).

[135] OF THE ANTIENT LAWES at [61],[65].

story of their common law and limited monarchic governance. Saltern continues his discussion by pointing out that no Saxon or Norman charter, not even Magna Carta, specifies a later grant of the right to hold jury trials to London, or any other cities. Those many charters "give them no new liberties," and if "any Law or Patent had been made of it in all that time; without question, they [(London)] would have pleaded the patent of Law, and not prescription." Saltern complements this point by also noting that in both the laws of Edward the Confessor and those of William the Conqueror there "is no new institution mentioned" other than "the ancient customs" in regards to the form of trials to be held within London. Therefore, if the form of trial by juries in London "had been by patent or Parliament of any *Saxon* Prince; without all question these two Princes would have known it." Saltern considers this highly significant because "in the *Saxon* times, not a piece of land passed from the Crown, and much less any liberties or Jurisdictions, which are parcel of the royal prerogative without Patent…." Since London "had this Liberty and Manner of trial" under both the Normans and the Saxons "not by Patent or new Law," they therefore "had it from a time whereof no proof could be made, that is, long before the *Saxons*."[136]

What is true of London for Saltern similarly applies to "all ancient Cities where they have like customs and Liberties; yea the ancient hundred, Courts, Shiremotes, Wardmotes, Swainmotes, Leets, and Wapentakes…." For Saltern, this effectively proves the ancient British origins of the core juridical institutions of England by prescription, thereby obviating any concerns that may arise due to the lack of any corroborating documentary evidence in official records. Should anyone "bring forth the trial by fire and water called *Ordeal*" to the contrary, Saltern as-

---

[136] *Id.* at [66]–[69].

serts that trials by ordeal were "by all likelihood but a superstitious invention" of the Saxons that was "used only in criminal causes where the truth could not otherwise be known…." Saltern then deftly acknowledges that "the Conqueror in his absolute command did something of his own head" in establishing laws for England after the Conquest, "yet it appears plainly that when by the earnest entreaty of his Nobles, he was persuaded to establish the former laws…." This re-establishment was only possible because, again "by the counsel of his Nobles, and according to the course and common Laws of the Realm," William I "impaneled twelve men of every Shire, to inquire & make a true presentment of the said ancient Laws and customs…." Saltern thereby coopts the Norman Conquest itself into a validation of the ancient origins of trial by jury. He then makes a rhetorical show of declining to elaborate upon the many "footsteps of this trial" in the native British chronicle histories in order to be able to once more recount the list of, now proven by prescription for Saltern, ancient British juridical institutions. Should anyone desire to, they could:

> read also of Parliaments, wapentakes, homages, fealties, descents from the Grandfather to the Nephew, *Escheats* to the King for want of heirs, in the days of *Aurelius Ambrosius*, and of *Arthur* the worthy, & straight way after, *Gildas* made mention of Courts, Judges, Freshsuit after thieves, & Judgements which could not be without trials.

This all leads Saltern to "think it is manifest that these points of common law, & namely these trials by twelve, are of most ancient antiquity, according to the common law…."[137]

---

[137] *Id.* at [69]–[71]. That trial by ordeal was unknown to pre-Saxon British law is supported by recent scholarship. *See generally, e.g.*

To deny these proofs by prescription which are recorded in "all the ancient and new records of Assizes, of Freshforce, of writs of right, and other trials in London" would require those proceedings to "be all falsified and many thousands of records besides, if we overthrow this prescription." Since Saltern's prescriptive proofs align with those of the British sources he has relied upon, he advises his readers to "leave Master *Polydore* & his followers which either never saw or did not understand, our ancient Histories and Records; let us leave them (I say) to their own imaginations…." Instead, Saltern admonishes "all discreet Antiquaries, that they be not over-hasty to believe either the *Roman* or other Authors, speaking of the *Britons* their enemies, but holding them suspect for partiality or ignorance…." Instead, "every judicial Reader" should "follow the true grounds confirmed by these faithful Monuments of our Laws, and the Histories thereunto agreeing."[138] In this Saltern is again echoing the same sentiment found in Coke's preface to the third part of *The Reports* that to "the grave and learned writers of histories, [his] advice is, that they meddle not with any point or secret of any art or science, especially with the laws of this realm, before they confer with some learned in that profession."[139] Should his reader follow this sage advice, Saltern is confident they will also clearly discern the lineal British descent of the common law and "conclude fully," as he does, "that all our common Laws was in use in the *Britons* time long before the *Saxons*, howsoever suppressed & the books thereof defaced by foreign invasions, and intestine dissensions."[140]

WATKIN, *supra* note 17 at 38, 40, 73 *and* DAFYDD JENKINS, THE LAW OF HYWEL DDA: LAW TEXTS FROM MEDIEVAL WALES TRANSLATED AND EDITED xxxii (1986).

[138] *Id.* at [71]–[72].

[139] COKE, *supra* note 70 at xx.

[140] OF THE ANTIENT LAWES at [72]–[73].

Saltern's treatment of the antiquity of Britain's common laws and of the British origins of trial by juries of twelve further demonstrates the persuasive use of mythical and historical elements one would expect to find in a work by a Jacobean literary lawyer. His recurring emphasis on the British origins of trial by jury is likely an attempt, albeit doomed to fail, to sooth Scottish fears of the introduction of English style jury trials into their legal system which did not provide such a forum in as many types of actions as the English legal system, and used 15 jurors who could reach a majority verdict rather than the unanimity required of English juries. Since the practice of using 12 jurors originated in the shared British antiquity of Scotland and England, even a total imposition of English practice in Scotland's courts would not be usurpation. It would instead, according to Saltern, be a restoration of the original 'ancient' British trial by twelve. In fact, such a restoration in Scotland would be most appropriate, because, as Saltern goes on to state in his concluding chapter: "the Laws of *Brechus* & *Fergussius* answer[] in time to *Molmutius* and *Mercia*, and [] the Laws of *Kennethus*, [are] not much distant from *Alfred*, and last of all [] their Books of *Regiam Majestatem* a principal book of Common Law amongst them, agree[s] in effect with our *Glanville*."[141]

Just as a minister would in a sermon, Saltern begins and ends his final chapter by praising God, echoing the manner in which he opens and closes the entire work. Chapter Eleven opens with Saltern extolling "the special providence of Almighty God, & of his infinite mercy to this Island" for preserving "yet certain remnants and

---

[141] *Id.*, at [75]. For general discussions of the history of Scottish jury trials, *see* DAVID M. WALKER, 3 A LEGAL HISTORY OF SCOTLAND 431–34 (1995) *and* IAN DOUGLAS WILLOCK, THE ORIGINS AND DEVELOPMENT OF THE JURY IN SCOTLAND (1966).

monuments, whereby to judge of those long past Antiquities" that have been obscured by the accretion of fantastic fables, destructive barbarian invasions, and contrarian chroniclers. It is only thanks to God, in Saltern's view, that those "remnants and monuments" survived so "that the truth found out might be the better confirmed. Some chroniclers of Britain's past "have given themselves to favor the *Roman* History so much, as to abrogate all faith and credit from the British [histories]." Other chroniclers went so far to the other extreme "as to favor all the vanities of the Poetical Bards, as if nothing could be denied, which they had once turned into Rhyme." These passages reveal both how Saltern views his own efforts and the extent to which he has attempted to find the proper balance between the two extremes. His guiding principle between the two is once again God's revealed truth, this time in Moses' instruction that "by the mouth of two or three witnesses every word shall be confirmed...." Since it is irrefutable that "truth cannot be so much oppressed as to be utterly destitute of proofs," Saltern suggests that he has let his proofs "rest upon witnesses and comparison of circumstances...." His star witness is "*Sir John Prise*," whose *Historia Britanniae Defensio* is among Saltern's most cited sources, and who "truly averred and learnedly proved, that the British Story is in many things more to be credited than *Caesar*, and *Polydore*, and other *Italians*." Saltern's most significant "comparison of circumstances" is "the Scottish History agreeing in many things with us...." Comparison with those Scottish sources not only clearly show the "Arrogance and vanity" of the Roman and Italian sources, they "prove the antiquity and sincerity of our common Laws" because "the same or others much like obtained in Scotland also, as well as here...." It is at this point that Saltern makes the comparative assertion quoted at the end of the last paragraph above, emphasizing the similarities to be found in both the twelfth century compilation of English writs known to posterity as *Glan-*

ville after its author and the Scottish *Regiam Majestatem* which was then believed to have been compiled at almost the same time.[142] He further notes that in "truth there was little difference in Laws and Religion, betwixt these two Nations, until the bloody wars, that began after the time of our King *Henry* the third...;" an effective way of eliding the instigator of those wars, Edward I, the Hammer of the Scots, in a work written to allay both English and Scottish fears of the proposed Union. Saltern's assertions that "the same or others much like obtained in Scotland also, as well as here..." is yet another indication that he is asserting a comparatively analogous relationship, not one of exacting correspondence between Scottish and English laws.[143]

Saltern then reiterates the running theme in his work that "the most ancient of the *Saxon* Princes, & lawmakers,

---

[142] OF THE ANTIENT LAWES at [73]–[75]. Alain Wijffels has noted that in 1605 it was still unclear which work was the more ancient, the English *Glanville* or the Scottish *Regiam Majestatem*. Furthermore, the fact that the most recent edition of *Glanville* from 1604 "had highlighted the parallels with *Regiam Majestatem* [] meant that, whichever text was deemed to be the more ancient one, the idea of a common historical foundation of both laws was strengthened." Alain Wijffels, *A British ius commune? A Debate on the Union of the Laws of Scotland and England during the First Years of James VI/I's English Reign*, 6 EDINBURGH L. REV. 315, 331 n.62 (2002). As Brian Levack observed, the early seventeenth century was fortuitously the one moment in the separate histories of Scotland and England that such similarities actually did exist to a sufficient degree to support such claims — "the time in which Scots law bore a close enough resemblance to English law that lawyers, judges, and members of parliament could reasonably discuss the possibility of reconciliation." BRIAN P. LEVACK, THE FORMATION OF THE BRITISH STATE: ENGLAND, SCOTLAND, AND THE UNION 1603–1707 97 (1986). *See also* Hector L. MacQueen, *Regiam Majestatem, Scots Law, and National Identity*, 74 Scot. Hist. Rev. 1, 13–19 (1995) ("In his *Of the Antient Lawes of great Britain*, published in 1605, George Saltern used the parallel of *Regiam* and *Glanvill* to argue for a closer union of the two laws on the English model").

[143] OF THE ANTIENT LAWES at [75].

do make mention of many things in our common Law, which we are forced to believe, that they received from the *Britons*...." The reason Saltern believes he is compelled to this opinion is that the Saxon sources "speak of them, as of things usual and common...." To emphasize this point, Saltern once again runs through these *usual and common* juridical monuments of ancient Britain that "*Ine*, *Alfred*, *Edgar* & other the *Saxon* law makers" refer to in their compilations of laws. The Saxons:

> speak of the Parliament, of Judgements, of Treason, of Sanctuaries, of Purgation, of execution by hanging, for theft, of freshsuit after thieves & homicides, of escapes, of Terms kept at London, of Recoveries, of Exchanges, of Feoffments, of entails, of Commons, enclosures, and the Law of *Curia Claudenda*, of the law of deceit, it in selling things corrupt or vicious; of dowers, Leases, Rents, Farms, services &c.

All of these, and more, are mentioned by the Saxons "as things then in use...," which the Saxons then preserved in their own legal compilations. Saltern then summarily reviews "certain of the notable *Saxon* laws, only to show the Godliness of those ancient *Saxons* and Scottish kings" in order to provide a final concluding proof of "how in that time the matters of our common Laws were usual and common."[144]

King Ine of Wessex, "about the year of our Lord 720," compiled "Laws for observation of the Sabbath, against theft, robbery, murder, & many other offences;" the laws of Ine also have provisions for "Land-lords, of Tenants, of Rents, and services." In Scotland shortly thereafter, "*Kennethus* [(MacAlpine)] the most worthy Scottish King also compiled laws. Among these was a

---

[144] *Id.* at [75]–[76].

provision that "in every Shire (this was before *Alfred*) Let skillful men in the Laws be appointed to reside...." Provision was also made that anyone who "blasphemes the name of God, of the Saints," the King or the chieftain of his clan "let his tongue be cut out." The latter presumably illustrates the godliness of the laws of Kenneth MacAlpine, the first king of both the Scots and the Picts. The laws of Alfred, "about the year 880...," included "certain laws against perjury, concerning Entails, against Sacrilege, Treason, Quarrelling, Fighting, Fornication, yea & against immodest touching of a woman; with other laws of great sincerity...." All of which made Alfred, for Saltern, "a manifest and approved Vicar and Lieutenant of God, a second *David*...," who was so godly and just he "translated the new Testament out of Latin into the Vulgar Saxon" for the edification of "his subjects...." After Alfred, "*Edward Anno Dom.* 920" began his laws by commanding "all *Greeves* that they give right Judgements to all according to their judgement Book." Saltern then jumps back to Alfred in order to link him to Aethelstan and give credit to "their league by act of Parliament" that, first and foremost, only "one God is to be loved & Worshipped." Furthermore, "humane Lawes are to be proclaimed as common to Christ and the King," which laws include those "for payment of Tithes, for observation of the Sabbaths &c." Subsequently, King Edmund prefaced his laws with a guiding purpose of advancing "the Christian faith" in order "that love and mutual kindness should be maintained amongst all men throughout [his] Kingdom." Only then did Edmund's laws command "that every man shall freely enjoy the benefit of the common Law." Saltern then pauses to "note the common law even then named, before St. *Edward* & the Conqueror," before proceeding to "*Canutus* the Dane...." Even the Danish Canute commanded all of his subjects to "observe one rule of Christian Religion...[,] with many other most Godly and Christian laws...." The laws of

Canute contained "many Footsteps of ancient Laws, which yet remain in use," and concluded "with a most ardent exhortation to all men to turn unto God and to obey his commandments." These godly laws made even the compiler of the Danelaw "another Lieutenant or viceregent of Christ." Once the English crown reverted to the Saxon line in the person of "*Edgar* the peaceable," that king also "confirmed the Liberties & rights of the Church, & amongst other things, enacted that every man shall enjoy the benefit of the common Law." This godly and just common law tradition was preserved by all subsequent rulers in Britain, even "*William* the Conqueror," who confirmed the common law and "has left them to us consecrated by his own oath, and the oath of all his successors." Should all other sources, especially those "confessions of strangers & enemies" like the Letter from Eleutherus (a Roman) and Polydore Vergil (an Italian), be deemed insufficient proof of "the sacred Majesty of our Imperial Princes," then "God has vouchsafed… [them] by these their Laws to be his Vicars & defenders of his faith."[145]

Saltern then summarizes his main points so far. First, not only Lucius but all of the "excellent Princes" of Britain Saltern has noted throughout his tract "sincerely and devoutly… followed the counsel of *Eleutherus* given to *Lucius*, in taking laws for their kingdom out of the word of God." Therefore, Saltern exhorts his fellow Britons, "how true it is that we affirm that our ancient common laws were begun in the times of the first *Britons*, grounded upon the laws of God, printed in Nature and Scripture." That original lawmaking process was "continued by the *Saxons* in their judgement books, & transmitted to us by Saint *Edward* and the Conqueror." Which in turn proves "the ground of Sir *John Fortescue's*

---

[145] *Id.* at [76]–[80].

testimony" that neither the "*Britons, Romans, Saxons, Danes,* and *Normans*" were "moved either with Justice or with reason, or affection" to replace the laws established by that godly and just process with their own laws or different procedures for making laws. How that godly and just process had been maintained over the long centuries is Saltern's third point concerning: "what direction and Precedents our Princes and Parliaments have had to follow in making Laws, and what Laws the whole Kingdom is bound to observe, by that solemn oath that is taken for the observation of St. *Edwards* laws and the Laws of the Realm…." For Saltern, the answer is to be found "partly [] noted [] unto us in the preface of that famous Statute, made against Provisors in the 25th year of King Edward the third."[146] That preface (which Saltern oddly fails to excerpt) recites all the troubles that have arisen, and were noted in "the Petition heard" in the final parliament of Edward I recounting how "the Bishop of *Rome*" had appropriated the right of granting appointments to English religious benefices in order to "give and grant the same Benefices to Aliens, which never did dwell in *England*…." Such ongoing misappropriation had resulted in:

> the first Fruits, and many other Profits, and a great Part of the Treasure of the said Realm [being] carried away and dispended out of the Realm…: Whereupon the said Commons have prayed our said Lord King, that sith [(since)] the Right of the Crown of *England*, and the Law of the said Realm is such, that upon the Mischiefs and Damages which happen to his Realm, [the King] ought, and is bound by his Oath, with the Accord of his People in his Parliament thereof to make Remedy and Law, and in removing the Mischiefs and

[146] *Id.* at [80]–[81].

> Damages which thereof ensue, that it may please him thereupon to Remedy.[147]

Finally, and building upon what must have been a familiar example to Saltern's fellow English lawyers, he recounts the reasons why these and other "manifold calamities, [were] sent by Almighty God, the most just and severe judge at sundry times upon this Realm..."[148]

These consist of, "namely the suppressing, and consequently the violation of this his Covenant, of these our ancient laws, and of the law of God, whereupon they are founded, by the predominant violence of Idolatry, superstition, injustice, uncleanness, Breach of faith, and loyalty, both before the *Norman* and since," by those "who suffered themselves and these laws to be overswayed by the supereminence of *Rome*...." A more fitting sentiment for a writer seeking an audience in post-Reformation Britain is difficult to imagine. In contrast to such apostate rulers, like "King *John* & King *Henry* the sixth," Saltern exhorts his readers to "consider the best means to establish the perpetual unity and felicity of these two mighty nations [(England and Scotland)], now again reunited...." Those best means "consist principally in conforming them, both as much as may be to the laws, of that God of unity which ordained the ancient Laws, of both kingdoms to be very like, & almost the same, as I have shown." Saltern holds up as paradigmatic examples to follow the historical line of kings in Britain he has already recounted multiple times as worthy of the appellation "Vicars of God in their kingdom," and adds to their number their rightful successors "*Edward* the 1st, the 3rd, and the 6th, *Henry* the 7th and the eighth, acknowledged by the enemy of our faith to be defender of the

---

[147] 25 Edw.3 st.6 (1350) (referring to 35 Edw.1 c.4 sect.3 (1307)).
[148] Of the Antient Lawes at [81].

faith, & the late most of all excellent *Elizabeth*...." To these worthies, Saltern then, of course, adds "the no less excellent Majesty of K. *James*, the true heir as well of the goodness as of the greatness of his Predecessors." He then follows this with a thunder and brimstone style jeremiad exhorting his readers to avoid the paths of those apostate rulers of Britain's past "whose Calamities because my heart does tremble to think, I will forbear my pen to write." Instead of further cataloging those recurring calamitous woes in Britain's history, Saltern winds up his juridical sermon by postulating what may happen in the future if the "two mighty nations" fail to fully follow through in implementing the Crown's proposal for creating a united British kingdom. Should the Union project fail, Saltern warns that the same "God [who] hath fed and directed us with the staff of Beauty, and with the staff of Bands... will break his staff of beauty, to disannul his covenant, made with all people, and he will break his staff of bands, to dissolve the Brotherhood between *Juda* & *Israel* [(i.e. Scotland and England)] except we repent of our manifold sins." In order to inspire the subjects of Scotland and England to avoid that woeful fate, Saltern "conclude[s] with the Godly words of one of our famous and learned Judges, *Bracton*, and one of our virtuous and Heroical Kings, *Canutus*...."[149]

The inspirational passage Saltern selects from *Bracton* is, of course, the well-known statement from Book 1, Chapter 8, that the king:

> himself ought not to be subject to man, but subject to God and to the law, for the law makes the king. Let the

---

[149] *Id.* at [81]–[83]. It is unclear why Saltern considered Henry VI to be an apostate, a monarch so devout he was considered highly ineffectual even by contemporaries during the Wars of the Roses. It is likely Henry's devotion to the Roman Church which Saltern is here deriding.

> king, then, attribute to the law what the law attributes to him, namely dominion and power, for there is no king where the will and not the law has dominion; and that he ought to be under the law, since he is the vicar of God, appears evidently after the likeness of Jesus Christ, whose place he fills on earth….

However, Saltern does not quote this passage in full. Instead he foreshortens it to "*Rex non debet esse sub homine, sed sub deo et Lege, ad similitudinem Iesu Christi, cuius vices gerit* [the king himself ought not to be subject to man, but subject to God and to the law, after the likeness of Jesus Christ, whose place he fills]." Perhaps he did so in order to craft a more succinct closing argument on the assumption that his intended primary audience of fellow English lawyers would likely have been at least as familiar with the fuller passage in *Bracton* as Saltern himself was. The full passage goes on to note that because of God's abiding interest in justice, God himself "was willing to be under the law, that he might redeem those who were under the law, for he was not willing to use his strength, but his reason and judgment" to redeem the world. Foreshortening the passage from *Bracton* essentially transforms the passage from a foundational statement of the rule of law in England to a statement that the king is "the vicar of God…," and that regal vicarage is what Saltern truly wants to emphasize here. He immediately follows this foreshortened version of Bracton's rule of law statement by asserting that "Judges do sit in the seat of the King himself, as in the throne of God, instead of the King as instead of Jesus Christ." The judges of Britain are therefore themselves also vicars of God, for "judgements are not the judgements of men, but of God; and therefore it is said that the heart of the King is in the hand of God," as are judges. Saltern then paraphrases an earlier passage from Book 1, Chapter 2 of *Bracton* to the effect that:

> into the seat therefore of judgement, which is as the Throne of the Divine Majesty, let no man unwise or unlearned, presume to ascend, lest he turn light into darkness, and darkness into light, and lest with an ignorant hand like a mad man, he strike the innocent & spare the offender, and lest he fall from above as from the Tribunal of God, by attempting to fly without wings to support him.

Saltern closes this exegesis of his chosen texts from *Bracton* by asserting that should either kings or judges fail to perform the duties of this regal vicarage in a godly and just manner, they shall suffer all the torments of the final day of judgement.[150]

Saltern's final example of a godly and just British king is not Lucius, his "lucid star of Britain," but the last of the major invaders of the pre-Norman era, "one of our virtuous and Heroical Kings, *Canutus*."[151] It seems likely that Saltern chose to close with Cnut in order to emphasize one final time that even the invaders and usurpers of Britain's history recognized the godly and just common laws and preserved them. According to Saltern:

> therefore said *Canutus* in the conclusion of his Laws I beseech all men in general, and command every man in particular in the name of the immortal God that sincerely, & with all their hearts they turn to God, and with all care and diligence, search what is to be done,

---

[150] *Id.* at [83]–[85]. Henrici de Bracton. De Legibus et Consuetudinibus Angliæ. Libri quinque in varios tractatus distincti. Ad diversorum et vetustissimorum codicum collationem typis vulgat 9, 38–41 (Sir Travers Twiss ed. & trans., London: 1878–1883) (ca. 1230). Coke had similarly quoted without attribution the now classic passage from Bk.1 Ch.8 that "the king is under no man, but only God and the law, for the law makes him king…" in the preface to his *Fourth Reports*. Coke, 2 The Reports *supra* note 71 at Pt. IV xix.

[151] OF THE ANTIENT LAWES at [54], [83].

> and what is to be avoided (as it is a thing most convenient for our salvation) that we love God & keep his commandments, & give diligent heed to the words of his messengers.

God's messengers in the context of Saltern's text are, of course, the godly and just king and judges of Britain, who "shall produce us before [God's] sight in the day, wherein the Lord shall come to judge every man according to his works." Saltern even exhorts "the Preachers and Ministers of God's word" to always encourage the subjects of Britain to be godly and just, "[s]o at length in the end we all abundantly shall obtain his gracious mercy." A final benediction to bless "the name of the Lord..." is followed by a closing motto to complement the one he opened his text with — "*Deus non deseret* [Desert not God];" a coda with a potential doubled meaning as a final exhortation to support the king's union proposal – Desert not the King – in light of Saltern's thematic emphasis on the king being the Vicar of God.[152]

The manner in which Saltern's concluding discussion of the pattern of devout British, Saxon, Scottish, and Danish monarchs from the history of Britain preserving godly and just laws in Chapter Eleven shifts from emphasizing examples of the "many Footsteps of ancient Laws" that can still be faintly discerned in the common law of his own time to a jurisprudential commentary upon the divinely ordained responsibilities of kings and judges illustrates two important features not just of Saltern's work, but of the mental world it was produced in. First, that it is the product of a writer thoroughly steeped in the prevailing paradigm of Cosmic Harmony and the Great Chain of Being that characterized all of medieval Europe and continued to significantly influence pre-Enlight-

---

[152] *Id.* at [85]–[86].

enment early modern Europe.[153] Within that paradigm everything and everyone had a divinely appointed place and function. The cosmos was "an interlocking and interdependent scheme of created things existing in a natural hierarchy."[154] At the turn of the seventeenth century there truly was no significant alternative paradigm, let alone a secular and purely rational one. Cosmic Harmony would soon, however, be challenged by the rising scientific revolution triggered by works like Galileo's 1610 *Siderius Nuncius* and the long-term effects of the Protestant Reformation itself. Nonetheless, the analogical reasoning and use of allegories so commonly employed within the paradigm of Cosmic Harmony would continue to influence British political thought well into the eighteenth century.[155] For writers at the turn of the seventeenth century like Saltern, however, those "Godly and devout admonitions, or secret footsteps of the ancient British constitutions, appearing yet in the body of our common Laws" were there to be found because God had ensured they would be; they were part and parcel of the divinely created harmonious natural order.[156]

Second, and perhaps most crucial for arriving at a proper understanding of the immemorial continuity of the

---

[153] *See generally, e.g.* James Daly, *Cosmic Harmony and Political Thinking in Early Stuart England*, 69 TRANSACTIONS AM. PHIL. SOC'Y 1, 14, *passim* (1979) (citing Saltern's Chapter Eleven in support of the assertion that "it seems to have been judges who most reflected the divine attributes along with the king; assize sermons were apt to endow them with nearly as much right as kings to be called gods, because they administered the king's law, which should resemble God's law.") *and* J.G.A. POCOCK, THE MACHIAVELLIAN MOMENT: FLORENTINE POLITICAL THOUGHT AND THE ATLANTIC REPUBLICAN TRADITION (1975) (discussing in detail the medieval mental world).

[154] Daly, *supra* note 153 at 3.

[155] *Id.* at 31–38.

[156] OF THE ANTIENT LAWES at [5].

common law asserted in ancient constitutionalist works like Saltern's, is that it is the godly and just British common law *tradition* that is allegedly continuous from ancient times to Saltern's present rather than a comprehensive survival of the precise substantive *content* of the specific provisions of the common law.[157] That continuity of *tradition* is the central theme of Saltern's work, and his juridical sermon closes with a zealous call to the subjects of Britain, especially his fellow lawyers, to best keep and preserve that godly and just common law tradition intact by supporting the Union proposal of King James. If the divinely preserved evidence of ancient British common laws was there to be found, then assuredly King James's union proposal was also divinely ordained because it effortlessly aligned with that evidence. In creating the unified kingdom of Great Britain they would be supporting the ancient constitution first granted by God's grace to the ancient Britons. Within the prevailing paradigm of Cosmic Harmony, that ancient constitution could be characterized thusly: the world is God's Realm, or Estate, harmoniously governed through the vicars, or vicegerents, of kings and judges, who are bound by their sacred oaths to establish, preserve, and improve upon, naturally occurring godly and just common laws.[158]

That this ancient constitution bound both sovereign and subject is seen in the excerpt from the preface to Edward III's Statute of Provisors of Benefices that Saltern

---

[157] *See* POCOCK, THE ANCIENT CONSTITUTION, *supra* note 44 at 275 ("[I]t was less (though it always could be) the content of the law than the juridical process itself – usage, judgment and statute – that was immemorial....").

[158] It is worth noting that the passages marked in either the 17th or early 18th centuries by one of the prior owners of Georgetown Law Library's copy of Saltern's *Of the Antient Lawes* that is reproduced in Appendix III of this volume are primarily those passages that emphasize this very paradigm.

references, but fails to quote, in his closing argument – "that upon the Mischiefs and Damages which happen to his Realm, [the King] ought, and is bound by his Oath, with the Accord of his People in his Parliament thereof to make Remedy and Law, and in removing the Mischiefs and Damages which thereof ensue, that it may please him thereupon to Remedy."[159] Whenever the subjects collectively petitioned the king to provide a new remedy, or improve an existing one, within the common laws of the realm, the king was bound by his oath to do so with their accord. This juridical process created "public law as enforced in the courts, and made in parliament, which partook of the divine will which it was blasphemy to dispute."[160]

The paradigm of Cosmic Harmony also suggests an explication of how Saltern could so readily gloss over what to a twenty-first century mind appears to be incompatible tension between the rule of law aspects of his chosen closing passage from *Bracton* and the implied absolute power of the monarch as a demi-god and regal Vicar through his seemingly intentional exclusion (again, from the perspective of historical hindsight) of the rule of law language from his quotation of the passage. That his celebrated "virtuous and Heroical Kings" of Britain's history could have used their absolute sovereignty to radically alter or abolish the "ancient British constitutions" would likely never have occurred to Saltern because:

> [t]he dominant political note of cosmic harmony was not the supremacy of the sovereign; it was the hierarchical chain, a chain of government as much as a chain of being, in which the absolutely necessary cooperation presupposed the respect of higher powers for the

---

[159] 25 Edw.3 st.6 (1350).
[160] Daly, *supra* note 153 at 11.

> legitimate roles of the lower, which were themselves just as necessary.[161]

There simply was no significant contradiction between absolute sovereign power and the common law's rule of law limitations within the harmonious ancient constitutionalism Saltern extolled. Rather than being seen as contradictory, such paradoxical relationships were themselves viewed as further evidence of the unitary and harmonious cosmos God had designed; "[t]he apparent paradox was congenial to cosmic harmony; it was a later mentality which was to find it ridiculous."[162] Saltern's "ancient British constitutions" story therefore defies categorization as either one of an immemorial rule of law or of an immemorial royal prerogative power. In this regard, Saltern's variant of the ancient constitution narrative can serve as a standard baseline of sorts for better understanding the influence ancient constitutionalism would come to have in early modern British political thought.

---

[161] *Id.* at 29.
[162] *See id.* at 21–31.

CHAPTER 3
The Juridical Genre of Ancient Constitutionalism

The harmonious mingling of mythic and historical authorities in the narratives of Saltern's *Of the Antient Lawes* and the other Union Tracts clearly reveals the extent to which myth and history functioned as a single discursive spectrum for reflecting upon the past and considering its relations to the issues and needs of the present in early modern Britain. The four literary lawyers whose works have primarily been examined herein provide a useful comparative sampling of ancient constitutionalist works by lawyers of different status within the legal profession of early seventeenth century Britain. Sir Edward Coke and Thomas Craig were among the leading jurists of the day in England and Scotland respectively. John Selden was still a student of the Inner Temple, and barely started on what would be a noteworthy career not only as a lawyer and jurist but as a leading critical antiquarian and highly influential Member of Parliament, when he wrote the *Jani Anglorum*.[163] George Saltern was by contrast, an average lawyer midway through his career practicing out of chambers in the Middle Temple. Although Saltern has been characterized as an "'ignorant populizer,'" this illustrates the extent to which "he had plenty of company in the early Stuart period."[164] Furthermore, surveying the works together demonstrates that

---

[163] Christianson, *Young John Selden*, *supra* note 45 at 272–273.
[164] GREENBERG, *supra* note 29 at 128–129 (quoting JOHANN SOMMERVILLE, POLITICS AND IDEOLOGY IN ENGLAND 1603–1640 91 (1986)).

in contrast to being the work of the ignorant and gullible, they are instead the product of authors searching for constitutional truths employing the developing critical standards of their day which by no means disparaged combining authoritative historical, mythical, literary and legal sources. These were literary lawyers writing not quite like genuine narrative historians, nor merely as catalogers of historical antiquities; their chosen "subject forced them to consider questions of the relevance of past to present and even (if in a rudimentary form) of historical development."[165]

Law in the Mental World of Cosmic Harmony

Coke, Craig, Selden, and Saltern were all products of late-sixteenth century modes of thought, not the increasingly more rationalist philosophies of later seventeenth century developments in British political thought. Of the four, only Selden was young enough that his mental world would potentially have been at least somewhat tempered by the barest beginnings of the transition to more recognizably modern patterns of political thought. It is therefore prudent to consider the early ancient constitutionalist works by these authors within that earlier milieu of the Great Chain of Being and Cosmic Harmony that still flourished in late Tudor Britain. That still markedly medieval cosmology viewed the entire universe as one of created perfection sustained by God. Only the sinful disobedience of Lucifer and then of Man marred that perfection; even those imperfections were post-creation and therefore exceptions to the original rule of perfection

---

[165] POCOCK, THE ANCIENT CONSTITUTION, *supra* note 44 at 29 (citing and discussing the relevance of Momigliano, *supra* note 25).

believed to characterize the very nature of the cosmos. The well understood historical origins of this cosmology of nesting celestial spheres of existence in pagan Greek philosophy was itself viewed as further proof of the immemorial perfection and harmonious order of God's Creation, for even those ancient pagans had discerned it. This was a cosmos of divinely ordained stable and harmonious perfection, not that of growth, change and adaptation more familiar to the modern mind. Such a paradigm encouraged teleological stabilizing processes of thought rather than the analytical and critical thought that would come to be so increasingly valued by later generations.

Every relationship in the cosmos, from the external hierarchies of the celestial spheres themselves to those internal to each sphere, illustrated the perfection and harmony of the Great Chain; "[f]rom God down to the tiniest grain of sand or insect, each link in the chain had its necessary role, its particular virtue and claim to importance, its lesson for the different links in the social chain." Humanity was seen as "the rather undependable but vital link which partook of both the higher and lower ranges of nature, and connected the two." The relationships of rulers and subjects, husband and wife, the family, and even those between the various parts of the human body itself were all used as metaphorical analogies to better understand the hierarchical and interdependent aspects of God's Creation. Such analogies were themselves employed in an interdependent manner; "the effect was cumulative, a process of constant mutual reinforcement." Within this prevailing world of thought all the learned disciplines were to be "found, not neatly compartmentalized, but blended into a whole where quantitative shades into qualitative, superstition marches with logic, and shrewd common sense is brought into the service of high-flown preachiness." While the analogical ratiocinations of the common law may have been beyond the average educated person's comprehension, these broader cosmological analogies were far more readily understood even when they were incompletely articulated (as some of Saltern's text undeniably is) because "the contemporary mind was steeped in the whole system, and would automatically supply whatever exact similarity was missing in a particular analogy by instant and unconscious reference to several similar ones." Generalities were preferred over detailed specifics, and imagination and emotive rhetoric were not only desirable, but essential, elements of the process of reasoning itself. The works surveyed herein reveal the extent to which late Tudor and early Stuart culture "still preferred to think in terms of intrinsically related images, and to *feel* those relations as well as *see* them." This was a culture steeped in thought processes that may seem "silly to more modern minds," but were in fact "comforting reminder[s] of the harmoniously ordered universe, with everything in its place and a meaning and a lesson for everyone." Saltern's *Of the Antient Lawes* paradigmatically shows the extent to which this prevailing mode of thought "encouraged thinking in wholes rather than parts, hence discouraging keen attention to detail" in a rhetorical style that was "always trying to reach the heart with an ethical conviction which would overcome self-interest." His text also illustrates the extent to which harmonist thought was far better at "convinc[ing] those who wanted to be convinced" than it was at changing opinions. While such rhetoric was "an excellent intellectual vehicle for expressing a yearning for unity," it could all too readily fall on deaf ears should that yearned for unity appear to be politically impractical as was the case with the Union Proposal of James VI and I.[166]

Law and legal rhetoric played a pivotal role in the mental world of Cosmic Harmony; it "was both the mainstay and the darling of this world-view." Law was viewed

---

[166] Daly, *supra* note 153 at 5–9, 36.

as being a primary and integral element of the cosmos; "not an arbitrary command representing power, but the expression of an intrinsic necessity, springing from the nature of things, and governing their harmonious operation." [167] God's law was seen as the connective constituent that governed the various celestial spheres and the interactions between them; a sort of cosmic constitutional law that even God obeyed: "'Of Law there can be no less acknowledged than that her seat is the bosom of God, her voice the harmony of the world: all things in heaven and earth do her homage, the very least in feeling her care and the greatest not exempted from her power.'"[168] Human laws were derived from that higher law in an imperfect manner due to humanity's intrinsic fallen nature. English lawyers were taught a legal hierarchy of six basic types of law: "the laws of God, the laws of nature (which in England are called the laws of reason), diverse general customs of the realm, maxims of the common law, diverse particular customs, and finally, parliamentary statutes." [169] The laws of nature were themselves viewed as the "*second law eternal*" just as God's laws were considered to be "*the first eternal law*."[170] The jurisprudential process of "right reason" by which human laws were to be properly derived from God's laws and the laws of nature was a fundamental

---

[167] *Id.* at 22.

[168] *Id.* at 6 (quoting RICHARD HOOKER, OF THE LAWS OF ECCLESIASTICAL POLITY Bk.1:xvi:8 (Everyman's Library reprint 1963) (1594).

[169] Christopher W. Brooks, *The Place of Magna Carta and the Ancient Constitution in Sixteenth-Century Legal Thought, in* THE ROOTS OF LIBERTY: MAGNA CARTA, ANCIENT CONSTITUTION, AND THE ANGLO-AMERICAN TRADITION OF THE RULE OF LAW 57, 62 (Ellis Sandoz ed. 1993) (discussing CHRISTOPHER ST. GERMAN, DOCTOR AND STUDENT 1–77 (T. F. T. Pucknett & J. L. Barton eds. 1974) (1523)).

[170] RICHARD HOOKER, 1 OF THE LAWS OF ECCLESIASTICAL POLITY 205 [Bk.1:iii:1] (Via Media reprint 1994) (1887 7th ed.) (1594)).

tenet of English jurisprudence.[171] Those laws which created and maintained an ordered society, the body politic, were considered "the Law of a Commonweal, the very soul of a politic body, the parts whereof are by law animated, held together, and set to work in such actions, as the common good requireth."[172] In the harmonious reasoning of the time, law "was the political counterpart of the soul."[173] Law was also likened to the human nervous system. As Fortescue described it:

> The law, indeed, by which a group of men is made into a people, resembles the nerves of the body physical, for, just as the body is held together by the nerves, so this body mystical is bound together and united into one by the law, which is derived from the word 'ligando', and the members and bones of this body, which signify the solid basis of truth by which the community is sustained, preserve their rights through the law, as the body natural does through the nerves.

This role of law in the body politic of the English nation was itself seen as the reason why the rule of law, which protected the liberties of the subject, and the absolute prerogative powers of the king could coexist without destroying the nation. No matter how absolute the powers of an English monarch might be, they were rendered incapable of ruling by will alone because:

> just as the head of the body physical is unable to change its nerves, or to deny its members proper strength and due nourishment of blood, so a king who is head of the body politic in unable to change the laws

---

[171] *Id.* at 63.
[172] HOOKER, *supra* note 170 at 239 [Bk.1:x:1].
[173] Daly, *supra* note 153 at 16.

> of that body, or to deprive that same people of their own substance uninvited or against their wills.[174]

While the king was undeniably the principal human source of the nation's laws, he "was both the source of law and subject to it, both above it and under it." This paradoxical relationship between English sovereign, subject, and laws was even incorporated in "the judges' oath to do justice 'notwithstanding the king's letters, or any other person's.'" Within a jurisprudence steeped in the paradigm of Cosmic Harmony, in establishing the oath by statute "[t]he king was ordering the judges to obey his rational will against his mere personal will."[175] Just as the human body only functioned properly when its various parts and humors were in balance so too a properly order society needed "a mixture of occupations, classes, estates, and powers within the body politic," which was commonly thought to require a balancing of monarchical, aristocratic, and democratic elements. Parliament was seen as the paradigmatic example of such a properly balanced institution of governance; as an analogical representation of all the estates of the realm Parliament was also a living metaphor for the whole nation. The harmonious ideal of "the king assisted by experienced advisors [and] informed by the people's elected representatives" was perfectly embodied by the king-in-parliament analogy. This organizing institutional "temperament of the body politic came to be called its *constitution*" in late Tudor and early Stuart juridical culture. That now standard meaning of the word *constitution* "sprang from the humeral correspondence in cosmic har-

---

[174] FORTESCUE, *supra* note 65 at 31–33.
[175] Daly, *supra* note 153 at 25 (discussing *The Oath of the Justices*, 18 Edw.3 s.4 (1344)).

mony," becoming an increasingly common usage in the first half of the seventeenth century.[176]

The English legal profession was fertile ground for the belief that this emerging rule of law concept that is now termed constitutionalism was the original form of government properly derived by right reason from those first and second eternal laws — God's laws and the laws of nature. Their revered predecessor Fortescue had stated a century earlier that England was a "political kingdom" wherein the king "is obliged to protect the law, subjects, and their bodies and goods," for which responsibilities "he has power to this end issuing from the people, so that it is not permissible for him to rule his people with any other power." Not only had "England blossomed forth into a dominion regal and political out of Brutus's band of Trojans" in ancient Britain, so too "Scotland, which at one time was obedient thereto as a duchy, grew into a kingdom political and regal." Fortescue had further asserted that the kings of Egypt and Ethiopia, "and other kings who reigned happily in ancient times" had ruled over similar political kingdoms. Kingdoms ruled solely by regal will were the aberrations of humanity's fallen nature. Fortescue had also referred to these different types of kingdoms as being ruled *jus regale* (solely by royal will) or *jus politicum et regale* (by royal and political will).[177] The nascent rule of law principle discussed

---

[176] *Id.* at 18–20.

[177] Fortescue, *supra* note 65 at 25–33. For the terms *jus regale* and *jus politicum et regale* see SIR JOHN FORTESCUE, THE GOVERNANCE OF ENGLAND: OTHERWISE CALLED THE DIFFERENCE BETWEEN AN ABSOLUTE AND A LIMITED MONARCHY 109–116 (Charles Plummer ed., 1885) (ca. 1471)). Plummer's editorial notes to the latter title underscore the extent to which the story of Brutus and other aspects of Galfridian history considered to be fantastic fables by a later age were instead considered as respectable sources: "nothing is less likely than that [Fortescue] should have disbelieved it." *Id.* at 185. In

by Fortescue as the binding ligaments of the English body politic and his substantiation that such political kingdoms were the original form of godly and just government by reference to mythic rulers of the ancient world became common themes of discussion in the Inns of Court. In "an anonymous reading on chapter 1" of Magna Carta "given at one of the Inns of Court either in the 1530s or early in the reign of Elizabeth" both of these elements are present. The Reader pointed out "that the laws of the land had continued in long use before the making of the Charter, and that some of these laws had been made by Lucius, some by Edward the Confessor, and some by William the Conqueror." This now unknown Barrister further "described law as the means by which the 'body politique' was bound together."[178] Later in the century, upon his promotion to Serjeant-at-Law in 1589, "Sir Christopher Yelverton told an audience at Gray's Inn" that law was not only "the devine gifte and invention of god, and the profound determination of wise men," law was also "the most strong synewe of a common wealth *and* the soule w[i]thout w[hi]ich the magistrate cannot stand…."[179] Ten years earlier a close associate of Lord Burghley's, James Morice, had asserted in a set of readings "at the Middle Temple" that the English form of government had been developed in order to best guard against the tendency of monarchy "to slip into

---

late 16th century Scotland, George Buchanan had written a similar ancient constitutionalist narrative extolling the rule of law limitations on royal power – *De Jure Regni apud Scotos* – in his capacity as tutor to the young James VI. *See generally, e.g.,* A DIALOGUE ON THE LAW OF KINGSHIP AMONG THE SCOTS: A CRITICAL EDITION AND TRANSLATION OF GEORGE BUCHANAN'S DE JURE REGNI APUD SCOTOS DIALOGUS (Roger A. Mason and Martin S. Smith eds. 2004) (1579).

[178] Brooks, *supra* note 169 at 77 (discussing BL Harleian MS 4990).

[179] *Id.* at 66 (discussing BL Additional MS 48, 109). Yelverton had been involved in the production of the historical tragedy *The Misfortunes of Arthur* the prior year. See discussion *supra* at 9.

tyranny and insolent oppression." According to Morice the view that the royal prerogative placed the king above the constraints of the law so "that he is not bounde to governe by the same but at his will and pleasure, is an Opinion altogether repugn[an]t to the wise and politique State of gov[er]nment established in this Realme, w[hi]ch placeth the Royall Majestie of The kynge as the Leiutenant of Almightie God in the Reverent Throne of Justice and true Iudgment."[180] While the juridical trope of the ancient constitution may not explicitly appear in any significant fashion "at least until the 1590s" as determined by Christopher Brooks, the constituent elements of harmonious natural law juris-prudence, assertions of the rule of law, and mythic figures from British chronicle histories had already long been present in English legal culture.[181]

Brooks has suggested several factors leading to the rise of ancient constitutionalism as an influential juridical trope in the early seventeenth century. First, the nearly exponential growth of both the English legal profession and the legal system itself, together with "a spectacular increase in the amount of litigation which came before the central courts," over the latter half of the Tudor era secured not only the political influence of the legal profession but of legal rhetoric in social and political thought as well. This unprecedented growth of law, lawyers and litigation led to increased criticism of lawyers "because they seemed unable to solve the administrative and professional problems associated" with it. Furthermore, the common law system itself characterized by "judge-made law was extremely susceptible to the charge that it was uncertain," and the standard explanation of the central role played by *right reason* in common law jurisprudence "raised suspicions that the law was nothing more than

---

[180] *Id.* at 71–72 (discussing BL Additional MS 36,081).
[181] *Id.* at 59, *passim*.

what a particular judge willed it to be at any given moment." The imminent succession to the English Crown by James VI, sovereign of the much derided and decidedly foreign legal system of Scotland, only added to this state of public uncertainty concerning the law and lawyers of England. That James was an unapologetic advocate for a view of the absolute powers of divine right monarchy barely constrained, if at all, by the rule of law further exacerbated these concerns. The new king's announcement in his first address to the English Parliament that his most cherished goal was to unify the two kingdoms into a new realm of Great Britain, which strongly implied a union of the two legal systems, focused this situation into a perfect storm. It was within this contextual perfect storm that Coke's ancient constitutionalist prefaces to *The Reports* and the Union Tracts themselves were written.

A further factor is the influential role likely played by the significant involvement of the lawyers of the Inns of Court in producing the masques and revels of the latter half of the sixteenth century that had so highly popularized the ancient constitutionalist aspects of British chronicle history. Themes of ancient traditions of the rule of law and an elective monarchy governing with the consent and advice of Council and Parliament, as well as the dangers of attempting to rule divided kingdoms, were recurring elements of the productions created by the collaborative efforts of the English legal and literary professions ever since the first performance of *Gorbuduc* in 1561. The ancient constitution trope would appear to have explicitly manifested in early Stuart Britain because it was so perfectly suited for rhetorical use as "a defense of the uniqueness of the common law became a politic means of opposing the union" as well as for opposing any assertions of an absolute royal prerogative power unbound by the rule of law.[182]

Ancient Constitutionalism and the Origins of the Rights of British Subjects in Jacobean Union Texts

Although Saltern's thorough use of ancient constitutionalist rhetoric in unequivocal and enthusiastic support of the king's proposal for union is a noticeable outlier among the Union Tracts, neither his discussions of the origins and development of laws, nor his use of ancient mythic elements from British chronicle histories would have been thought exceptional by his contemporary readers. Myth-history and natural law jurisprudence were not merely potentially useful tools of juridical rhetoric in their cosmically harmonious world, they were essential lodestones for the Tudor and early Stuart mental world. Several examples from Coke's works are relevant to these points and also further illustrate the extent to which ancient constitutionalist tropes permeated not just the Union Tracts but were also used in other juridical narratives to facilitate and maintain the limited union achieved by the accession of James VI and I. In Coke's Fourth Institutes written long after the Union proposal failed, he begins Chapter 75, *Of Scotland*, with the words of the very first English statute of James's reign to state the first of "many things worthy of observation: 1. That these two mighty, famous, and ancient kingdoms, viz. England and Scotland (I use the words of the Act of Parliament) were anciently but one." Coke then proceeds to state, "[t]hat as there is one language in both, so there was one kind of government and one law in ancient time that ruled both

---

[182] *Id.* at 59–60, 83–86.

with many unanimous agreements between them," employing an analogical style that could almost have been cribbed from Saltern's tract. "First," Coke asserts, "the Laws of Scotland are divided as the Laws of England be into the Common laws, Acts of Parliament, and Customes." He then notes that the common laws of Scotland were compiled into two books, the *Regiam Majestatem* and *Quonia Attachiamenta*, observing that the former "doth in substance agree with our Glanvil." After stating the exception to primogeniture in allowing royal daughters to inherit the kingdom in the absence of a direct male heir, Coke goes on to note the similarities of Parliaments "consisting of the same Members, viz. Lords Spiritual, Lords Temporal, and the Commons." Both realms "have the same degrees of Nobility… the same great Officers…, and the same Ministers of Justice." Furthermore, both kingdoms have "the same laws for the most part," and "the like writs." Even certain aspects of Scottish law "agree with Magna Carta concerning Wardships, &c." Coke further notes that "[t]he same Vocables of art are used in the laws of both kingdoms." If the two kingdoms were "anciently but one," then where had the current differences in laws come from? For Coke these divergences only came about "by reason of their Acts of Parliament." It was through the same process as had happened in England that the old common laws of Scotland were "altered, diminished, and abrogated," and new ones made that had led to "the distinct kingdoms as they now stand hav[ing] many different Lawes."[183] This is the same basic rhetorical pattern used by Saltern and other pro-union tract

---

[183] SIR EDWARD COKE, THE FOURTH PART OF THE INSTITUTES OF THE LAWS OF ENGLAND: CONCERNING THE JURISDICTION OF COURTS 345 (London, 1644), (citing 1 Jac.1 c.1, "two mighty, famous and ancient kingdoms (yet anciently but one) of England and Scotland…."). [hereinafter FOURTH INSTITUTE]

authors to demonstrate that England and Scotland had shared a legal unity in antiquity.

Earlier in Chapter 48, *Of Wales*, Coke had extolled the need and value of at least the spirit of union within and amongst the various domains of the British multiple monarchy. After recounting the recurring trouble brought upon Welsh attempts to maintain a union under a system of partible inheritance until finally brought under one monarch again (a unity which had in fact never actually fully existed in Welsh history) by the conquest of Edward I, Coke asserts that "the royall dignity of a Monarch or King, from whence all other subordinate dignities… are derived, without any diminution, will suffer no division. He then references not a legal source, but the story of *Gorbuduc*, the highly popular first British history play in the history of English theatre produced by the Inner Temple in 1561:

> The most wofull event that fell out in this Realm, when Gorbuduc divided this Kingdome between his two sons, Ferrex and Porrex, and what heavy event came to pass untill it was reduced again under one Monarch, let our Histories tell you: And letting passe others, I cannot over-pass the miserable state within this Kingdom under the Heptarchy until all was reunited under one Sovereign. And this is the reason, that in England, Scotland, and Ireland, the royall dignity is descendible to the eldest daughter or sister, etc.[184]

As well as further illustrating the persuasive authority of non-historical sources for our authors, the highly non-contextual references to Scotland and Ireland in the *Of Wales* chapter also reveals that Coke likely continued to believe in the benefits of an eventual more complete un-

---

[184] *Id.* at 243. See discussion of *Gorbuduc*, the Inns of Court, and early English theatre *supra* at 8–11.

ion of the multiple monarchies long after James VI and I's union proposal had for the most part failed in that the need to guard against those risks transcended the reach of the common law of England to affect the other British dominions as well.

Coke's report of *Calvin's Case* twenty-five years earlier had included a claim that a form of genuine union had in fact already occurred. Following after his lengthy discussion of the relevance of the law of nature to the issues involved in *Calvin's Case* (which will be more fully discussed below), Coke stated:

> [I]t is first to be understood, that as the law hath wrought four unions, so the law doth still make four separations: The first union is of both kingdoms under one natural liege Sovereign King, and so acknowledged by the Act of Parliament of recognition [(the very first English statute of James's reign)]. The 2d is an union of ligeance and obedience of the subjects of both kingdoms, due by the law of nature to their sovereign: and this union doth suffice to rule and overrule the case in question: and this in substance is but a uniting of the hearts of the subjects of both kingdoms one to another, under one head and sovereign. The 3d union is a union of protection of both kingdoms equally belonging to the subjects of either of them: and therefore the two first arguments or objections drawn from the two supposed several ligeances were fallacious, for they did *disjungere conjungenda*. The 4th union and conjunction is of the three lions of England, and that one of Scotland, united and quartered in one escutcheon.
>
> Concerning the separations yet remaining: – 1. England and Scotland remain several and distinct kingdoms. 2. They are governed by several judicial or municipal laws. 3. They have several distinct and separate Parliaments. 4. Each kingdom has several nobilities: for albeit a *postnatus* in Scotland, or any of this posterity, be the heir of a nobleman in Scotland,

> and by his birth is legitimated in England, yet he is none of the peers or nobility of England....[185]

This passage from *Calvin's Case* helps makes sense of an otherwise easily misread passage in Coke's *Of Scotland* chapter from the *Fourth Institutes* discussed above: "I never read of any union of divided kingdomes, and therefore I conceive it to be without president [(precedence)]. And in this union many things would fall into consideration, and those of great weight, other than the union of lawes, though that be a maine one...."[186] Read in isolation this passage would seem to indicate that Coke believed no union had in fact taken place because the kingdoms were still divided. However, read in the context of his report of *Calvin's Case* it instead reveals Coke's lasting pride in the successful and unprecedented union of divided kingdoms that had in his view occurred as a matter of law upon James VI's succession to the English crown as James I. The limited extent to which James's proposal had succeeded was thanks in large part to Coke himself, specifically the lasting influence of his report of *Calvin's Case*.

Calvin's Case had come about after it had become clear in 1607 that neither the Scots nor English Parliaments were willing to do more than repeal comparatively minor statutes limiting trade and commerce between the realms. James's English Privy Council then contrived *Calvin's Case,* which is perhaps the first constitutional test case in the history of British-American law. The efficacy of the limited union of the crowns at the heart of the seventeenth century British multiple monarchy required that subjects of the different royal domains should be able to avail themselves of the different legal systems within those

---

[185] *Calvin's Case*, *supra* note 12 at 394; 14b–15a.
[186] FOURTH INSTITUTE *supra* note 183 at 347.

domains. If the subjects of the various domains were considered to be aliens outside their own domain, the potential for even minimally productive cooperation and unity would be virtually nil. Since both Parliaments had refused to resolve this issue, the King and Council turned to the English courts. Two English estates were conveyed to a Scottish child born after James' accession to the English Crown in 1603. The child, Robert Calvin, was then allegedly dispossessed of the estates by English subjects.

In order to have the case decided upon by the entire English judiciary, separate cases were brought in King's Bench and Chancery. Each estate's dispossession was challenged in a different court in order to allow each to be adjourned into Exchequer Chamber so that the ultimate holding should have the force of both the common law and the royal prerogative power. In this combined action, the plaintiff Calvin was represented by both Attorney-General Henry Hobart and Solicitor-General Francis Bacon while the defendants were represented by two of the leading Serjeants-at-Law, Laurence Hyde and Richard Hutton. The two Serjeants had also been among the leaders of the opposition to the Union measures in the English Parliament.[187] With all the judges hearing the cause and some of England's highest ranking barristers on both sides, no doubts would arise concerning the weight of the issue and its importance to the Crown. In the end only two of the judges ruled against Calvin with the remainder holding that those born in Scotland after James' accession were to be considered as natural born subjects in England. The corollary of this, that all English subjects born after the accession were to be considered

---

[187] *See* Le Case del Union, del Realm, D'Escose, ove Angleterre, 72 ENG. REP. 908 (n.d.), 2 STATE TRIALS 561–562.

natural born subjects in Scotland was transmitted by royal letter to the Scots Privy Council.[188]

In rhyme with his fellow lawyer Saltern's narrative, Coke's report of *Calvin's Case* relied upon both mythical and historical sources. Coke's use of myth-history commences at the very outset of his discussion of the issues in *Calvin's Case* including, among other mythical sources, the story of the Trojan Horse, and a discussion of Moses as "the first reporter or writer of law in the world."[189] Most telling of all, the narrative features Arthur prominently as the originator of the practice of requiring oaths of allegiance from the lowest levels of society — "this oath of ligeance at the torn and leet was first instituted by King Arthur …."[190] This anchoring of the reciprocal bonds of allegiance and obedience in the reign of Arthur is perhaps the most crucial ancient constitution trope in Coke's narrative as it aligns the holding of the case with the cycle of literature that had been used repeatedly for over 500 years to justify claims to a unified suzerainty over Britain by successive English monarchs — the *Matter of Britain*. Elements from the *Matter of Britain* would continue to be incorporated into legal texts well into the nineteenth century.

While a complete survey of these later texts is beyond the scope of this work, a small sampling illustrates the range of such texts. In 1614 John Selden discussed as historical both Arthur's seal and the Round Table in *Titles of Honor*. In his 1641 *Treatise of the Antiquity, Authority, Uses and Jurisdiction of the Ancient Courts of Leet* Robert Powell discussed the origins of Courts Leet and the oaths of ligeance taken therein, and of Parliament in Arthur's reign. William Hughes similarly included the

---

[188] *See, e.g.*, GALLOWAY, *supra* note 96 at 148–150.
[189] *Calvin's Case*, *supra* note 12 at 399, 392; 18b, 13a.
[190] *Id.* at 385; 7a.

origins of the oaths of Homage and Fealty in Arthur's reign in his 1662 *Grand Abridgment of the Law*. Sir George Mackenzie noted "the exclusion of Mordredus, son of Lothus" from the rightful descent of the British monarchy in his 1684 *Jus Regium, or the Just and Solid Foundation of Monarchy*. Humphrey Hody mentioned Ambrosius, Uther Pendragon, and Arthur in the context of origins of the granting of charters to churches in his 1701 *History of English Councils and Convocations*. The anonymous author of a 1715 *Book of Oaths* saw fit to include the "The Oath of the Knights of the Round Table, in the time of King Arthur." Giles Jacob would similarly include an entry for "CALIBURNE, the famous sword of the great King Arthur" in his *Law Dictionary*; and entry maintained by every subsequent editor of Jacob's dictionary. Among such works in the nineteenth century was the discussion of both Vortigern and Arthur as examples of the origins of the rule of law and oaths of allegiance in T.H.B. Oldfield's 1816 *Representative History of Great Britain and Ireland*.[191]

---

[191] SELDEN, TITLES OF HONOR, *supra* note 88 at 160, 365–366; ROBERT POWELL, A TREATISE OF THE ANTIQUITY, AUTHORITY, USES AND JURISDICTION OF THE ANCIENT COURTS OF LEET, OR VIEW OF FRANK-PLEDGE, AND OF SUBORDINATION OF GOVERNMENT DERIVED FROM THE INSTITUTION OF MOSES, THE FIRST LEGISLATOR: AND THE FIRST IMITATION OF HIM IN THIS ISLAND OF GREAT BRITAINE, BY KING ALFRED AND CONTINUED EVER SINCE 19 [leaf D2], 174–75, 199 (London, 1641); WILLIAM HUGHES, 2 THE GRAND ABRIDGMENT OF THE LAW 1049 (London, 1662); SIR GEORGE MACKENZIE, JUS REGIUM, OR, THE JUST AND SOLID FOUNDATIONS OF MONARCHY 165 (Edinburgh: 1684); HUMPHRY HODY, A HISTORY OF ENGLISH COUNCILS AND CONVOCATIONS 16, 59 (London, 1701); THE BOOK OF OATHS, AND THE SEVERAL FORMS THEREOF, BOTH ANCIENT AND MODERN, FAITHFULLY COLLECTED OUT OF SUNDRY AUTHENTICK BOOKS OF RECORDS 64–65 (London, 1715); GILES JACOB, THE LAW-DICTIONARY : EXPLAINING THE RISE, PROGRESS, AND PRESENT STATE OF THE ENGLISH LAW, IN THEORY AND PRACTICE; DEFINING AND INTERPRETING THE TERMS OR WORDS OF ART; AND COMPRISING

In another of those later texts, the 1675 case of *Witrong v. Blaney*, the *Matter of Britain* had found its way back in to the juridical narrative of the common law itself. The report of this case also provides further insight into the question of how a unified kingdom of Great Britain could be defended as a restitution when the various kingdoms that had in fact existed in Britain's long history had never actually been unified under a single sovereign power. The issuance of a *testatum scire facias* on a debt judgment into Wales was challenged in *Witrong*. It was held that:

> *Scire facias* or other exception on the like reason may issue into Wales. Originally Wales and England were but one nation, so the union is but a restitution, both have the same descent, religion, government and laws before the Romans, and till the time of the Saxons, as all histories of Cesar [sic], Tacitus, and the poets *divisos orbe Britannos* testifie [sic] that they were taken as one; but when the Romans left Britain to pursue the Goths, the Britains King Arthur and Kadwallader to govern; but on the Saxons success the Britains retyred westward, and *Saxo Wallios nuncupavit*, as distinct from other parts of Britain then divided into Heptarchy....

The report of the decision also echoes the celebration of James VI and I uniting the sundered bloodlines of the ancient British monarchy found in various Jacobean Union texts by noting that "in H.7 the British, Northern and English blood were united...." One notable difference is that while such a statutory union of Scotland and England

---

COPIOUS INFORMATION, HISTORICAL, POLITICAL, AND COMMERCIAL, ON THE SUBJECTS OF OUR LAW, TRADE, AND GOVERNMENT (T. E. Tomlin ed., London, 1797); *and* T.H.B OLDFIELD, THE REPRESENTATIVE HISTORY OF GREAT BRITAIN AND IRELAND: BEING A HISTORY OF THE HOUSE OF COMMONS, AND OF THE COUNTIES, CITIES, AND BOROUGHS OF THE UNITED KINGDOM, FROM THE EARLIEST PERIOD 14 (London, 1816).

had yet to occur by 1675, there had in fact been a statutory union of Wales and England — "27 H.8, cap.26, makes the absolute union...[;]" which statute was "but an Act of Restitution...."[192] The crucial element in common with the Jacobean Union texts is the assertion of an ancient union when no such ancient union had actually existed in the history of Britain. Nonetheless, a restitution was legally held to have happened based upon the statutory recitation of that historically non-existent union within the earlier statute of Henry VIII.

There is a remarkably similar discussion of how and why Wales had always been part of England in Coke's report of *Calvin's Case*. Coke discusses Wales in order to further emphasize the extent of the bonds of natural ligeance throughout the multiple domains of the now British sovereign authority, James VI and I. However, rather than citing to Arthur, Cadwallader, or any other purported ancient British kings, Coke instead notes that "in this respect in divers ancient charters, Kings of old time styled themselves in several manners, as King Edgar, *Brittanniae* [*Basileus*]; *Ethelredus, totius Albioni' Dei povidentia Imperator*; *Edredus Magn' Britann' Monarcha*, which among many other of like nature I have seen."[193] As with the assertion by Thomas Craig of a restitution discussed earlier in Chapter One, these passages in *Witrong v. Blaney* and *Calvin's Case* were juridically valid precisely because mythic and chronicle sources and prior mere claims of unitary sovereignty were the equivalent of historical sources in terms of persuasive authority. Such sources conveyed culturally significant constitutive and moral symbolic truths.

---

[192] *Witrong v. Blaney*, 84 ENG. REP. 789, 790–792; 3 KEBLE 401, 404–407 (1675).

[193] *Calvin's Case, supra* note 12 at 403; 21b.

In addition to such primary components of the *Matter of Britain*, Coke's report of *Calvin's Case* and Saltern's *Of the Antient Lawes* share two other telling elements that provide helpful clues into the basic nature of ancient constitutionalism. The first concerns how conquests could affect the ancient laws without disrupting the basic continuity of the common law over time. The second is an assertion of faith and fidelity to the divinely crafted law of nature as a foundational concept. In *Calvin's Case* Coke explains in dicta that there is a profound difference between the conquest by a Christian king over "a kingdom of an infidel" and when such a king "come[s] to a Christian kingdom by conquest…." In the former case all of the pagan realm's laws are immediately set aside in favor of the laws of the conquering Christian king. In the latter case the conqueror "may at his pleasure alter and change the laws… but until he doth make an alteration of those laws the ancient laws of that kingdom remain." Furthermore, "if a King hath a kingdom by title of descent, there seeing by the laws of that kingdom he doth inherit the kingdom, he cannot change the laws of himself, without consent of Parliament."[194]

That mitigating effect of claiming a crown by title of descent renders the Norman Conquest potentially moot for Coke and Saltern in that Duke William of Normandy

---

[194] *Id.* at 398; 17b–18a. *See also* KEN MACMILLAN, THE ATLANTIC IMPERIAL CONSTITUTION: CENTER AND PERIPHERY IN THE ENGLISH NEW WORLD 16 (2011) (noting that Coke drew upon medieval jurisprudence to assert that inherited domains "were required to be governed according to the laws and constitutions already in operation in those lands.") *and* Gavin Loughton, *Calvin's Case and the Origins of the Rule Governing 'Conquest' in English Law*, 8 AUSTL. J. LEG. HIST. 143 (2004) (discussing the extent to which Coke's report of *Calvin's Case* changed the medieval English law of conquest in order to accommodate both the limited union of English and Scottish subjects and the establishing of common law legal systems in the emerging colonial dominions).

only resorted to conquest in order to enforce his claim to be the rightful heir of Edward the Confessor. The earlier conquests of the Romans, Saxons, and Danes could also be considered as having no lasting effect on the continuity of the common law because they were pagan conquerors whose alterations would have been remedied by subsequent Christian kings of England like Alfred the Great, if not stymied entirely by the successful initial resistance "of *Aurelius Ambrosius*, and of *Arthur* the worthy…."[195] Coke and Saltern were hardly alone in finessing the consequences of ancient conquests on the development of the common law. Even Sir Henry Spelman, who relied upon the Norman Conquest to refute "the existence of hereditary tenures before William I" and the pre-Norman existence of Parliament, nonetheless also asserted an ancient pre-Norman origin of the institution of tithes by referring to King Edgar confirming the payment of tithes as a legal obligation "'in a great parliament about the yeare 959….'"[196] There simply was no uniform view in early modern Britain as to "antiquity of the law and its relationship to the successive conquests not just of the Normans, but of Romans, Anglo-Saxons, and Danes…," which is why "neither proved to be the occasion of an early Stuart historical controversy, either among prose historians or lawyers."[197] Deriding ancient constitutionalist authors like Coke and Saltern for neglecting or dismissing the effects of prior conquests on the continuity of the common law's development is the product of much later authors, especially of late nineteenth century and twentieth century writers caught up in the de-mythologizing historiography of their own times.

---

[195] OF THE ANTIENT LAWES at [71].
[196] WOOLF, THE IDEA OF HISTORY IN EARLY STUART ENGLAND, *supra* note 24 at 29, n.79.
[197] *Id.* at 29.

The assertion of faith and fidelity to the divinely crafted law of nature as a foundational concept is seen in Saltern's perception of the continued existence of the "secret footsteps of our ancient British constitutions" in the English common law of his day as deriving from the extent to which "the principles thereof [(of the common law)] will appear to be the very Laws of the eternal God, written in the two immortal tables of nature & Scripture." This is a continuity not of unchanging substance, but one of faith and fidelity to the common law's guiding spirit and inspiration. This tradition of continuity is most fully discussed in Saltern's fifth chapter about the laws King Lucius supposedly derived from the laws of the ancient pagan Britons. Any laws deemed by Lucius and his Council to be "against right & good reason, which God in nature & Scripture hath described, … they procured to be amended, or patiently suffered, if it were incurable, least the whole common good … should be stirred in hope of some particular…." The goal of this ongoing process was to stabilize rather than "shake and weaken the public estate…." It is this never-ending process of revision and amendment faithfully guided by the light of reason as revealed in the divine law of nature "whereby all our questions, and controversies, all our arguments and judgements, all our Statutes and customs, are ruled and overruled, enlarged and corrected."[198] Saltern primarily

---

[198] OF THE ANTIENT LAWES at [5], [23]–[24]. This process of legal continuity also aligns well with the rules of settlement and conquest derived from *Calvin's Case* and codified in a Privy Council Memorandum of Aug. 9, 1722, which stated that "upon an appeal to the King in Council from the foreign plantations:– 1st. That if there be a new and uninhabited country found out by English subjects, as the law is the birthright of every subject, so wherever they go, they carry their law with them, and therefore such new found country is to be governed by the law of England, though after such country is inhabited by the English, Acts of Parliament made in England, without

extols an unbroken fidelity in Britain to this common law process in his tract, not a perfect preservation of the exact substantive rules of the ancient common law itself. Although Saltern does not expressly use the terms fidelis or fidelity, fidelity is the underlying theme of continuity for the ancient constitutions in his tract.

The birth-right ligeance at the heart of *Calvin's Case* is likewise originally the product not of man-made laws, but of harmonious fidelity to the sacred law of nature itself. As for Saltern, for Coke the law of nature is eternal, having existed long before any man-made laws. "This law of nature," Coke states, "which indeed is the eternal law of the Creator, infused into the heart of the creature at the time of his creation, was two thousand years before any laws written, and before any judicial or municipal laws." For Coke, faith (*fidem*) and allegiance (*ligeance*) are equivalent terms — "[s]ometimes ligeance is called faith, *fides, ad fidem Regis, &c.*," and, later, "[*i*]*n fide*, in faith or ligeance nothing ought to be feigned, but ought to be *ex fide non ficta*."[199] In another passage he states: "he that is sworn in the leet, is sworn to the King for his lige-

---

naming the foreign plantations, will not bind them, for which reason it has been determined that the Statute of Frauds and Perjuries, which requires three witnesses, and that these should subscribe in the testator's presence in the case of a devise of land, does not bind Barbadoes: but that 2ndly. Where the King of England conquers a country, it is a different consideration; for there the conqueror, by saving the lives of the people conquered, gains a right and property in such people, in consequence of which he may impose upon them what law he pleases: but 3dly. Until such laws given by the conquering prince, the laws and customs of the conquered country shall hold in place, unless where these are contrary to our religion, or enact any thing that is *malum in se*, or are silent; for in all such cases the laws of the conquering country shall prevail." 24 ENG. REP. 646 (Privy Council, 1722).

[199] *Calvin's Case, supra* note 12 at 383, 389; 5a, 10b. There are multiple uses of, and references to, *fidem* and *fidelis* throughout Coke's report of *Calvin's Case* at 383, 385, 387–389, 391–392, 397, 403, and 410; 5a–5b, 6b–7b, 8b–10b, 12b–13b, 16b, 22a, and 27b.

ance, that is, to be true and faithful to the King," and, "it appeareth, that ligeance, and faith and truth which are her members and parts, are qualities of the mind and soul of man."[200] This is not precisely the faith of religious belief. It is faith in the sense of loyalty and fidelity; a juridical analogy of religious faith. It is this definition of ligeance as those "qualities of the mind and soul of man" that leads Coke to conclude that ligeance and its associated oaths are therefore owed to the natural body of the monarch rather than to the political body of the monarch because the latter has no soul — "which oath[s] he taketh in his natural person: for the politic capacity is invisible and immortal; nay, the politic body hath no soul, for it is framed by the policy of man." Having demonstrated that ligeance is owed to the natural body of the monarch, Coke goes on to reiterate "that the ligeance or faith of the subject is due unto the King by the law of nature: secondly, that the law of nature is part of the law of England: thirdly, that the law of nature was before any judicial or municipal law: fourthly, that the law of nature is immutable."[201] Fidelity to the sacred law of nature since time

---

[200] *Id.* at 385; 7a–7b.

[201] *Id.* at 389; 10b. For a thorough discussion of the medieval political theory of the King's Two Bodies, *see* ERNST H. KANTOROWICZ, THE KING'S TWO BODIES: A STUDY IN MEDIAEVAL POLITICAL THEOLOGY (1957). The concept had first been expressed as part of the common law of England in *Plowden's Commentaries*: "The King has in him two Bodies, *viz*, a Body natural, and a Body politic. His Body natural (if it be considered in itself) is a Body mortal, subject to all Infirmities that come by Nature or Accident, to the Imbecility of Infancy or old Age, and the like defects that happen to the natural Bodies of other People. But his Body politic is a Body that cannot be seen or handled, consisting of Policy and Government, and constituted for the Direction of the People, and the Management of the public weal, and this Body is utterly void of Infancy, and old Age, and other natural Defects and Imbecilities, which the Body natural is subject to, and for this cause, what the king does in his Body politic, cannot be invalidated or frus-

immemorial is the underlying theme of legal continuity through the long centuries for both Saltern and Coke.

Anchoring the bonds of allegiance that connect the sovereign and the subject in the law of nature, and asserting that they were owed not to the political body of the monarch but to the natural body, also supported the growth of extra-territorial colonial British dominions. If the "ligeance of both kingdoms [(Scotland and England)], is due to their sovereign by one law, and that is the law of nature," then by definition the bonds of British allegiance are capable of expanding along with the dominions of the British sovereign.[202] Coke follows his discussion of the origins of the bonds of allegiance in the law of nature with a discussion of the legal meanings of the term *alienigena*, or alien, within English law. Coke states that "[a]n alien is a subject that is born out of the ligeance of the King, and under the ligeance of another...." Such an alien "can have no real or personal action for or concerning land" in England. Coke follows this explication of legal alienage with detailed examples of how in prior centuries when the English Crown still held extensive continental dominions, "all men born in Normandy, Gascoin, Anjou, and Britain [(Britanny)]," as well as the Welsh and Irish, and those born within domains conquered from the French (referring to the example of Calais), "were inheritable within this realm as well as Englishmen." Coke then states that "the reason thereof was, for that they were under one ligeance due to one sovereign."[203]

---

trated by any Disability in his natural Body." EDMUND PLOWDEN, THE COMMENTARIES OR REPORTS 213 (London, 1779) (1548) (reporting the *Case of the Dutchy of Lancaster*). Coke cites to this case and to the case of *Willion v. Berkley* reported in *Plowden's Commentaries*. *See Calvin's Case*, *supra* note 12 at 389; 10a.

[202] *Calvin's Case*, *supra* note 12 at 394, 399; 14b, 18b.

[203] *Calvin's Case*, *supra* note 12 at 399–406, 402; 18b–25a, 20b.

It is for this same reason that all Scots subjects born before the accession of James VI of Scotland to the English Crown as James I, the *antenati*, were aliens in English law, "(for that at the time of their birth they were under the ligeance and obedience, of another king)," whereas those subjects of both realms born after the accession of James VI *and* I, the *post-nati*, were subjects within both England and Scotland.[204] The *post-nati* all owed ligeance to the same natural body. James Stuart, King of Scotland, and James Stuart, King of England, shared the same natural body but had two separate political bodies. Therefore, from the date of James' English accession in 1603 every *British* subject born thereafter owed ligeance to James's natural body regardless of which British dominion in either the Old or New Worlds each subject happened to be born. This is the seed from which the British-American legal doctrine of birthright citizenship would ultimately be born.[205]

The significance of *Calvin's Case* cannot be overstated. In addition to authoritatively defining the parameters of the relationship of allegiance and obligations between subject and sovereign in a multiple monarchy, it remained the foundation of British, and later American, birthright citizenship until the twentieth century. Through its holding that every subject born owing allegiance to the King of England, whether born within or without territory within the dominion of the king, was a natural born subject in all of the king's dominions, *Calvin's Case* became the bedrock upon which successive generations of British colonists would claim all the rights due natural born Eng-

---

[204] *Id.* at 396; 16a.

[205] *See generally* CLIVE PARRY, BRITISH NATIONALITY: INCLUDING CITIZENSHIP OF THE UNITED KINGDOM & COLONIES AND THE STATUS OF ALIENS (1951) *and* Polly J. Price, *Natural Law and Birthright Citizenship in* Calvin's Case *(1608)*, 9 YALE J.L. & HUMAN. 73 (1997).

lishmen, enabling the eventual growth of the British Empire. The rule of *Calvin's Case* would eventually ensure that the increasingly far-flung subjects of the developing British Empire would not be considered aliens when travelling in other imperial dominions. In a very significant sense, then, the fundamental right to travel also stems from *Calvin's Case*.[206] The beginnings of the conviction that separate states with different legal systems and fundamental liberties could be successfully united under a single sovereign power while still retaining their own laws and liberties lie in the limited British Union secured by the decision in *Calvin's Case*.

The United States and the Commonwealth nations would all grow from this nascent British constitutionalism that began to develop in early Stuart Britain. Without the limited union secured by *Calvin's Case* both American constitutionalism and Commonwealth constitutionalism would have developed along starkly different lines, if at all. *Calvin's Case* should therefore be viewed as part and parcel of the body of texts known to posterity as the Jacobean Union Tracts, the closing tract if you will. Indeed, as a product of all the judges of England sitting the in Exchequer Chamber, the various printed reports of *Calvin's Case* can be viewed as constitutionally serving a jurispathic function by excising certain narratives of the common law tradition's origins, historical development, and meaning in order to judicially secure a limited union of British subjects through the shared bonds of allegiance based on birthright out of the ashes of King James' original proposal. The term *jurispathic*, first coined by Robert

---

[206] *See* DANIEL J. HULSEBOSCH, CONSTITUTING EMPIRE: NEW YORK AND THE TRANSFORMATION OF CONSTITUTIONALISM IN THE ATLANTIC WORLD, 1664–1830 23 (2005) ("But the doctrine of ligeance was radical for its time because it encouraged mobility throughout the king's composite monarchy.").

Cover in his now classic *Nomos and Narrative* article, refers to the essential role courts serve in meeting the societal "need to suppress law, to choose between two or more laws, to impose upon laws a hierarchy" in the all too common situation where there are variant juridical narratives being asserted in order to resolve a legal dispute. [207] The context of *Calvin's Case* provides a paradigmatic example of such a situation. As David Martin Jones has suggested, the official accounts of *Calvin's Case* were "designed to legitimize an official understanding of the Crown's lawful political authority, which had been evolving since the oath [(of allegiance)] attached to the act of succession had established the outlines of a formally incorporated English body politic[;] *Calvin's Case* filled in the outline." The decision reached by all but two of the judges of England sitting en banc in Exchequer Chamber "thus performed the inestimable service of producing a version of the ancient constitution which legitimated the English state's evolving use of the oath since the Reformation." The political significance of *Calvin's Case* was two-fold. On the one hand, "it married the government's view of allegiance, promulgated in recent state oaths, to the law and ancient constitution of the realm."[208] The decision also effectively ended the political discourse related to the King's Union Proposal.

That the reports of *Calvin's Case* did indeed successfully bring the Jacobean Union Debates to a close with definitive finality is suggested by a contemporary manuscript wherein the anonymous author, writing circa 1610 about recent political issues, decries the result:

---

[207] Robert Cover, *The Supreme Court 1982 Term – Foreword: Nomos and Narrative*, 97 HARV. L. REV. 4, 40 (1982).
[208] DAVID MARTIN JONES, CONSCIENCE AND ALLEGIANCE IN SEVENTEENTH CENTURY ENGLAND: THE POLITICAL SIGNIFICANCE OF OATHS AND ENGAGEMENTS 69, 74 (1999).

> Three things have been debated in this parliament that have much concerned the right of our whole nation, of which every one of them have exceeded the other by a gradation in weight and moment.
>
> [....]
>
> The second was the union, a question of greater moment for it concerned the freehold of our whole nation not in so high a point of division and participation. That is whether we should enjoy the benefits and liberties of the Kingdome ourselves onely as we and our ancestors had done, or admit our neighbour nation to have equal right of them. And so make our own part the less by so much the greater the number should be among whom the Division was to be made. This was adjudged against us both legally and solemnly.
>
> [....][209]

It is because of this jurispathic function that *Calvin's Case* can, and should, be read as the final and authoritative Jacobean Union Tract, or Union Text, contrived in response to the Union proposal of James VI and I.[210]

---

[209] ANONYMOUS, COLLECTION OF COPIES OF DOCUMENTS RELATING LARGELY TO CONSTITUTIONAL AND LEGAL CONTROVERSIES OF 1610–CA. 1621 [MANUSCRIPT], COMPILED CA. 1625. This manuscript codex is held by the Folger Shakespeare Library at call number V.a.121.

[210] The term Union Texts is offered as a potential alternative to Union Tracts when referring to this larger body of works. In addition to Coke's report of Calvin's Case, the Exchequer Chamber speeches of Lord Chancellor Ellesmere and Solicitor-General Bacon in favor of Calvin's suit were also printed in 1609 and 1641 respectively. THOMAS EGERTON, BARON ELLESMERE, THE SPEECH OF THE LORD CHANCELLOR OF ENGLAND, TOUCHING THE POST-NATI (London, 1609) *and* FRANCIS BACON, THREE SPEECHES OF THE RIGHT HONORABLE, SIR FRANCIS BACON KNIGHT, THEN HIS MAJESTIES SOLLICITOR GENERALL, AFTER LORD VERULAM, VISCOUNT SAINT ALBAN. CONCERNING THE POST-NATI, NATURALIZATION OF THE SCOTCH IN ENGLAND, UNION OF THE LAWES OF THE KINGDOMES OF

Calvin's Case is still cited as authority to this day. A survey of just American federal cases reveals over 20 cases relying in part or in whole upon it as authoritative precedent. It is not cited just for resolving issues of citizenship, but also issues of inheritance, and the effect of a conquest on the existing legal system of a conquered nation. While most of these American cases are from the Founding period, or shortly thereafter into the early 19th century, several date from the late 19th century and 20th century. The most recent is a 2015 District of Columbia Circuit birthright citizenship case, *Tuaua v. United States*. *Calvin's Case* is the first precedent cited in the opinion's discussion of birthright citizenship.[211] Among these authoritative uses of *Calvin's Case* in American law, there is a telling early challenge to its authority in the case of *M'Ilvaine v. Coxe's Lessee* from 1805.[212] An intriguing aspect of *M'Ilvaine* for the purpose of discussing the role played by myth-history in the juridical narratives of the law is that the plaintiff's challenge to the authority of *Calvin's Case* stresses that "[t]he authority of that case is much shaken by the many absurdities it contains."[213] The absurdities recounted by plaintiff's counsel specifically deride the notion of believing "that Moses was the first reporter," among others.[214] What is not so specified is the

---

ENGLAND AND SCOTLAND. PUBLISHED BY THE AUTHORS COPY, AND LICENSED BY AUTHORITY. (London, 1641). These two works and Moore's report of the earlier Parliamentary debates were later combined with Coke's report of *Calvin's Case* as the version included in *Cobbett's State Trials*. 2 COBBETT'S COMPLETE COLLECTION OF STATE TRIALS AND PROCEEDINGS FOR HIGH TREASON AND OTHER CRIMES AND MISDEMEANORS FROM THE EARLIEST PERIOD TO THE PRESENT TIME 560 (London, 1809–1828). The Union speeches and proclamations of James VI & I should also be included within this larger body of Union Texts.

[211] *Tuaua v. United States*, 788 F.3d 300, 304 (D.C. Cir. 2015).

[212] *M'Ilvaine v. Coxe's Lessee*, 6 U.S. 280 (1805).

[213] *Id.*, at 290.

[214] *Id.*

belief in the origins of oaths of allegiance in the reign of King Arthur. The failure to include Arthur's existence as one of the absurdities complained of strongly suggests that such a belief was not yet considered either foolish or utterly non-historical at this point in the development of American constitutional jurisprudence. This together with the fact that plaintiff's arguments in this regard apparently carried little weight in failing to persuade the Court to abandon *Calvin's Case* as binding authority indicates that the presence of myth and fable in judicial opinions — in other words, in the narrative fabric of law itself — was still fairly unremarkable in the juridical discourse of early America. A cogent reminder that one century's myths are often the cherished history of another; and, that myths are capable of continuing to influence a culture long after their historicity is called into question.

Alain Wijffels comparative study of the Union Tracts quite rightly concluded that the combination of a mytho-historical "medieval legal heritage of 'ancient liberties' and the early-modern concept of sovereignty" was integral to "[t]he most successful legal developments of' early seventeenth century Britain. As Wijffels suggests, Saltern's work "[m]ore adequately than all the pamphlets on the union … illustrates how allegedly historical findings could contribute to the manipulation of the political debate on a union of laws."[215] This is why Bruce Galloway could justifiably, but somewhat misleadingly, note that: "Saltern's work does not, however, appear to have had much influence on popular beliefs, or royal policy!"[216] Galloway has this exactly backwards. Saltern's narrative aligned perfectly with the existing and developing popular beliefs, juridical culture, and royal policy of

---

[215] Wijffels, *A British ius commune?*, *supra* note 142 at 316, 330.
[216] GALLOWAY, THE UNION OF ENGLAND AND SCOTLAND, *supra* note 96 at 40.

early modern Britain. Pointing out that it did not significantly influence "popular beliefs, or royal policy" and implying that it failed to help bring about the full union of Scottish and English laws is akin to pointing out that adding a bucket of water to the ocean failed to appreciably alter the sea level. Saltern's assertions of a common British legal history, and of common elements in the laws of Scotland and England as still discernible evidence of those 'ancient British constitutions, appearing yet in the body of our common Laws' in 1605, resonated with analogous statements in Craig and other tracts, parliamentary debates, and *Calvin's Case*, as well as the initial 1603/04 Royal Proclamation.[217]

Wijffels study also supports the view that Craig in particular well understood the constitutive value of such juridical historiography, in that he "argued for a new British historiography" as a vital step towards ultimately bringing the Union of Great Britain to fruition.[218] Craig not only suggested that "the public annals of the two countries should be revised" because "[e]rrors and irritating expressions must be expunged ..., and a new history of Britain should be written with the utmost regard to accuracy" to further the aim of a British union. His work also provided examples of possible revisions that are sufficiently pseudo-historical to cast doubt on his commitment to historical accuracy unless pseudo-mythic history is somehow accurate according to the criteria of a literary lawyer. The clearest example of this is his attempt to shift the Druidic Colleges that Caesar stated were to be found in Britain and Tacitus identified as being on the Isle of Mona northwards to the Isle of Man, rather than the more traditional location of Anglesey off the coast of northern Wales. Relying on Boece, Craig asserted "that

---

[217] OF THE ANTIENT LAWES at [5].

[218] *See* Wijffels, *A British* ius commune*?*, *supra* note 142 at 333.

the Brigantes and Silures were Scots, that the island of Mona, the ancient abode of the Druids, belonged to the Scots and formed part of Scotland ...." After a lengthy exposition of why this must be true, he suggests that the reason why English authors refuse to accept this history lies in "the almost invariable fault of English writers, who care little what they say if there is a chance of speaking ill of the Scots."[219] Another example from a later work of Craig's is his assertion that the Kingdom of Scotland was not only more ancient than that of England, the Scots Kingdom was in his estimation "the most ancient kingdom in Europe."[220] He was clearly aware of several, from his perspective, erroneous elements in English accounts of British history. He must have also been aware of the rising popularity of works by Camden, Selden and others on both sides of the Scottish and English border. Perhaps Craig's call for a new model of British history arose because he was on some level aware that the English, whose emerging ancient constitutionalist discourse drew on far more varied chronicle history traditions than did that of Scotland's, were better positioned to inextricably align the emerging British identity with English culture than his fellow Scots were. Colin Kidd has convincingly argued that it was just such a comparative lack in the mytho-historical traditions of the Scots that enabled

---

[219] CRAIG, *supra* note 50 at 365–368.

[220] THOMAS CRAIG, THE RIGHT OF SUCCESSION TO THE KINGDOM OF ENGLAND: IN TWO BOOKS; AGAINST THE SOPHISMS OF PARSONS THE JESUITE, WHO ASSUM'D THE COUNTERFEIT NAME OF DOLEMAN: BY WHICH HE ENDEAVOURS TO OVERTHROW NOT ONLY THE RIGHTS OF SUCCESSION IN KINGDOMS BUT ALSO THE SACRED AUTHORITY OF KINGS THEMSELVES. WRITTEN ORIGINALLY IN LATIN ABOVE 100 YEARS SINCE BY SIR THOMAS CRAIG AND NOW FAITHFULLY TRANSLATED INTO ENGLISH, WITH A LARGE INDEX OF THE CONTENTS, AND A PREFACE BY THE TRANSLATOR, GIVING AN ACCOUNT OF THE AUTHOR AND OF HIS ADVERSARY 425, *passim* (London, 1703).

an Anglo-British identity to completely displace any sense of Scoto-British identity even in early nineteenth century ancient constitutionalist works by Scottish authors.[221] Craig's wish for a new genre of British public history would most assuredly be fulfilled, albeit without eliminating the historical inaccuracies he and so many others have bemoaned. The genre of ancient constitutionalism would live on well past its origins in early seventeenth century British juridical discourse to continue influencing British and American juridical thought through the eighteenth century and well into the nineteenth. As will be seen, it has even potentially survived into the twenty-first century.

---

[221] *See generally* COLIN KIDD, SUBVERTING SCOTLAND'S PAST: SCOTTISH WHIG HISTORIANS AND THE CREATION OF AN ANGLO-BRITISH IDENTITY, 1689–C.1830 (1993).

CONCLUSION

Constitutional Antiquarianism from the Letter of Eleutherus to American Originalism

The Union Debates and the explicit juridical conflicts between absolute royal power and the limitations of the rule of law which developed in the decades following the accession of James VI of Scotland to the English Crown as James I had provided fertile soil for ancient constitutionalism to take root and flourish in. Reading Saltern's *Of the Antient Lawes* together with Coke's report of *Calvin's Case* as the final authoritative Union Tract suggests an alternative way of understanding how the trope of the ancient constitution subsequently developed into a popular cultural narrative of immemorial juridical continuity that would allow ancient constitutionalism to grow far beyond its roots in the Union Texts. Rather than focusing in on those alleged substantive survivals cited by the authors of ancient constitutionalist texts that have since been demonstrated to be historically inaccurate, the focus should be on the claims of a continuous survival of the common law tradition and its associated juridical institutions. As Pocock has aptly stated:

> it was less (though it always could be) the content of the law than the juridical process itself — usage, judgment, and statute — that was immemorial; [and] the reform of obsolete laws and the making of new ones were perfectly compatible with the view that the common law rested in ancient usage...[222]

---

[222] POCOCK, THE ANCIENT CONSTITUTION, *supra* note 44 at 275.

This is a theme of continuity based on a commonplace view of the common law in this period "not as static but as in perpetual flux." As one of Coke and Saltern's fellow lawyers, Thomas Hedley, stated in Parliament in 1610, "the common law grew with England as the skin with the hand."[223] Others, inspired by "medieval Romanists such as Accursius and Baldus," compared the ancient constitution to "a ship which retained is essential form even though its planks and sails had been continuously replaced over the years."[224] The connective tissue, so to speak, maintaining that original ancient "essential form" with the juridical institutions of early modern Britain was fidelity to that essential form irrespective of the inevitable, and often clearly evident, changes to its substance wrought over time.

This is an ancient constitution of faithful process, not of perfectly preserved substantive details; "it is not a vision that is in any obvious way unsophisticated or inconsistent."[225] Selden's 1610 *Jani Anglorum* conveyed that vision of juridical continuity in "a detailed historical model of the ancient constitution in which the fundamental form of mixed government endured while particular laws, practices, and institutions slowly changed over time

---

[223] GREENBERG, *supra* note 29 at 33 (citing and paraphrasing 2 PROCEEDINGS IN PARLIAMENT IN 1610 50 (Elizabeth Read Foster ed., 1966)).
[224] *Id.* (citing Selden's *Notes on Fortescue, in* SIR JOHN FORTESCUE, DE LAUDIBUS LEGUM ANGLIAE (Robert Mulcaster trans., London: 1672) (1616)). This is, of course, the well-known "Ship of auncient Theseus which had only the forme of it and made of new boards clapt on at severall times…." William Klein, *The ancient constitution revisited, in* POLITICAL DISCOURSE IN EARLY MODERN BRITAIN 41 (Nicholas Phillipson & Quentin Skinner eds., 1993) (quoting THOMAS OWEN, OF THE ANTIQUITIE AMPLENES AND EXCELLENCE OF THE COMMON LAWES OF ENGLAND [Brit. Lib. MS Harley 1572] f. 250b (ca. 1615–1616)), cited in GREENBERG, *supra* note 29 at 33.
[225] Klein, *supra* note 224 at 41.

to accommodate various shifts in society" without the sermonizing exhortations to support the king and his judges as the vice-regents of God emphasized throughout Saltern's *Of the Antient Lawes.*[226] The basic historical narratives of Saltern's and Selden's texts are nonetheless virtually identical, which strongly suggests that the basic story of juridical continuity must have been a fairly common theme in the pedagogical environment of the Inns of Court. As the product of "humanist philological historical method" by an author who would soon earn a reputation as a noted early historian of English law Selden's text "contained the most persuasive historical account of the English constitution published before" the parliamentary disputes that commenced in the late 1620s and culminated in the civil wars of the 1640s fueled an exponential growth of ancient constitutionalist literature that included reprints and an English translation of Selden's original Latin text.[227]

Criticizing Saltern as "an ignorant populizer" and Coke, Craig, Selden and so many others as deliberate inventors of juridical fiction obscures the undeniable fact that their stories of an immemorial ancient constitution were utterly conventional products of a culture that implicitly believed the Bible to be a sacred and therefore inerrant primary source for historical narratives that aligned their revered chronicle histories with that sacred history and the cosmically harmonious natural world.[228] That resonance had encouraged the development of ancient constitutionalist narratives throughout late medieval Europe, but nowhere did they flourish with the diversity

---

[226] Christianson, *Young John Selden*, *supra* note 45 at 272.
[227] *Id.* at 274, 282–283.
[228] JOHANN SOMMERVILLE, POLITICS AND IDEOLOGY IN ENGLAND 1603–1640 91 (1986).

they did in late Tudor England and early Stuart Britain.[229] The harmonious resonance between chronicle histories and sacred history is also apparent in the later royalist variants of the ancient constitution purporting to trace the divine right powers of the monarchy back through the Biblical Patriarchs to Adam produced by Robert Filmer, Sir Edward Hyde, and Robert Brady later in the seventeenth century.[230] Even once that strong harmonious cultural resonance between chronicle histories and biblical sacred history began to tail off by the late seventeenth century, variants of the ancient constitution trope continued to arise. In a very real sense, every British work of political theory produced after the Jacobean Union Texts firmly secured the central place of ancient constitutionalism in the emerging constitutional jurisprudence of Britain can be viewed as an attempt to definitively explicate the nature of that ancient constitution. The narratives of an original all-powerful sovereign forging a secure society out of the turmoil of the state of nature in Thomas Hobbe's 1651 *Leviathan*, the origins of the feudal constitution in the Gothic balance in Ricahrd Harrington's 1658 *Common-wealth of Oceana*, the initial grant of governmental power to Adam from God after the expulsion from Eden in Filmer's 1680 *Patriarcha*, or those of an immemorial Parliament in William Prynne's 1643 *Soveraigne power of Parliaments and Kingdomes* and William Petyt's 1680 *Antient Right of the*

---

[229] *See* POCOCK, THE ANCIENT CONSTITUTION, *supra* note 44 at 15–32 (discussing how this wide-spread culture of "constitutional antiquarianism" developed in late medieval Europe, and why the English common-law mind was such fertile ground for it to so fully flower in).

[230] For a general discussion of the royalist variants of the ancient constitution, see Greenberg, *supra* note 29 at 192–194, 256–257. *See also* POCOCK, THE ANCIENT CONSTITUTION, *supra* note 44 at 148–151 (discussing how "many royalists even as late as the [Glorious] Revolution … may be found turning to the concept of an immemorial constitution to support the doctrine of an immemorial prerogative.").

Commons of England Asserted, to name just a few of the most influential, are all to varying degrees attempts to anchor each author's political theory in an immemorial foundation.[231] Only John Locke's *Two Treatises* would appear to be a notable and significant exception to the dominant culture of early modern British political thought wherein "the attempt to understand English politics through the history of English law was an all but universal pursuit of educated men" to the extent "that to discover a man who did not engage in it is to discover something of a rarity."[232]

Yet, even Locke was arguably not completely immune to the ancient constitutionalism's quest for an immemorial origin point. Locke's *First Treatise* was specifically written to refute the royalist divine right ancient constitutionalist variant of Filmer's *Patriarcha*. The underlying immemorial origin discursive bedrock of Locke's work is also suggested by the very subtitle of the *Second Treatise*, "an essay concerning the *true original*, extent, and end of civil-government." Furthermore, Locke refers several times in the *Second Treatise* to "the Indians in America" being "a pattern of the first ages in Asia and Europe…" in his discussions of the state of nature, the origins of property rights, and how human societies in the state of nature develop sufficiently to be able to enter into a social compact. Nor is the *Second Treatise* untouched by the earlier political thought of Cosmic Harmony. Locke cites to and quotes extensively from none other than the paradigmatic Tudor era English treatise of harmonious juridical principles — Hooker's *Of the Laws of*

---

[231] *See* POCOCK, THE ANCIENT CONSTITUTION, *supra* note 44 at 124-180 (discussing how narratives of immemorial origins came to characterize both sides in the debates between royalists and parliamentarians in seventeenth century Britain).
[232] *Id.* at 237.

Ecclesiastical Polity — throughout his chapters on: *Of the State of Nature*, *Of paternal Power*, *Of political or civil Society*, *Of the Beginning of Political Societies*, *Of the Extent of the legislative Power*, and *Of the Dissolution of Government*. While Locke's work undeniably lacks the tell-tale signatures of precedents drawn from British chronicle histories, he nonetheless asserted an ancient and immemorial origin point for *all* political societies:

> Thus we see that the kings of the Indians in America, which is still a pattern of the first ages in Asia and Europe, whilst the inhabitants were too few for the country, and want of people and money gave men no temptation to enlarge their possessions of land, or contest for wider extent of ground, are little more than generals of their armies; and though they command absolutely in war, yet at home and in time of peace they exercise very little dominion, and have but a very moderate sovereignty; the resolutions of peace and war being ordinarily in the people, or in a council. Though the war itself, which admits not of plurality of governors, naturally devolves the command into the king's sole authority.[233]

---

[233] JOHN LOCKE, TWO TREATISES OF GOVERNMENT: IN THE FORMER, THE FALSE PRINCIPLES AND FOUNDATION OF SIR ROBERT FILMER, AND HIS FOLLOWERS, ARE DETECTED AND OVERTHROWN. THE LATTER IS AN ESSAY CONCERNING THE TRUE ORIGINAL, EXTENT, AND END OF CIVIL-GOVERNMENT (London, 1698) (ca. 1680) (italicized emphasis added). The quoted passage is from "Chapter VIII: Of the Beginning of Political Societies." *Id.* at 248:§108. Locke's other references to American Indians are in that chapter, "Chapter V. Of Property" and "Chapter II. Of the state of nature." *Id.* at 176:§14, 185:§26, 187:§30, 242:§102. The references to and quotes from Hooker are at 167–168:§5, 176:§15, 208-10:§60–61, 220:§74, 232–233:§90–91, 237:§94, 251:§111, 268–270:§134–136, and 355:§239. *See also* FORREST MCDONALD, NOVUS ORDO SECLORUM: THE INTELLECTUAL ORIGINS OF THE CONSTITUTION 62 (1985) (discussing Locke's use of "tribes of American Indians and Africans" in order to prove that

Hobbes, it should be noted, had also referred to "the savage peoples in many places of America" as living in the "condition of Warre" that characterized his far more violent definition of the pre-societal state of nature.[234] The works of Hobbes and Locke essentially transcended the British ancient constitutionalist tradition's reliance upon British chronicle histories and ancient laws by instead asserting global immemorial origins for all human societies. To use the terms from Fortescue's works which were so favored within ancient constitutionalist discourse, Hobbes asserts an immemorial origin point of *jus regale* rule by absolute royal power, and Locke an immemorial origin point of *jus politicum et regale* rule by delegated

---

every "organized political society" arose out of such original pre-political, but nonetheless organized, society in the 'state of nature'). While it was dogma over the following centuries that the *Two Treatises* had been written specifically in defense of the Glorious Revolution, that view "has been conclusively debunked by Peter Laslett and Richard Ashcraft who established that the bulk of it had in fact been written almost a decade earlier, so that, whatever its purposes, justifying the Glorious Revolution was not among them." Ian Shapiro, *Introduction: Reading Locke Today, in* JOHN LOCKE, TWO TREATISES OF GOVERNMENT AND A LETTER CONCERNING TOLERATION (Ian Shapiro ed. 2003) (citing Peter Laslett, *Introduction* to JOHN LOCKE, TWO TREATISES OF GOVERNMENT 61, 123–126 (Peter Laslett ed. 1988) *and* RICHARD ASHCRAFT, JOHN LOCKE'S TWO TREATISES OF GOVERNMENT (1987)).

[234] THOMAS HOBBES, LEVIATHAN: OR THE MATTER, FORME, AND POWER OF A COMMONWEALTH ECCLESIASTICAL AND CIVIL 63 (London: 1651). Hobbes also saw fit to bemoan the failure of King James's Union proposal, "[w]hich if he could have obtained, had in all likelihood prevented the Civill warres, which make both [England and Scotland], at this present, miserable." *Id.* at 101. It also bears noting that no historian of political thought has ever dismissed Hobbes work as unworthy of serious study in the same manner that so many scholars have dismissively derided the literature of ancient constitutionalism due to the fact that he discusses "the Kingdome of Faeries" found in "the old wives *Fables* of England" as a worthy analogy to the Roman Catholic Church in his final chapter. *Id.* at 386–387.

royal power granted by the people limited by political institutions and the rule of law.

This British national pastime of expounding upon ancient constitutionalist immemorial origins would continue well into the eighteenth century after being redirected by the political rhetoric of the Glorious Revolution, especially the public printing of Locke's *Two Treatises of Government* (which had privately circulated before then only in manuscript) as a sort of official standard bearer, into a search not for the original form of human governance but for the original British social contract.[235] Just shy of a century after Saltern had crafted his definition of an ambiguously bilateral ancient constitution based upon the preface to Edward III's Statute of Provisors of Benifices, the ancient and immemorial British social compact was by then "identified with the coronation oath, an oath to observe the ancient constitution – which, it seems probably, binds the people as well as the king."[236] Over the course of the eighteenth century "the concept of the ancient constitution was itself transformed, to a considerable extent, by being based on reason rather than custom;" a discursive transition that nonetheless still found many British writers clinging to the notion that their cherished laws and liberties were an ancestral inheritance from the distant past.[237] As John Pocock aptly imagined an eighteenth century Briton stating:

> 'Our constitution is rational', it might now be said; 'that substantially the same constitution existed among our Saxon ancestors proves both that the principles of reason on which it is founded are eternal, and that our

---

[235] *See* POCOCK, THE ANCIENT CONSTITUTION, *supra* note 44 at 229–251 (discussing how the constitutional settlement of the Glorious Revolution altered the trajectory of ancient constitutionalist narratives).
[236] *Id.* at 231. *See* discussion of Saltern's text *supra* at 103–104.
[237] POCOCK, THE ANCIENT CONSTITUTION, *supra* note 44 at 241.

> ancestors in their unpolished way were rational beings too, as all free men should be.' Something like this must have been the thought underlying many of the appeals to the ancient constitution made in the age of political rationalism; and in so far as this was the character of eighteenth-century constitutional antiquarianism, it was clearly unlike that of the seventeenth-century.[238]

One of the best examples of such a thoroughly rational ancient constitution variant from the early eighteeenth century is found in Roger Acherley's 1727 *The Britannic Constitution: or, the Fundamental Form of Government in Britain.*

Acherley's narrative of the origins of Britain's ancient constitution reads much like Saltern's basic story of an ancient British ruler consulting with his wise and noble councilors to create the original constitutional compact, but rather than being guided by the advice of Bishop Eleutherus they seem instead to have somehow been given a copy of Locke's *Two Treatises* by a kindly time-traveler. Acherly begins by noting that while "[i]t is proper here to distinguish between the *Original* Forms and Constitutions, and the *Original* Contract," once those "Constitutions and Forms of that Law are *first made*, and after that a *Contract* is Enter'd into, to *Observe* them; the Words *Original Contract*, and *Original Constitutions*, become Synonymous Terms, and mean the same Thing." Following this Acherley states his foundational proposition — "That the GOVERNMENT of this Nation was at first founded upon certain *Original* Constitutions and Forms Agreed on, and Insituted, and upon an *Original Contract* reciprocally Entered into, to Observe them…." Instead of then recounting that original constitutional council by reference to chronicle histories, Acherley asserts that:

---

[238] *Id.* at 239.

> In a *Matter* of this Nature, where the *Usage* of Specific Forms of Government hath been Constant, Clear, and Certain, and the *Commencement* of those Forms is *Antient*, and beyond the Time of Memory, and all *Memorials* of that Commencement have been Lost; Presumptions are of Necessity to be make Use of, and Allowed;....

He then proceeds to craft a narrative within which an ancient "Lord, or Nobleman; [whose] Name was *Britannus*," commences the original "GENERAL ASSEMBLY" held out of "Necessity" in order "to Debate, and Resolve, and take proper Measures to redress those *Confusions*" arising out of the initial state of nature of God's creation. In this task, Britannus, after expounding upon the origins of property and the need to protect the nation and its people from the struggles that inevitably ensued over it, is joined by two other leaders — "*Agricola*, an Eminent Commoner," and "*Mercator*, another eminent Commoner."[239] These three then lead the assembly through a detailed debate that tracks the political theory of Locke's *Second Treatise* as if it were a script.

Nearly a hundred pages later, Acherley acknowledges that "some *Objectors* will Treat this *Presumptive* Commencement of the Constitution, with the Characters of *Visionary*, *Romantic*, *Utopian*, *&c.* and as subsisting,

---

[239] ROGER ACHERLEY, THE BRITANNIC CONSTITUTION: OR, THE FUNDAMENTAL FORM OF GOVERNMENT IN BRITAIN. DEMONSTRATING, THE ORIGINAL CONTRACT ENTERED INTO BY KING AND PEOPLE, ACCORDING TO THE PRIMARY INSTITUTIONS THEREOF, IN THIS NATION. WHEREIN IS PROVED, THAT THE PLACING ON THE THRONE KING WILLIAM III. WAS THE NATURAL FRUIT AND EFFECT OF THE ORIGINAL CONSTITUTION. AND, THAT THE SUCCESSION TO THIS CROWN, ESTABLISH'D IN THE PRESENT PROTESTANT HEIRS, IS DE JURE, AND JUSTIFY'D, BY THE FUNDAMENTAL LAWS OF GREAT BRITAIN. AND MANY IMPORTANT ORIGINAL POWERS AND PRIVILEGES, OF BOTH HOUSES OF PARLIAMENT, ARE EXHIBITED 22–33 (London: 1727).

only in *Imagination*." To this potential criticism, he answers: "That the Facts, or Things Made and Formed, are present with us, and are *Visible* and *Undeniable*; all that is Presumptive is, the Names and Qualities of the *Actors*, or *Makers*." Acherley then recounts the sacred history of Noah's Flood and how his family survived to repopulate the world and challenges any who would raise such objections to "Please to give and Account, How these People, from so small an Original, as Eight Persons, came to Increase into such vase Multitudes, and to Divide" in order to be in Britain, let alone to be "Planted in *America*…." If the answer is, as he expects, that "[i]t must be *Presumed*, That the secret Effluxes of God's Power, Will, and Providence" was sufficient to the task, "then the same *Presumptions*, are of equal authority, to Prove, and Manifest every Thing" that has been asserted about the origins of the British Constitution. Therefore, "since these Human Constitutions are real Facts, and from themselves, in a manner, Self-evident, though of the greatest Antiquity, why is it not Proper, or Rational, to Represent in an Allegory, the Origination of them?" After all, Acherley asks, "since it must be (by the most Sceptical) owned, That these Original Constitutions, did not happen by Chance; but were the Results of Thinking, Rational, and Free Agents, such as *Britannus*, *Agricola*, *Mercator*, and the Assembly, are supposed to be…." It is only through such allegorical speculation that "[t]he Antiquity of the Original Constitution [can be] thus Illustrated, and, in a manner, Proved…."[240] The bulk of Acherly's work is devoted to recounting the various breaches of that original constitution by acts of arbitrary rule from the Norman Conquest until the restoration of it by the Glorious Revolution. Only then does he recount the oft-told tale from Fortescue that none of the ancient invaders of Britain, not

---

[240] *Id.* at 112–115.

even the Normans, ever "*Imposed* or Introduced their Foreign Institutions, but Preferred and Embraced the *British*; which is an *Evidence* of the Strongest Nature, to prove the Excellency of our Fundamental Form of Government...."[241] Other than his allegorical origin story, at no point in his extensive narrative had Acherley ever wandered before the Norman Conquest, nor does he ever do so other than this short paraphrase of the by then nearly sacrosanct passage from Fortescue, yet he is perfectly assured in restating the same basic assertion found a century earlier in the works of Coke and Saltern. *The Britannic Constitution* is a paradigmatic example of how within a culture that widely believed it had been definitively proven that the British "mode of government [was] the most conformable to reason and abstract justice, there [was] at least an illustrative value in showing that this constitution [had] been normally observed in the past — even in time immemorial."[242]

It seems clear that by this time the essential trope of the ancient British constitution was a cultural article of faith. So much so that even a work praised for its systematically rational and analytical treatment of the laws of England, Blackstone's *Commentaries on the Laws of England*, incorporated the core elements. Blackstone first briefly notes at the commencement of his introductory chapter, *Of the Laws of England*, that "the British as well as the Gallic Druids committed all their laws as well as learning to memory; and it is said of the primitive Saxons here, as well as their brethren on the continent, that *leges sola memoria et usu retinebant* [*they retained their laws solely by memory and practice*]." He then continues to recount how "[o]ur ancient lawyers, and particularly Fortescue, insist with abundance of warmth, that these

---

[241] *Id.* at 690-91.

[242] POCOCK, THE ANCIENT CONSTITUTION, *supra* note 44 at 238-39.

customs are as old as the primitive Britons, and continued down, through the several mutations of government and inhabitants, to the present time, unchanged and unadulterated." However, Blackstone cautions with a reference to the notes from Selden's 1616 edition of Fortescue:

> this assertion must be understood with many grains of allowance; and ought only to signify, as the truth seems to be, that there never was any formal exchange of one system of laws for another: though doubtless by the intermixture of adventitious nations, the Romans, the Picts, the Saxons, the Danes, and the Normans, they must have insensibly introduced and incorporated many of their own customs with those that were before established: thereby in all probability improving the texture and wisdom of the whole, by the accumulated wisdom of divers particular countries.

He then states that "indeed our antiquaries and first historians do all positively assure us, that our body of laws is of this compounded nature," before commencing to summarily recount essentially the same sequence of juridical transmissions found in the works of Coke and Saltern. First, "in the time of Alfred the local custom of the several provinces of the kingdom were grown so various, that he found it expedient to compile his *dome-book* or *liber judicialis*, for the general use of the whole kingdom." Next, "the irruption and establishment of the Danes in England, which followed soon after, introduced new customs, and caused this code of Alfred in many provinces to fall into disuse; or at least to be mixed and debased with other laws of a coarser alloy." Finally, "Edward the confessor extracted one uniform law or digest of laws, to be observed throughout the whole kingdom," drawing upon the "*Mercen-Lege*, or Mercian laws… very probably intermixed with the British or Druidical customs[,] [t]he *West-Saxon-Lage*, or laws of the West Saxons…[, and] [t]he *Dane-Lage*, or Danish law...." Edward the Confessor's compilation were the laws "which our ancestors struggled so hardly to maintain, under the first princes of the Norman line; and which subsequent princes so frequently promised to keep and restore, as the most popular act they could do, when pressed by foreign emergencies or domestic discontents." It was through those laws, "that so vigorously withstood the repeated attacks of the civil law; which established in the twelfth century a new Roman empire over most of the states of the continent,... while the free constitution of England, perhaps upon the same account, has been rather improved than debased." The very authority of the common law lies in the fact that "in our law the goodness of a custom depends upon its having been used time out of mind; or, in the solemnity of our legal phrase, time whereof the memory of man runs not to the contrary."[243]

Blackstone's concluding chapter, *Of the Rise, Progress, and gradual Improvements, of the Laws of England*, commences with a similar discussion. He asserts, "[p]articularly, the very notion itself of an oral unwritten law, delivered down from age to age, by custom and tradition merely, seems derived from the practice of the Druids....." This is followed by a more nuanced explication of how "it is morally impossible to trace out, with any degree of accuracy, *when* the several mutations of the common law were made, or what was the respective original of those several customs we at present use, by any chemical resolution of them to their first and component principles." Blackstone's nuanced explication nonetheless recounts the same ancient constitutionalist

---

[243] 1 WILLIAM BLACKSTONE, COMMENTARIES *63–*67. The translation of the Latin is from Wayne Morrison's excellent 2001 edited edition. 1 BLACKSTONE'S COMMENTARIES ON THE LAWS OF ENGLAND 47 (Wayne Morrison ed., 2001).

chronology.[244] It should also be noted that Blackstone's acknowledgement of the extreme difficulty, and likely impossibility, of accurately tracing the precise origins of the ancient common laws as well as any contemporary remnants is not too far removed from similar cautionary notes in *Of the Antient Lawes*. Saltern opened his work by acknowledging that such evidence was "no less fit and necessary for this time to be known, then obscure and difficult to expound." He further prefaced the discussion of the laws of the ancient Britons in his penultimate chapter by cautioning that "particularly which of these laws or institutions now extant were enacted by *Lucius*, it is hard to say…."[245] That Saltern nonetheless devotedly attempted to substantiate those ineffable links should not obscure the honesty with which he presented his opinions. Nor was Blackstone any less keen on ensuring that the basic assertion that there were still ancient common law remnants extant in his day was authoritatively conveyed to readers of his *Commentaries* regardless of whether or not such remnants could be clearly identified. In a time when the indexing of books was still far from common, and assuredly not required by standards of scholarly respectability, the *Commentaries* included a commendably thorough index. Within that index there are matching entries for "Britons, ancient, their laws. I. 63. IV. 401" and "Druids, their customs. I. 63. IV. 401."[246]

---

[244] 4 WILLIAM BLACKSTONE, COMMENTARIES *407–*413. The cover image to this case study of a color-coded timeline of British history from the 1753 volume of *Gentleman's Magazine* also reveals the extent to which the basic chronology of the ancient constitution was still being revered well into the eighteenth century.

[245] OF THE ANTIENT LAWES at [4], [57].

[246] 4 WILLIAM BLACKSTONE, COMMENTARIES ON THE LAWS OF ENGLAND leaves Iii recto, I[iv] verso (London: 1769). The now standard starred pagination based upon the 9th edition shifted 4:401 to 4:*408.

While Blackstone's ancient constitutionalist narrative may have been comparatively truncated, in style it is remarkably similar to Saltern's basic theme of noble and just adaptive continuity. Blackstone undeniably viewed the ancient constitution as a foundational subject necessary for students of the English common law to learn, likely because of his conviction:

> that the liberties of Englishmen are not (as some arbitrary writers would represent them) mere infringements of the king's prerogative, extorted from our princes by taking advantage of their weakness; but a *restoration* of that ancient constitution, of which our ancestors had been defrauded by the art and finesse of the Norman lawyers, rather than deprived by the force of the Norman arms.[247]

Perhaps inspired by the inclusion of these ancient constitutionalist elements in Blackstone's *Commentaries*, Edward Brooke saw fit to commence his 1788 supplementary Part II for John Worrall's popular *Bibliotheca Legum Angliae* reference book with a "General Account of the Laws and Law-Writers of England From the earliest Times to the Conquest" that begins with none other than "Brutus, or Brute, the first king of this land" and progresses through all the notable rulers recounted by Saltern nearly two centuries earlier including Dunwallo Molmutius and Queen Marcia. Brook's "General Account" seems to have been crafted as much to sell popular ancient constitutionalist works as much, if not more so, than to provide a useful reference tool for practitioners and those interested in the law.[248]

---

[247] 2 WILLIAM BLACKSTONE, COMMENTARIES *52 [emphasis added]

[248] EDWARD BROOKE, BIBLIOTHECA LEGUM ANGLIÆ, PART II. CONTAINING A GENERAL ACCOUNT OF THE LAWS AND LAW-WRITERS OF ENGLAND, FROM THE EARLIEST TIMES TO THE REIGN OF EDW. III. AS

Saltern's *Of the Antient Lawes* would itself be reprinted in serialized form with editorial annotations in 1803 by two barristers of the Inner Temple, John Morgan and Thomas Walter Williams, in their *The Law Journal for Hilary and Easter Terms, 1803*. Saltern is described in an introductory paragraph as being "a lawyer, eminently distinguished in the reigns of Q. Eliz and Jac. I. not only by his great learning, but for exemplary piety...." It is hardly surprising, therefore, that the editorial annotations, far from being critical of Saltern as a historian are even more strongly ancient constitutionalist than Saltern's text (if that is even possible). One annotation in particular confirms that Blackstone's *Commentaries* was indeed, as suggested above, viewed as a restorative ancient constitutionalist text by at least some members of the English legal profession: "[t]he learned and elegant commentator on the laws of England, (Blackstone) adopts in every part of that excellent elementary book, which may be presumed to be in the possession of every student, the same reasoning as *Saltern* did near two centuries back." Another annotation emphasizes the juridical role played by the ancient British Druids as adjudicators of the laws, who "were, very properly, deemed safer depositaries of them, than men of the sword." There is even an annotation commending the *Mirrour of Justices* to law students because: "[w]e are inclined to think, if he attends to it, he may have an advantage over many of the profession." In addition to serializing *Of the Antient Lawes*, John Morgan also provided "Commentaries on Selden's *Jani Anglorum Facies Altera*," which includes a notation that: "[w]e recommend to our student, to get some ac-

---

ALSO OF THE PUBLIC RECORDS, AND OTHER AUTHENTIC LAW MSS. THE STATUTES, AND THE SEVERAL COLLECTIONS AND EDITIONS THEREOF; THE REPORTS, OR COLLECTIONS OF ADJUDGED CASES IN THE COURTS OF LAW AND EQUITY; TOGETHER WITH AN ACCOUNT OF THE PRINCIPAL WORKS UPON THE LAW AND CONSTITUTION, PUBLISHED DURING THE PRESENT REIGN 1–6 (London: 1788) (citing Blackstone's *Commentaries*).

quaintance with the History of the Druids[;] [n]o English lawyer should be unacquainted with their laws, customs, and government." A further section contains "Observations upon a Dissertation on the Judicial Customs of the Saxon and Norman Age, by James Ibbetson, Barrister at Law. Published by White, Fleet-street, anno. 1780," which also includes ancient constitutionalist annotations and recommends that law students study the *Mirrour of Justices*. The caption title under which *Of the Antient Lawes* was serialized, "Ancient and Scarce Authors", and the running title of "Ancient Authors," further illustrates the variant contemporaneous meanings of the term *ancient* discussed above at the end of Chapter One. The editorial annotations, commentaries, and the serialization of Saltern's text further supports the suggestion made at the beginning of this chapter that the basic ancient constitutionalist narrative was a standard story learned by English law students. Morgan and Williams stated that they were inspired to reprint Saltern's work by "having been favored with a literal transcript, from the printed book, which may also be seen in the Inner Temple Library…." *Of the Antient Lawes* was also held by the libraries of Lincoln's Inn, the Birmingham Law Society, and Harvard Law Library in the nineteenth century. This strongly suggests that Morgan and Williams were far from alone in considering it to be a work worthy of study.[249] Little wonder that Maitland would so vigorously

[249] JOHN MORGAN AND THOMAS WALTER WILLIAMS, THE LAW JOURNAL FOR HILARY AND EASTER TERMS, 1803 72, 83, 84, 189, 275, 475–476 (London: 1803). CATALOGUE OF LINCOLN'S INN LIBRARY PRINTED BOOKS (London: 1858); CATALOGUE OF THE LIBRARY OF THE BIRMINGHAM LAW SOCIETY, ARRANGED ALPHABETICALLY, WITH A SUBJECT INDEX, 1880 (Birmingham: 1880); CATALOGUE OF THE LIBRARY OF THE LAW SCHOOL OF HARVARD UNIVERSITY (Cambridge: 1909). John Morgan had previously edited the 9th, 10th, and 11th editions of Jacob's *Law Dictionary*,

seek to extirpate such ancient constitutionalist elements from the proper study of English legal history later in the nineteenth century.

The ancient constitutionalist elements in British jurisprudence had inevitably found their way across the Atlantic into early American political discourse. Thomas Jefferson and others in the American founding generation viewed their British constitutional origins with near reverential awe, and routinely employed ancient constitutionalist rhetoric of both the earlier Brittanic and later Gothic variants.[250] In *A Summary View of the Rights of British America* Thomas Jefferson compared the settlement of the British colonies in America to the Saxon

---

and written several legal treatises: *A Digest of the Common Law* in 1767; *The Attorney's Vade Mecum* in 1787; a three volume set of *Essays upon I. The law of evidence. II. New trials. III. Special verdicts. IV. Trials at bar. And V. Repleaders* in 1789; and, *The Modern Pleader* in 1793. *The Law Journal* itself would be restyled as a periodical and published through 1806. T. W. Williams finished his *Abridgment of Cases* from the reign of George III to 1803 in 1803; and then published *The Practice of the Commissioners, Assessors, Surveyors, Collectors and other Officers, under the authority of the several Acts relating to the Assessed Taxes* in 1804; a collection of *Original Precedents in Conveyancing* in 1808; *A Digest of the Statute Law, from Magna Charta, to the 49 Geo. III* and *The Whole Law relative to the Duty and Office of a Justice of the Peace, also the Authority of Parish Officers* in 1812; *The Jurisdiction of Justices of the Peace, and Authority of Parish Officers* in 1814; and, *A Compendious and Comprehensive Law Dictionary* in 1816. *See* JOHN GAGE MARVIN, LEGAL BIBLIOGRAPHY, OR A THESAURUS OF AMERICAN, ENGLISH, IRISH, AND SCOTCH LAW BOOKS 529, 737 (Philadelphia, 1847). Marvin's *Legal Bibliography* also listed Saltern's *Of the Antient Lawes*. *Id.* at 627.

[250] *See generally, e.g.* MCDONALD, *supra* note 223 at 6 (discussing how delegates to the 1787 Constitutional Convention frequently "cited British constitutional practice as being instructive concerning the tasks at hand) *and* JOHN PHILLIP REID, THE ANCIENT CONSTITUTION AND THE ORIGINS OF ANGLO-AMERICAN LIBERTY 8–12 (2005) (discussing the common usage of ancient constitutionalist rhetoric in the Founding period).

migrations into ancient Britain that established "that system of laws which has so long been the glory and protection of that country," and defends the American colonists' assertion of free allodial tenures in land by likening them to "the Saxon laws of possession, under which all lands were held in absolute right." Jefferson also proposed adding Hengist and Horsa to the new nation's seal as they were "the Saxon chiefs from whom we claim the honor of being descended, and whose political principles and form of government we have assumed."[251] British juridical works were singularly influential on Revolutionary era American jurisprudence as they had formed the core of American legal studies since the earliest colonies in New England and Virginia due to a profound lack of colonial legal treatises and case reports.[252] Coke was the preferred authority for earlier generations of American lawyers, and Fortescue's *De Laudibus* was also considered to be an authoritative historical legal treatise. Once Blackstone's *Commentaries* were published, however, they eclipsed such earlier works by becoming so popular that early "American lawyers cited Blackstone in American courts as today they cite opinions of their state's highest court."[253] Ancient

---

[251] *A Summary View of the Rights of British-Americans, in* THOMAS JEFFERSON, WRITINGS 105, 106, 118–119 (1984) (1774); 1 THE PAPERS OF THOMAS JEFFERSON, 1760–1776 495 (Julian P. Boyd ed. 1950).

[252] *See generally, e.g.* ANTON-HERMANN CHROUST, 1 THE RISE OF THE LEGAL PROFESSION IN AMERICA 18–19 (1965) *and* LAWRENCE FRIEDMAN, A HISTORY OF AMERICAN LAW 88 (1973) *and* HERBERT JOHNSON, IMPORTED EIGHTEENTH CENTURY LAW TREATISES IN AMERICAN LIBRARIES, 1700–1799 ix–xxvi (1978) *and* Morris L. Cohen, *Legal Literature in Colonial Massachusetts, in* LAW IN COLONIAL MASSACHUSETTS 243 (1984) (all noting the common reliance upon and influence of British legal works due to the lack of such works by pre-Revolutionary era colonial Americans).

[253] ARTHUR E. SUTHERLAND, THE LAW AT HARVARD: A HISTORY OF IDEAS AND MEN, 1817–1967 24 (1967). Regarding Coke's earlier

constitutionalism was so widely accepted in the late eighteenth century that it has been aptly described by John Phillip Reid as "the cornerstone of the arch supporting the various rules, rights, maxims, and dogmas that, collectively, can best be summarized as the *jurisprudence of English and American liberty*." This influence was so noticeably pronounced in America's Founding period that it became a common subject of political discussion in Britain, leading the Earl of Abingdon to "note[] in 1777 and 1780, 'that the Constitution and Form of Government established by our wise Forefathers in America, was precisely, in Principle, the Constitution and Form of Government of the Saxon Heptarchy.'"[254] This early American cultural affinity also suggests a potential alternative meaning for the Anti-Federalist pseudonym of *Brutus*. Not the Brutus so memorably involved in the as-

---

influence, Jefferson wrote to Madison concerning the proper criteria for selecting the University of Virginia's first law professor: "You will recollect that before the Revolution, Coke Littleton was the universal elementary book of law students, and a sounder Whig never wrote, nor of profounder learning in the orthodox doctrines of the British constitution, or in what were called English liberties. You remember also that our lawyers were then all Whigs. But when his black-letter text, and uncouth, but cunning learning got out of fashion, and the honeyed Mansfieldism of Blackstone became the students' hornbook, from that moment, that profession (the nursery of our Congress) began to slide into toryism, and nearly all the young brood of lawyers now are of that hue." Letter to James Madison (Feb. 17, 1826), *in* 7 THE WRITINGS OF THOMAS JEFFERSON 432, 433 (Washington, D.C.: 1853).

[254] Reid, *supra* note 250 at 9 (quoting WILLOUGHBY BERTIE, EARL OF ABINGDON, DEDICATION TO THE COLLECTIVE BODY OF THE PEOPLE OF ENGLAND, IN WHICH THE SOURCE OF OUR PRESENT POLITICAL DISTRACTIONS ARE POINTED OUT AND A PLAN PROPOSED FOR THEIR REMEDY AND REDRESS xlii (note) (Oxford, 1780) *and* THOUGHTS ON THE LETTER OF EDMUND BURKE, ESQ.; TO THE AFFAIRS OF AMERICA (Oxford, 6th ed. ca.1770)). *See also id.* at 24 ("The most celebrated practitioners of ancient-constitution history during the eighteenth century were the American founding fathers.").

sassination of Julius Caesar, but the eponymous founder of Britain's ancient constitution of *jus politicum et regale* governance.

The basic ancient constitutionalist narrative of the origins of the common law tradition among the ancient Britons also found its way into American legal education through the *Lectures on Law* of Supreme Court Justice James Wilson delivered at the College of Philadelphia's law school in the winter terms of 1790 and 1791. Justice Wilson noted that "[a]mong the ancient Britons also, no written laws were known: they were ruled by the traditionary — and if traditionary, probably, the customary — laws of the Druids." Wilson subsequently cited both Fortescue and Blackstone in an extensive recounting of the basic ancient constitutionalist narrative of adaptive continuity in his lectures on the ancient origins of the common law and the British Constitution. According to Wilson the Saxons, far from extirpating the ancient Britons, were gradually civilized by the remaining Britons and "entirely blended together" along with their laws into "a mingled mass of Saxon Britons and British Saxons." After commending the Anglo-Saxon kings Alfred, Edgar, and Edward the Confessor for preserving and improving upon that ancient blended Anglo-Britannic common law, Wilson stated that "[t]he common law, as now received in America, bears, in its principles, and in many of its more minute particulars, a stronger and a fairer resemblance to the common law as it was improved under the Saxon, than to that law, as it was disfigured under the Norman government." Wilson then asserted that American constitutionalism was of similarly ancient Anglo-Britannic lineage:

> The original frame of the British constitution, different, indeed, in many important points, from what it now is, and bearing, to some of the constitutions which have been lately formed, and established in America, a de-

> gree of resemblance, which will strike and surprise those who compare them together — this venerable frame may be considered as of Saxon architecture.[255]

The *Legal Lectures* were published posthumously by his son, Bird Wilson, in 1804.[256] The inclusion of the standard ancient constitutionalist narrative in Justice Wilson's legal lectures provides a cogent example of how the commonly held view "that liberty had been more nearly perfect during ancient than in more recent times" led to the adoption of "Gothicism and Saxonism standards for measuring the liberty of currently existing government institutions" in early American juridical discourse.[257]

That such ancient constitutionalist criteria prevailed in Antebellum America to the extent that they were not only acceptable, but preferred, led William Sampson, a New York lawyer, to bemoan such a state of juridical affairs in the 1820s:

> If there be such a pure fountain, and that we have profanely troubled it, or foolishly strayed from it, we cannot too soon retrace our steps, and return with penitent devotion, "Fonti divino et Genio numinis fontis:" we must prostrate ourselves before the offended genii of the common law; appease the celestial and infernal

---

[255] Kermit L. Hall, *Introduction* to THE COLLECTED WORKS OF JAMES WILSON xx-xxi (Kermit L. Hall & Mark David Hall eds. 2005) *and* James Wilson, *Lectures on Law, in* THE COLLECTED WORKS OF JAMES WILSON 494, 677–678, 750–771 (Kermit L. Hall & Mark David Hall eds. 2005).

[256] THE WORKS OF THE HONOURABLE JAMES WILSON, L.L.D. LATE ONE OF THE ASSOCIATE JUSTICES OF THE SUPREME COURT OF THE UNITED STATES, AND PROFESSOR OF LAW IN THE COLLEGE OF PHILADELPHIA (Bird Wilson ed., Philadelphia: 1804). *See also* Mark David Hall, *Bibliographic Essay History of James Wilson's Law Lectures, in* THE COLLECTED WORKS OF JAMES WILSON, *supra* note 255 at 401–413.

[257] Reid, *supra* note 250 at 10.

> deities of our wise ancestors, the druids; soothe the angry sun and moon with human victims; and propitiate both Thor and Woden with costly offerings. The frowning oaks, the troubled fountains, and the dreadful thunder, must be placated by all the arts of magic astrology and augury, known and practiced in the times of the "pristine vigor" of the common law.[258]

Sampson's exceptional ire was likely fueled by the fact that such rhetoric had utterly failed his clients in the 1810 trial "of the Journeyman Cordwainers, indicted for a conspiracy at *Common Law*, in combining to raise their wages." In that trial, Sampson had argued before the Mayor of New York City and the two sitting Justices of the Session, asking:

> Why did our constitution repeal the English statutes, and declare that nothing of the common law, repugnant to that constitution, should remain, if antiquated barbarities were still to be revived and visited upon us; and if we are not to be allowed even to inquire whether they are attacks upon our rights or not? We should then be worse off than the English people are: for many of the old common law doctrines are abrogated by English statutes, but in which the colonies were never named, and with which the colonial legislators never meddled, not supposing them to have force of law on this side of the Atlantic. Our case would be singular on the earth. Our judges might then unlearn all they had studied of national or congenial institutions, to make themselves proficient in Mercian lage and Dane lage. They might study *more majorum*

---

[258] SAMPSON'S DISCOURSE, AND CORRESPONDENCE WITH VARIOUS LEARNED JURISTS, UPON THE HISTORY OF THE LAW, WITH THE ADDITION OF SEVERAL ESSAYS, TRACTS, AND DOCUMENTS, RELATING TO THE SUBJECT 8 (Pishey Thompson compiler & publisher, Washington City, 1826).

in hollow trees and caverns, till they forgot to read or write, and became Druids at common law.[259]

Such rhetoric had no effect whatsoever on the steadily increasing use of Blackstone's *Commentaries*, with its underlying ancient constitutionalist foundation, in American legal education. Appeals to continue basing the education of American lawyers on Blackstone would continue well into the twentieth century, ensuring that multiple generations of American lawyers would be exposed to Blackstone's condensed ancient constitutionalism.[260] Little wonder the ancient constitution trope has remained sufficiently popular and influential in American juridical culture that rhetorical calls to be faithful to an original constitutional moment still resonate to this day; a resonance that is quite clear among the proponents of the American theory of constitutional interpretation known as *Originalism*. This should hardly be an objectionable proposition in that ancient constitutionalism has always been more "a method of legal argumentation" utilizing forensic historiography than an objective and precise historiographical method.[261]

As the United States progresses into its third century of existence, there are signs that the paradigm of constitutional antiquity is once again becoming an influential part

---

[259] *Id.* at 149–150.

[260] This American devotion to Blackstone's *Commentaries* can even be found in law school student newspapers of the otherwise reform minded 1960s. In 1969, Georgetown Law's Dean Paul R. Dean noted that the advocates for retaining the traditional model of American legal education regularly "call[ed] for a return to Blackstone, to his orderly thought, his admirable arrangement." Paul R. Dean, *G.U. "Unbeguiled By The Trumpet Of The False Progressive"*, 2 GEO. L. WEEKLY 3 (Apr. 29, 1969). Blackstone's "admirable arrangement" begins, of course, with the origins of the common law among the Druids of ancient Britain.

[261] REID, *supra* note 250 at 13, *passim*.

of American political and constitutional discourse. Recent cases involving the First Amendment rights of free expression and petition, the Sixth Amendment right to confrontation, the Fourth Amendment rights against unlawful search and seizure, and the Second Amendment right to bear arms prominently feature the term *ancient* in their analysis and discussion of constitutional rights secured by events of just over two centuries ago; "*Austin* was a significant departure from ancient First Amendment principles..." is a particularly telling example.[262] Such a statement can only be true by the more generous standards of aesthetic and moral truth. The First Amendment itself is barely over 200 years old. The principles of freedom of the press, freedom of expression, religious liberty, and the rights of assembly and petition are by even the most generous standards no more than just over

---

[262] Federal Election Comm'n v. Wisconsin Right to Life, Inc., 551 U.S. 449, 490 (2007)) (Scalia, J., concurring in part and concurring in judgment); *See also, e.g.,* Borough of Duryea, Pa. v. Guarnieri, 564 U.S. 379, ____, 131 S. Ct. 2488, 2498 (2011) (Kennedy, J.) ("Petition, as a word, a concept, and an essential safeguard of freedom, is of ancient significance in the English law and the Anglo–American legal tradition."); District of Columbia v. Heller, 554 U.S. 570, 599 (2008) (Scalia, J.) ("Federalists responded that because Congress was given no power to abridge the ancient right of individuals to keep and bear arms,..." *and* "The prefatory clause does not suggest that preserving the militia was the only reason Americans valued the ancient right; ..."); McDonald *v.* City of Chicago, 561 U.S. 742, 744, (2010) (Alito, J.) ("Self-defense is a basic right, recognized by many legal systems from ancient times to the present day, and in Heller, we held that individual self-defense is "the central component " of the Second Amendment right."); Hudson *v.* Michigan, 547 U.S. 586, 602 (2006) Kennedy, J. concurring in part and concurring in judgment) ("[T]he knock-and-announce requirement protects rights and expectations linked to ancient principles in our constitutional order."); *and* Crawford *v.* Washington, 541 U.S. 36, 43-49 (2004) (Scalia, J.) (discussing the right of confrontation as being of ancient origin).

400 years old. Those principles first arose in the late Tudor privilege of freedom of political speech for members of Parliamentary debate while Parliament was itself in session, the extension of highly limited religious tolerance to non-conforming Protestants under Elizabeth I and James VI and I, with the remainder beginning to develop during the highly contentious struggles between Parliamentarians and Royalists later in the seventeenth century. By the standards of twenty-first century historical accuracy First Amendment principles are assuredly not *ancient*, the revered and cherished principles underlying the First Amendment can only justifiably be considered ancient by the more forgiving standards of ancient constitutionalism.

Most telling of all is the persistent influence of Originalism as an accepted theory of constitutional interpretation despite repeated scholarly efforts to debunk the central premise of a unitary founding original intent as historically inaccurate. Although arguably distinguishable from ancient constitutionalism by the written nature of the U.S. Constitution and ample documentary evidence of its origins and subsequent development, Originalism in its essence as well as its practice shows notable "parallels linking ancient constitutionalism in the seventeenth and eighteenth centuries with today's doctrine of 'original intent'."[263] Originalism came to prominence shortly after the American constitutional bicentennial amid a chorus of despair over the progressing woeful state of historical awareness of the average citizen and resolute efforts to remedy that lack. The most ardent adherents and practitioners of Originalism routinely rely on and produce erroneous or partial accounts of constitutional history as well. Just as ancient constitutionalism spawned multiple

---

[263] REID, *supra* note 250 at 122.

variants, so too has Originalism.[264] Calls for fidelity to the original American constitutional moment or design characterize every variant of Originalism. The thesis articulated in the introductory chapter – *Fidelity to Text and Principle* – of one such variant, Jack Balkin's 2011 *Living Originalism*, resonates with the central role of fidelity in Saltern's text and Coke's report of *Calvin's Case* by proposing an interpretive methodology that "requires fidelity to the original meaning of the Constitution, and in particular, to the rules, standards, and principles stated by the Constitution's text."[265] The title and thesis of another originalist work, *Restoring the Lost Constitution*, by the libertarian legal scholar Randy Barnett exemplifies the extent to which originalism echoes the restorative aspects of ancient constitutionalist rhetoric.[266] Libertarian originalists may also be echoing those ancient constitutionalist variants that posited an immemorial natural law origin of appropriate principles of law and governance when human society first emerged from the state of nature before later ineffective and oppressive forms of government arose. Originalism has also been used both to assert the rule of law, the strongest parallel noted by John Philip Reid, and absolute executive power just as ancient constitutionalism produced parliamentarian and royalist variants.[267]

---

[264] *See generally e.g.,* DENNIS J. GOLDFORD, THE AMERICAN CONSTITUTION AND THE DEBATE OVER ORIGINALISM (2005); JOHNATHAN O'NIELL, ORIGINALISM IN AMERICAN LAW AND POLITICS: A CONSTITUTIONAL HISTORY (2005); ORIGINALISM: A QUARTER-CENTURY OF DEBATE (Steven G. Calabresi ed. 2007); *and* JACK M. BALKIN, LIVING ORIGINALISM (2011).
[265] BALKIN, *supra* note 245 at 3.
[266] *See generally* RANDY BARNETT, RESTORING THE LOST CONSTITUTION (2004).
[267] *Compare* REID, *supra* note 250 at 81, 122–123 (noting in an aside that "supporters of prerogativism occasionally used changeless constitutionalism in much the same way for opposite purposes" only to then gloss over that fact by discussing only the rule of law limitations

Another paradigmatic aspect of ancient constitutionalist thought is the pre-Enlightenment sense of historical consciousness wherein history inevitably illustrates the fall from an ancient golden age of divinely established law and governance into a present moment of comparatively lawless and sinful barbarity. The leading proponent of originalism on the Court, the late Justice Antonin Scalia, has stated that "[a] society that adopts a bill of rights is skeptical that 'evolving standards of decency; always 'mark progress,' and that societies always 'mature,' as opposed to rot," a statement that resonates with the mental world of ancient constitutionalism.[268] Originalism has also been likened to ancestor worship.[269] These tell-tale characteristics were markedly evident in British ancient constitutionalist texts as well. Saltern's use of the story of Lucius and his successors devotedly following the godly and just general principles contained in the Letter of Eleutherus, and all the woes that ensued each time subsequent generations of British kings and subjects failed to do so, is a cogent and paradigmatic ex-

---

of ancient constitutionalism, especially in relation the parallels he notes with American Originalism) *and* JOHN YOO, CRISIS AND COMMAND: THE HISTORY OF EXECUTIVE POWER FROM GEORGE WASHINGTON TO GEORGE W. BUSH (2009) (asserting an originalist argument for the Unitary Executive theory of unbridled American executive power).

[268] ANTONIN SCALIA, A MATTER OF INTERPRETATION: FEDERAL COURTS AND THE LAW 40–41 (1997).

[269] *See, e.g.*, Michael Kirby, *Constitutional Interpretation and Original Intent: A Form of Ancestor Worship?*, 24 MELB. U. L. REV. 1 (2000) *and* Christopher Schmidt, *The Tea Party and the Constitution*, 39 HASTINGS CONST. L.Q. 193, 209 (2011) ("A central reason for this phenomenon of populist originalism can be traced to the cultural resonance of originalism as a form of ancestor worship and search for stable values.") *and* Edward J. Sullivan & Nicholas Cropp, *Making it Up: 'Original Intent' and Federal Takings Jurisprudence*, 35 URB. LAW. 203, 215 ("[I]f Justice Kirby's "ancestor worship" analogy is followed to its logical conclusion, the judiciary becomes a kind of High Priesthood for this ancestral worship.").

ample of such calls to be faithful to the *original* inspirational constitutive intent of the enactor(s) of the original constitutional moment(s). The strong parallels between ancient constitutionalism and Originalism suggest that the latter can appropriately be thought of as yet another variant of constitutional antiquarianism; like ancient constitutionalism, the underlying spirit of American Originalism is undeniably "a form of reverential conservatism."[270] In the United Kingdom and Commonwealth nations, cultural echoes of ancient constitutionalism are, at the very least, reasonable explanations for the devotion to keeping a now constitutionally non-essential and powerless monarchy as well as for their ardent pride in maintaining the traditions of Magna Carta, the rule of law, and parliamentary governance. All of these are undeniably cherished and revered juridical institutions within these nations. There is clearly something more to the British-American ancient constitutionalist tradition than a mere early modern literary or juridical trope.

Perhaps ancient constitutionalism is a juridical meme. The concept of cultural memes first proposed in the 1970s by the evolutionary biologist Richard Dawkins in his book *The Selfish Gene* is useful concept for more fully appreciating this enduring power of ancient constitutionalism. Dawkins suggested that at least some cultural concepts were capable of transmitting themselves over multiple generations in much the same way that the genes of biological organisms do. In order to emphasize the analogy to genes, Dawkins termed these cultural replicators *memes*. Like genes, memes replicate quite independently from the intentions, desires, or even the well-being and survival, of the culture they are a part

---

[270] GALLOWAY, *supra* note 96 at 38.

of.[271] Cultural memes undoubtedly exist; "there is nothing mythical or hypothetical about" them, although many myths and hypotheses do in fact become replicating memes. Replication is the "core definition" of memes; "tunes, ideas, catch-phrases, fashions, and ways of making things are all spread from person to person by imitation." Memes undeniably "exist, for unless you deny that anything is ever copied from person to person, they must." Those memes that are simple, memorable, and beneficial to a culture tend to survive the longest; however, destructive or harmful memes are also capable of thriving. The enduring survival of memes is not determined by their benefit to the culture they symbiotically exist within. Rather, it is determined by whether replication benefits the meme itself:

> Some survive predominantly because they are useful to their hosts (e.g., effective financial institutions, scientific theories, or useful technologies); others depend on fulfilling human desires and preferences (e.g., the arts, music, and literature); and still others are positively harmful, tricking their hosts in propagating them… such as chain letters, e-mail viruses, and pyramid schemes.

Memes are most "effective when they are copied with high fidelity (accuracy of copying), fecundity (number of

---

[271] *See generally* RICHARD DAWKINS, THE SELFISH GENE (1976); SUSAN J. BLACKMORE, THE MEME MACHINE (1999); JOHN CARTWRIGHT, EVOLUTION AND HUMAN BEHAVIOR: DARWINIAN PERSPECTIVES ON HUMAN NATURE 327–342 (2008); *and* COSMOS AND CULTURE: CULTURAL EVOLUTION IN A COSMIC CONTEXT (Steven J. Dick & Mark L. Lupisella eds. 2009). *See also* Michael S. Fried, *The Evolution of Legal Concepts: The Memetic Perspective*, 39 JURIMETRICS 298–300 (1999).

copies made), and longevity (lifetime of the copies)."[272] The evolutionary development of cultural memes are also susceptible to the human influences of *methodical selection*, or selective breeding for particular traits, and *unconscious selection*, or breeding using the healthiest and strongest animals or hardiest plant strains. It has further been suggested that major unique aspects of human culture, like music and language, the evolutionary origins of which have long been contentious, arose due to the imitative memetic habits of early hominids quite apart from whatever benefits may have accrued to humanity. Music in particular is an enduring mystery to evolutionary biologists because "it is manifestly complex, intricately designed, an expensive consumer of time, energy and materials" without contributing any clear benefit "to the genetic fitness of those who make and participate in the proliferation of music."[273] The obvious benefits of music, art, language, religion, and to bring the discussion back to the subject of this study, law are cultural rather than genetic.[274]

Ancient constitutionalism has clearly benefitted from imitative repetition in order to survive despite recurring attempts to prove its historical inaccuracy and to demonstrate the extent to which its many variants had reduced it to an almost meaningless tautological absurdity that the

---

[272] Susan Blackmore, *Dangerous Memes; or, What the Pandorans Let Loose, in* COSMOS AND CULTURE: CULTURAL EVOLUTION IN A COSMIC CONTEXT 297, 300–303 (Steven J. Dick & Mark L. Lupisella eds. 2009) (citing DAWKINS, *supra* note 254). Blackmore suggests the term *temes* to differentiate technologically enhanced memes like computer viruses and internet 'memes' from those transmitted solely by human beings themselves. *Id.* at 304–306.

[273] Daniel C. Dennett, *The Evolution of Culture, in* COSMOS AND CULTURE: CULTURAL EVOLUTION IN A COSMIC CONTEXT 125, 132–35 (Steven J. Dick & Mark L. Lupisella eds. 2009).

[274] *Id.* at 131–132 *and* Blackmore, *supra* note 255 at 302–304.

nation should be ruled by a particular constitution because the nation had been thereby ruled ever since (more or less) its moment of origin. Reduced to its essence ancient constitutionalism asserts that a culture should be faithful to its original constitutional moment and that disaster ensues whenever the culture is unfaithful to its noble origins. This is a remarkably simple, memorable, potentially useful, and often beneficial meme of juridical culture. The various imitative repetitions of which have clearly accrued to the ancient constitutionalist meme's own long-term survival. What human society could fully resist the alluring notion that they should continue to follow the noble intentions of their distant ancestors because the design of fundamental laws establishing the original form of governance by those ancestors was faithful to the highest ideals of justice guided by either divine inspiration or rational deliberations (and perhaps both)? To rephrase that in the context of British-American constitutional history, what British society, as well as those cultures which developed out of the British traditions of law and governance, could be totally immune to being influenced by the core principles of the *Matter of Britain* that the essential duty of the sovereign is to forge a society of law and justice, not of mere will and power that inevitably leads to disorder, violence and vengeance?

Whether it is the early seventeenth century immemorial common law constitutionalism of Coke and Saltern; the immemorial origins of Parliament crafted in defense of the Long Parliament's actions in the 1640s and then recrafted in support of the Glorious Revolution Parliament; the immemorial and indefeasible divine right constitutionalism crafted by royalist supporters in the Restoration period; the rational, and potentially allegorical, ancient constitutionalism of Acherly, Blackstone, and the American Revolution and Founding in the eighteenth century; or, American Originalism today, every variant of ancient constitutionalism utilizes the power of that basic cultural meme of faith and fidelity to a foundational constitutional paradigm nourished by forensic mytho-historical rhetoric. The meme of ancient constitutionalism has been sustained over the centuries by the extent to which those uses of forensic mytho-historical rhetoric have bordered on the edges of analogical believability, if not always precise historical accuracy.

The story of King Lucius's exchange of letters with Pope Eleutherus in the second century is a cogent final example of the need to not read the juridical historiography of the ancient constitution from a twenty-first century awareness of their historical accuracy. The British stories of King Lucius have recently been shown to have arisen due to a misreading of a reference in the sixth century *Liber Pontificalis* [*Lives of the Popes*] by the Venerable Bede or one of his continental colleagues when Bede was writing his *Historia Ecclesiastica Gentis Anglorum* [*Ecclesiastical History of the English People*] in the eighth century. Under the entry for Pope Eleutherus was a notation: "'This pope received a letter from Lucio Britannio rege [which he interpreted to be a British King Lucius] asking for assistance in converting his lands to the Faith.'" Bede's *Historia* was subsequently used as the earliest available primary historical source by every chronicler and historian of Britain. In that "every British historian and clergyman read Bede[,] [h]is non-existent King Lucius of Britain thus became an important 'reality' as the king who brought the Faith to Britain in the second century." It was only after "Biblical scholar Adolf Harnack first noticed in 1904 that the interpolated King Lucius in the Liber Pontificalis was really King Abgar VIII, full name Lucius Aelius [Aurelius] Septimius Megas Abgarus VIII (177–212), first Christian king of Edessa and the only King Lucius who espoused Christianity in the late second century time of Pope Eleutherus" that the historical inaccuracy of Saltern's "lucid starre of Britain" began to become patently obvious. More recent scholarship has shown that

Bede's mistake likely arose due to the fact that the region of Syria where Edessa was located was then known as *Birtha*, which was rendered into Latin as *Britium* and which all too easily became *Britannio*.[275]

Should Saltern's extensive use of the story of King Lucius of Britain and his reliance upon Lucius's correspondence with Pope Eleutherus lead to a dismissal of *Of the Antient Lawes* as an utterly fabulous work by a gullible and ill-informed author, or worse as a deliberately fraudulent work by a lawyer writing as an advocate for King James's Union proposal? Assuredly not. Well over a thousand years of British historical scholarship, including the comparatively pristine humanist *Historia Anglorum* of Polydore Vergil, relied upon Bede and later sources that in turn had relied upon it. By the standards of twenty-first century historical accuracy much of the British historiography produced over the course of that millenia would now also be dismissively suspect, not just Saltern's work and those of other ancient constitutionalist writers.

Whether ancient constitutionalism is a juridical meme or merely an enduring tradition of forensic historiography used by constitutional lawyers and judges, it is best evaluated not by the strict standards of historical accuracy but by the more forgiving and contextually appropriate measures for determining the truths of constitutional fictions or myths. Read as stories that are "'more or less' true" that reveal aspects of our constitutional history that are "'strange and wonderful'," the many variants of ancient constitutionalism undeniably exhibit a high degree

---

275 Daniel Scavone, *Edessan Sources for the Legend of the Holy Grail*, PROC. INT'L WORKSHOP ON SCI. APPROACH TO ACHEIROPOIETOS IMAGES 3 (2010), http://www.acheiropoietos.info/proceedings/ ScavoneGrail-Web.pdf. *See also* Daniel Scavone, *Joseph of Arimathea, the Holy Grail, and the Edessa Icon*, 9 Arthuriana 1 (1999) *and* Alan Smith, *Lucius of Britain: Alleged King and Church Founder*, 90 Folklore 29 (1979).

of aesthetic truth.[276] There indeed were other literary cultures of law and lawyers in ancient Britain than those traditionally recounted in contemporary Anglo-American legal history. While each of these legal cultures were undeniably insular, interactions between them that influenced each were "a constant feature of the history of the British Isles." There were also recurring cycles of rulers considered lawful, or legitimate, who preserved and maintained traditions of law and justice punctuated by periods of rule by monarchs who were considered unlawful, or illegitimate, and who were perceived as having ruled solely by their own will and regal power within the various realms of Britain. The various societies of ancient northwestern Europe had also in fact been governed by remarkably similar, albeit not precisely identical, systems of law and juridical institutions.[277] That the actual juridical history of Britain is far more complex, nuanced and anachronistic (especially in terms of continuity over time) than that does not diminish the high degree of aesthetic truth conveyable by the traditions of ancient constitutionalism. The many variants of ancient constitutionalism were also highly effective at conveying symbolic moral truths, and to a lesser (but still culturally significant and influential) degree constitutive moral truths. Ancient constitutionalism would not have survived to the extent it

---

[276] West, *supra* note 38 at 996. *See also* discussion *supra* at 21–24 .

[277] RICHARD S. TOMPSON, ISLANDS OF LAW: A LEGAL HISTORY OF THE BRITISH ISLES 2 (2000). *Compare generally, e.g., id. and* RICHARD S. TOMPSON, THE ATLANTIC ARCHIPELAGO: A POLITICAL HISTORY OF THE BRITISH ISLES (1986) *with* NORMAN DAVIES, THE ISLES: A HISTORY (1999) *and* WATKINS, *supra* note 17 *and* STACEY, *supra* note 17. The early chapters of Davies' *The Isles* in particular provide an excellent comparative summary of what we now know (more or less) about the societies of what he aptly terms the Celto-Germanic peoples of ancient Europe; a term which harmonizes nicely with the Anglo-Brittanic culture of ancient constitutionalism.

clearly has if it were not such an excellent vehicle for conveying such cultural truths. That this cultural meme (or, if one prefers, tradition of forensic historiography) has not only survived, but positively flourished through imitative and unconscious selection over the centuries since it was first methodically 'cultivated' as courtly entertainment and official juridical propaganda by the late Tudor and early Stuart royal courts is itself a testament to the remarkable capacity of ancient constitutionalism to convey culturally significant aesthetic and moral truths.

As the works of Selden, Craig, Coke, and Saltern illustrate, the Union Texts were clearly produced by writers who epitomize the characteristics of literary lawyers crafting the constitutional trope of fidelity to ancient British laws and constitutions out of myth and history. Saltern's *Of the Antient Lawes* was written and published at a pivotal moment in the development of ancient constitutionalism. His text would appear to be the first explicit use of the plural phrase *ancient British constitutions* and is most assuredly the first work to assert its historicity in such a concerted and methodical fashion. Other Union Texts, including those of Coke, undeniably include a multitude of references to ancient laws, ancient kingdoms, ancient names, ancient officers, and so on, without actually using the phrase *ancient constitution.* Prior to Saltern's text, ancient constitutionalism was primarily implicit in the juridical traditions of the common law. After Saltern's text, the phrase *ancient constitution* begins to appear more frequently until it becomes the predominant rhetorical device of early modern British juridical thought. While it is too much to credit Saltern alone for that development, it clearly shows how pivotal the historical moment was when *Of the Antient Lawes of great Britaine* was printed in 1605. The works of Pocock and others have demonstrated that this rhetorical device of ancient constitutionalism became considerably varied as it developed after those origins in the early seventeenth century and has continued to influence British, and later American, juridical thought ever since.[278] Variants were developed later in the seventeenth century by both Royalists and Parliamentarians to support their positions, effectively bifurcating the core paradox of medieval British political thought – the coexistence of an absolute royal prerogative power and the limitations of the rule of law and representative political institutions into the opposing dogmas of early modern British political thought. By the eighteenth century ancient constitutionalism had become the dominant rhetorical device of British and American juridical discourse. The variety and enduring influence of the myth of Britain's ancient constitutions clearly merits a status as a cycle of constitutional myth "so worn and domesticated with constant varying use that it may be described as belonging to [the] traditions" of British-American constitutionalism.[279] Saltern's illustrative survey of the "secret footsteps of the ancient British constitutions" is itself now an ancient footstep of that long-lived tradition of ancient constitutionalism. The juridical meme of the "ancient British constitutions" may indeed be aptly described not merely as an enduring monument of the mental world of the Jacobean Court, but of the common law mind of British-American constitutionalism writ large.

---

[278] *See generally, e.g.*, POCOCK, THE ANCIENT CONSTITUTION, *supra* note 44; GREENBERG, *supra* note 29; Paul Christianson, *Royal and parliamentary voices on the ancient constitution, c. 1604–1621, in* THE MENTAL WORLD OF THE JACOBEAN COURT 71 (Linda Levy Peck ed., 1991); *and* REID, *supra* note 250.

[279] *Time, Institutions and Action; An Essay on Traditions and Their Understanding, in* J.G.A. POCOCK, POLITICS, LANGUAGE AND TIME: ESSAYS ON POLITICAL THOUGHT AND HISTORY 233, 243 (1973).

APPENDIX

APPENDIX I

Translation of the Letter of Eleutherus to Lucius[1]

Pope Eleutherus to Lucius King of the Britons.

You required that we should send you the Roman and Imperial laws, that you might use them in your kingdom of Britain, but those laws we may disprove, but not the laws of God. You have received lately through God's goodness in your kingdom the faith and law of Christ; you have there in your kingdom both Testaments; out of them by God's grace and the advice of your realm, take a law, and thereby patiently govern your kingdom. You are the Vicar of God in your kingdom; according to the Kingly Prophet, 'The earth is the Lord's, and his fullness is the whole world and all that dwelt therein.' And again: 'Thou shalt love righteousness and hate iniquity, wherefore God, even thy God, hath anointed thee with the oil of gladness above thy fellows.' They are the King's children — Christian nations and peoples of your kingdom that live and exist under your protection and peace, according to the Scripture, 'As a hen gathereth her children under her wings.' The people and nations of the kingdom of Britain are yours. Such as are divided you should gather them together to the law of Christ, his holy Church to peace and concord, and cherish, maintain, protect, govern, and defend them from the injurious, malicious, and their enemies. Woe be to that kingdom whose king is a

---

[1] *Glastonbury Abbey, Past and Present. The Rise and Influence of English Monachism*, 66 DUBLIN U. MAG. 631, 640 (Dublin: 1865).

child, and the princes eat early in the morning. I do not call a king a child for his youth or minority, but for his folly, iniquity, and madness. According to the Kingly Prophet, 'The bloodthirsty and deceitful men shall not outlive half their days.' By eating we shall understand gluttony; by gluttony luxury; by luxury all filth, wickedness, and mischief; according to King Solomon, 'Wisdom will not enter into the spiteful soul, nor inhabit in a body subject to sin.' A king has his name of governing not of his kingdom. You will be king so long as you rule well, otherwise you will not be so named, but lose that name, God forbid. God grant that you may reign with Him everlastingly, whose Vicar you are in the said kingdom. To whom with the Father, &c., &c.

APPENDIX II

Works Cited by Saltern

Aug. de Ciuit. Dei.	St. Augustine, The City of God (ca. 430).
Bed.	Bede, Ecclesiastical History of England (ca. 730)
Brac./Bracton	Henrici de Bracton. De Legibus et Consuetudinibus Angliæ. [The Laws and Customes of England] (London: 1569) (ca. 1230).
Camden	William Camden, Britanniae, or a Chorographicall description of the most flourishing Kingdomes, England, Scotland, and Ireland, and the Islands adjoyning, out of the depths of Antiquitie (London: 1586).
Caesar	Caesar, Commentarii de Bello Gallico [Commentaries on the Gallic War]
Decret.	Pseudo-Isidore, Decretals (ca. 9th century).
De. Leg./Cic. Leg.	Marcus Tullius Cicero, De Legibus (On the Laws) (ca. 50 BCE)
Diodor Sic./Dio	Diodorus Siculus, Bibliotheca historica (ca. 50 BCE)
Ethic.	Aristotle, Nicomachean Ethics (ca. 4th century BCE)
Fitz. N.B.	Anthony Fitzherbert, La Novvelle Natura Breviũ [The new Natura Brevium] (London: 1567)

Fortescue	Sir John Fortescue, De Laudibus Legum Angliae [In Praise of the Laws of England] (ca. 1470)
Fox	John Foxe, Actes and Monuments [Book of Martyrs] (London: 1583).
Gen./Psal./(Etc.)	The Bible
Gildas	Gildas, De Excidio et Conquestu Britanniae [On the Ruin and Conquest of Britain] (ca. 580).
Gra. Dist.	Gratian, Decretum Gratiani (Concordia discordantium canonum) (ca. 1150)
Higden.	Ranulf Higden, Polychronicon (sive Historia Polycratica) (ca. 1350)
Huntindõ.	The chronicle of Henry of Huntingdon; comprising The history of England, from the invasion of Julius Cæsar to the accession of Henry II. Also, The acts of Stephen, King of England and Duke of Normandy. (ca. 1154).
Hooker.	Raphael Holinshed, The first and second volumes of Chronicles comprising 1 The description and historie of England, 2 The description and historie of Ireland, 3 The description and historie of Scotland: first collected and published by Raphaell Holinshed, William Harrison, and others: now newlie augmented and continued (with manifold matters of singular note and worthie memorie) to the yeare 1586. by Iohn Hooker aliàs Vowell Gent and others. With conuenient

	tables at the end of these volumes. (London: 1587).
Ingulfus	Ingulphus, Historia Monasterii Croylandensis [Croyland Chronicle] (ca. 1300)
Hist. Ely	Historia Eliensis [History of Ely] (ca. 1180).
Lãb. Archaion.	William Lambarde, Archaionomia, siue de priscis anglorum legibus libri sermone Anglico, vetustate antiquissimo, aliquot abhinc seculis conscripti, atq[ue] nunc demum, magno iurisperitorum, & amantium antiquitatis omnium commodo, è tenebris in lucem vocati. (London: 1568).
Livy	Livy, Ab Urbe Condita [History of Rome] (ca. 20 BCE)
Malmesbury	William Malmesbury, Gesta Regum Anglorum [The Deeds of the English Kings] (ca. 1127)
Monemuthens	Geoffrey of Monmouth, Historia Regum Britanniae [The History of the Kings of Britain] (ca. 1136).
Polidor.	Polydore Vergil, Anglica Historia (Basel: 1555)
Polit.	Aristotle, The Politics (ca. 4th century BCE)
Pontic. Vir.	Ponticus Virunnius, Doctissimi Britannicae Historiae (1534)
Sir John Prise	Historiae Brittanicae Defensio [A Defence of the British History] (London: 1573).
Riuall. in hist. Iur. de Iustiniana	Aymari Rivalli, Historia Juris Civilis (1539)

Stanf.	William Staunford, Les plees del coron [The Pleas of the Crown] (London: 1574)
Vlpianus	Ulpian, Domitii Ulpiani fragmenta (Paris: 1549).
Wesembech	Pandectas Iuris Civilis Et Codicis Iustinianei (ca. 1575).
Xenophon	The Works of Xenophon

APPENDIX III

OF THE ANTIENT LAWES OF great Britaine.

Seruato Ius, metue Mortalis Deum.

George Saltern.

LONDON

Printed for *Iohn Iaggard*, and are to bee ſolde at his Shop in Fleeteſtreete, at the Signe of the hand and Starre. 1605.

De Antiquis Britanniæ Legibus.

Cap. 1.

IN *all actions, in euerie* election, in euery counsell and deliberation, it is to bee held for a certaine and vndoubted principle, that, Onely thinges Godly, just, & necessarie are to be done, & that with due inuocation of Diuine assistance, without the which nothing can be done. So the first consideration ought to bee of the end, the second of the meanes, the third of the effectuall working power, which cannot be hindred, which is onely the spirit of God all sufficient. By this wee may see how that ground is to be vnderstood, which some haue taken, namely that in al innouations there ought to be vrgent necessitie, or euident vtilitie. A ground which if it had bin vsed onely as it was first proposed by a *Pagan*, I would

Gen. 17.1

Vlpianus.

B.

De Antiquis

I would ſay that it were altogether vnperfect & defectiue, ſeeing the conſideration of Godlines & juſtice, is quite omitted; but ſeeing the ſame is now taken and preſſed by Chriſtians, I will deſire them to admit a Chriſtian expoſition, & to ſay that Religion, Piety & Iuſtice, doe carry the waight of neceſsity and vtility, and whatſoeuer is Godly and juſt, the ſame is neceſſarie & proffitable, according to the ſaying of the A-
1. Tim. 4. poſtle: Godlyneſſe is proffitable to all things & hath the promiſes of this life and of the life to come. And againe whatſoeuer is not Godly & juſt, the ſame is not to be done whatſoeuer neceſsitie or vtilitie may ſeeme to bee in it: as it is
Mat. 10. 37 writtē. He that loueth Sonne or daughter more thē me, is not worthy of me. And ſo that groūd is much more perfect & abſolute which out of a *Pagan*, is thus expreſſed:

Seruato ius et metue mortalis Deum.

How Godly and juſt a thing it is to eſtabliſh a perfect Vnitie in theſe Kingdomes, for the confirmation of an euerlaſting peace betweene them, and by conſequence thereof, for the increaſe and propagation of Gods truth and his Goſpell, in a former treatiſe I haue ſhewed according to the beſt of my vnderſtanding.

Now

Britanniæ Legibus.

Now I take in hand to ſpeake of our auncient Lawes, and God is the beginning and end of my worke. The thing it ſelfe is no leſſe fit and neceſſarie for this time to be knowne, then obſcure and difficult to expound. For whether we conſider our Statutes enacted ſince the *Norman*, wee ſhall finde them grounded vpon moſte juſt and prudent jntentions: or the remnants of our Actes made by the *Saxons*, we ſhal ſee them ful of Godly & deuout admonitions, or the ſecret footeſteps of the auncient Britiſh conſtitutions, appering yet in the bodie of our common Lawes, the principles thereof will appeare to be the verie Lawes of the eternal God, written in the two immortal tables of nature & Scripture. The reaſon heereof ſurbordinate vnder the gracious ordinance of the Almightye, was either the bleſſed diſpoſitiō of our Princes, whoſe matches for Godlineſſe and vertue no countrie but the Cradle of our Sauiour could euer affoord (as our eyes now doe witnes,) or the natiue inclination of our people moſt apt to be led by piety and deuotion, as the greateſt number of examples doe prooue: or the religious & happie counſell of *Elutherius* to *Lucius* King of Brittain, who hauing publikely receaued in his

B 2 kingdome

De Antiquis

kingdome the faith & Gospel of our Lord, and studying to amend his Lawes then vnperfect, sent vnto the said *Elutherius* for a Coppy of the *Romane* Lawes. The Christian Bishop made such an answere to the first Christian King, as betweene two such persons ought to passe; As the most high God answereth his most faithful

Exo. 25.40 seruant. Make al thinges according to the patterne &c. So writeth this good Bishop. *Petistis a nobis leges Romanas et Cæsaris vobis transmitti, quibus in regno Britanniæ vti voluistis: Leges Romanas et Cæsaris semper reprobare possumus, Legem Dei nequaquam. Suscepistis enim nuper miseratione diuina, in regno Britanniæ Legem et fidem Christi. Habetis penes vos in Regno vtramque paginam. Ex illis dei gratia, per consilium regni vestri sume legem, et per illam Dei patientia, vestrum rege Britanniæ regnũ. Vicarius vero Dei estis in Regno iuxta Prophetam regem.*

Inter Leges St[i]*. Edwardi Lãb. Archaion. Fox ex Antiquo codice See also Monemuthens. Bed. Li. 1. Pontic. vir.*

Psal. 24. *Domini est terra, et plenitudo eius, orbis terrarum et vniuersi qui inhabitant in eo. Et rursum*

Psal. 45. *iuxta prophetam Regem, Dilexisti iustitiam, et odisti iniquitatem, Propterea vnxit te Deus tuus oleo Lætitiæ, præ consortibus tuis. Et rursus iuxta*

Psal. 72 *prophetã regem. Deus iudiciũ tuũ regi da, et iustitiam tuã filio regis. Non enim Iudiciũ neque iustitiam dm Cæſaris Filij enim Regis gentes Chriſtiane et populi regni ſunt qui ſub veſtra protectione, et pace et regno degunt et conſiſtunt iuxta Euangelium, quemadmodum gallina congregat pullos ſub alis, &c. Gentes vero regni, pulli veſtri ſunt, quos diuiſos debetis in vnum ad concordiam, et pacem, et ad fidem, et ad legem Chriſti, et ad ſanctam eccleſiam congregare. &c.* This counſell I ſay might bee the reaſon, and by all likelyhood was the reaſon that our common lawes are ſo much grounded vppon the lawe of God, which I am the rather mooued to beleeue, for that I ſee our learned Iudge Mr. *Bracton* ſo oftentimes inculcating the ſentence of this Epiſtle, and namely that *Rex eſt vicarius Dei*, and deriuing ſuch excellent conclusions from it, as of Godlines in the Prince and of dutie and obedience in the ſubiect &c. And the effect heereof hath been that which is written in the Scriptures: *Verbum Dei manet in æternum*. Theſe lawes ſaith the learned Sir *Iohn Forteſcue* haue been in the times of the *Brittaines*, *Romaines*, *Saxons*, *Danes* and *Normanes*, and if they were not the beſt Lawes, ſome of thoſe Kings (eſpecially the *Romans*) would haue changed them. Of theſe thinges therfore I haue to ſpeake matters farre aboue the mediocritie

Lib.1.C.2.

Lib.3.C.9.

Forteſcue de laudibus Legum.

B 3 of

of my knowledge: but that I may the better do it, I humbly beseech thee O true light of eternitie! to whome all ages and times are present, to reuiue the memorie of thy glory established by thee in our auncient Lawes, lighten my vnderstanding, confirme my judgement, & leade mee in the wayes of truth and justice, seeing that without thee neither any man can doe, nor I can speake any thing.

Cap. 2.

ORder of learning, and of the said Epistle doth require, that before I enter into the discourse of our auncient Britaine lawes, I speake somewhat concerning the *Romane* Lawes, that it may appeare that neither the reuerend *Elutherius* was deceiued in judgement, nor the Godly *Lucius* in his choise, nor the learned *Fortescue* in his testimony: but that our said auncient Lawes were, indeed, as well as by the *Romanes* owne confession (in that they did not change them) better then their owne. I speake as a Christian, for asmuch as *Brittain* receaued the Lawes of Christ before it knew the gouernmēt of *Rome*; but because I wold be loath to offend,

Britanniæ Legibus.

offend,I will remit the reader that is deſirous to know,what may be ſaid of the Authors & composers of the firſt *Romane* Lawes:to St.*Auguſtin* and of theſe now extant to *VVeſembechius Rivallius*,*Procopius*,and others: And for the principles and groundes,I will referre them to conſider the particulars of the twelue tables yet in parte remayning, and to meaſure and examine the rules of the Inſtitutes by the wordes of the Authors,out of which they ſeeme to bee taken: *Ariſtotle*, *Tully*, *Iſidorus. &c.* and both by the Scriptures : a woorke worthy the vacation of a learned man. But for the Lawes of *Brittaine*, my principall intention before I come to ſpeak of them, I will intreate a little leaue to ſpeake ſomewhat firſt of lawe in generall,and ſecondly of the auncient inhabitantes of this Ile. For by knowing what they were, wee ſhall the better knowe their Lawes and manners.

Aug.de Ciuit.Dei.L.3 *Weſembech prefat in Iſag.* *Riuall. in hiſt. Iur. de Iuſtinian.*

Cap. 3.

THe Lawe by *Ariſtotle* is called a couenant of the ſocietie of men. By *Tully* the reaſon and minde of God diſcerning juſt and vniuſt: If we joyne theſe two and call it the couenant made

Polit. 1. *De Leg.*

De Antiquis

dystinitio legis made by God with the societie of men, according to his owne reason, discerning just & vniust:it agreeth with the words of *Moses*, and will be as I take it a perfect definition.

Ex. 34. 27 & 20. v. 5. 6 Deut. 5. 2

The end as *Tully* saith is manifest, *Ad salutem ciuium, ciuitatumque incolumitatem vitamque omnium quietam et beatam.* Agreeing also with *Moses*, if *Salus et Incolumitas et Beatitudo*, bee taken for all the blessing of this life, and the life to come. Lawes are called Diuine or Humane. The deuine Lawes are those which God immediately made, first written in nature, secondlye described in the ten commaundements, & the Scriptures. Humane Lawes are Lawes deriued out of the diuine Lawes by applycation of the generall commaundements, First to the principal parties *viz.* to God, to the common estate, and to priuate men according to the diuision of the twelue Tables: secondlye to particular circumstances of Persons, thinges, actions, times, places, Penalties and such like, as the Institutes are deuided.

De Leg. 2.

Auson.

Heerehence followeth a conclusion obserued also by *Tully*; that if a Law be made contayning any thing contrary to the Lawe of God, it is not to be called a Lawe, (though all the world in a

ioynt

Britanniæ Legibus.

ioynt Parlamẽt confirme it. For neither is it deriued out of the general precepts, nor partaketh of the common definition, ſeeing it is not a couenant of God, but a confederacy againſt God.

The property and effect of the Lawe is firſt to make a diſtinction of juſt from vniuſt. Secondlye to commaund and forbid. Thirdlye to punniſh and rewarde. Theſe thinges are performed originallye and gennerally by the Lawe of God, and ſecondarily and particularly by the Lawe of men. The quallities of a true Lawe are reckoned vp by *Iſidorus* and others. *Eſſe debet Lex Honeſta, Iuſta, poſſibilis, ſecundum naturam et conſuetudinem, Loco et tempori conueniens, neceſſaria vel vtilis manifeſta. &c.* A Lawe muſt bee honeſt, juſt, poſsible, agreeable to nature and cuſtome, to time and place, neceſſarie or profitable and manifeſt: & of this proceedeth another ground alſo, *jus nemini violare vel ignorare Licet. Item* lex *obligat ad ſcientiam, ad obedientiam, ad pænam.* The Lawe bindeth to knowledge, obedience, & puniſhment: no man may breake it, no man may be ignorant of it, and that which I*ſidore*, ſaith, when Lawes are made, no Man may judge of them but according to them. The exact per-

Decret. Part.1 Weſemb.

C. formance

De Antiquis

5 *Ethic.* formance of the Lawe is called Iuſtice, the moderation of the Lawe vppon conſideration of circumſtances, is called equitie, the contraries to the law are iniurie, iniuſtice, iniquity, wrong, force, fraud & ſuch like. Whatſoeuer is ſaid of the Law of God abſolutely, may proportionally be applyed to the Lawe of men. The end of the Lawe of God is al happines. That happines which is the end of Humane Lawes, conſiſteth *Pſal.72.85.* chieflie in the conſeruation of Religion, Peace, and Iuſtice, all which thinges are comprehended by St. *Auguſtin*, vnder the name of peace, *De Ciuitate Dei.li.19* which alſo he maketh the finall end of the Citie of God. The matters which the Lawes doe handle, are chiefly perſons, things, places, times, contracts, offences and actions. In this Iland, perſons appointed ſpecially for the procuration of Religion, are the Archbiſhops, Biſhops & Miniſters; for the preſeruation of Peace are the Nobilitie, Sheriffes, and Iuſtices of peace. For the adminiſtration of Iuſtice, the Iudges, profeſſors and Officers of Lawe. And the King hath from God ſupreame authoritie ouer all, according to the ſentence, *Rex eſt Vicarius Dei.*

Other diſtinctions there be of Perſons, but it is not my intention to ſpeake of euery difference,

Britanniæ Legibus.

rence, but onely ſo much as may ſerue to giue light to the Diſcourſe intended.

Things alſo haue many diuiſions, whereof I meane to touch but one, which is that ſome may paſſe by courſe of inheritance, as Landes and tenements: ſome cannot, as Chattelles.

Of places, ſome haue ſacred priuiledge, as Temples, repreſenting God by his woord. The Kinges preſence and Iudiciall Courtes, repreſenting God in power and Iuſtice; othersare ordinarie and common, and of them ſome are publique: as Markettes, Wayes: Some priuate, as Houſes, Shoppes. &c. Times are likewiſe diuided into ſacred and common, the Day, the night, and ſuch like diuiſions. Contracts haue manifold Diſtinctions, which ſee in *Bracton*. *Bracto.L.3*

Crimes, are either againſt Religion, Peace, or Iuſtice, and againe are conſidered as publike offences, & ſo *Rex pro pace ſequi debet*, in which *Bracton.* all the Pleas of the Crowne are contayned, or as ſome particular perſon is intereſſed, who is to ſue accordingly. Againe, they may be purſued ciuilly or criminally. Laſtly, actions are diſtinguiſhed for the moſte parte according to the things which they demaund, or the perſons plaintifes or defendants, or the Courts wherin,

C 2 or

De Antiquis

or the times whē.&c. In actions,are these principall partes: Sūmons, or Citations,triall,Iudgement,and execution: These points as fitter to be sought in other places,& as to learned men, and as my selfe not halfe learned, I doe briefely passe ouer,hasting to speake somewhat of the Inhabitants of this Lande, and so to that which I intend.

Cap.4.

AMongst the seueral opinions that haue bin conceiued cōcerning the first possessors of this Isle,I cannot see any more consonant to diuinity, to reason, and the testimonies of best approoued Antiquaries, then that which maintaineth the Nations of *Brittaine* to be descended of *Gomer* the Sonne of *Iaphet*, whose children,after the diuision of tongues,at *Babel*, spred throughout al *Europe*, & so replenished this Island, *De tractu Armoricano (vt fertur) in Britanniā aduecti* saith the venerable *Bede*. And to say that any multitude of *Chams* posterity arriued heere to inhabit,is in my vnderstanding cōtrary to the grounds aforesaid. For first there is no probabilitie to maintaine that the Children or families, descended of one sonne: as of

Bed. Hist. Lib. 1.

Iaphet,

Britanniæ Legibus.

Iaphet, were mixed with the Children of the other. For then how ſhould the accompliſhmēt of the Prophecye be obſerued, which God pronoūced before by the mouth of *Noah*? that *Chanaan* ſhould be a ſeruant both to *Sem* & *Iaphet*, and that *Iaphet* ſhould dwel in the tents of *Sem*: Gen. 9. Secondly, it is euident, that almightie God gaue to euery famely of the Sonnes of *Noah* his ſeuerall Language, & his ſeuerall Country, by theſe reaſons: *viz.* by the ſuruay of all Nations the Sonnes of *Iaphet*, *Madai* the *Medes*; *Iauan* the *Ionians*; *Tubal* the *Iberians*; *Meſchech*, the *Moſcouites*; *Gomer*, the *Cymbri*; *Ashkenas*, the *Tuiſcones*. The Sonnes of *Cham*, *Cush*, the *Aethiopians*, *Miſraim* the *Aegiptians*, *Canaan* the *Canaanites*: the Sonnes of *Sem*, *Ashur*, *Elā*, *Arachshad*, *Lud* and *Aram*, euerie one had his language and his Countrie, and as I take it the contrarie cannot be ſhewed.

And this is confirmed by the expreſſe words of *Moſes*, or rather of God himſelfe, the trueſt Author: where hauing named, firſt the Sonnes Gen. 10. of *Iaphet* by themſelues, *Gomer* and the reſt, hee addeth this concluſiō; Of theſe, were the Iles of the *Gentles* diuided, in their Landes euery man after his tongue, and after their families, in their

C 3 nations.

De Antiquis

nations. So hauing reckoned the Children of *Cham*, euerie one by name, hee addeth the like conclusion: These are (saith hee) the Sonnes of *Cham*, according to their families, according to their tongues in their Countries, & in their nations. The like conclusion he maketh after the ennumeration of the Sonnes of *Sem*. And the same point is prooued by the Historie of *Abraham*, where he is commaunded to goe from his Country, from his Kindred, & from his Fathers house: and againe by the Song of *Moses*, & diuers other places of Scripture. So as it is apparant by the wordes of the Scripture, that howsoeuer the languages were confounded, yet the seuerall kindreds, and families descended from the Sonnes of *Noah*, were not confounded together; but that euerie familie had his particular tongue and country, and were seuered from other Families. And it is also likely, that howsoeuer their speeches were confounded, and their families deuided: yet the Sonnes of *Iaphet* had amongst thẽselues more intelligence one of an others language, then they had of the languages vsed by the natiõs descended of *Cham*, or *Sem*. For wee see the *Assirians*, *Persians*, *Syrians*, and *Hebrewes* descended of *Sem*, had more similitude

Vers. 20. | Gene. 12 | Deut. 32. 8. | *Vid. Augus. Lib. 16. de Ciuit. Dei.*

Brit annia Legibus.

tude of ſpeech, and writing among themſelues, then they had with any the nations of *Europe*. And ſo the *Aegiptians*, *Aethiopians*, *Libians*, & other deſcended of *Cham*; which vicinityes (as I may call it) of ſpeech, being greater in thoſe original times, then now it is, cauſed thoſe families that had beſt intelligence one with another to ſorte themſelues together, in places of neerer neighbour-hood, And thereof it came, that the Children of *Sem* remained in *Asia*, The children of *Cham* went into *Africa*, & the children of *Iaphet* went northward into *Europa*; as wee ſee the *Moſcouits*, the *Thracians*, *Ionians* and *Iberians*, the Sonnes of Iaphet to be round about vs. Of all which premiſſes reſteth this concluſion, that all the inhabitants of *Britaine* are deſcended from ſome one of I*aphets* Children.

Other teſtimonies of the Scriptures incline the ſame way, for *Gomer* and *Togarmath* his ſonne are called the ſides of the North; & learned men doe agree, that the auncient *Kimbri* or *Gomeri*, the Sonnes of *Gomer* did reigne farre & wide in one neighbor Countries; and the auncient *Brittaines* doe yet call their countrie *Gimbri*. So that in Diuinitie and reaſon we cannot chooſe but acknowledge our ſelues to be bran-

Ezech. 38.

Camden.

Sir Iohn Priſe.

ches

ches of the ſame ſtocke, namelye the *Cimbri* of *Gomer*, & likewiſe the *Saxons* & *Danes* of *Ashkenas*, and the *Scots*, If *Iberi* of *Tuball*, and al of *Iaphet*: But if the *Scotti* wil confeſſe themſelues to be *Getæ*, according to the opiniõ of the moſt learned M^r^. *Camden*, then are they deſcended from *Gether*, the Sonne of *Sem*, as *Melanchton* ſheweth. And to theſe opinions the reaſons and authorities of beſt antiquaries doe concur, which he that deſireth to ſee, may peruſe them in M^r^. *Camden* and others, neither will I preiudicate any mans opinion, (though to me ſomewhat improbable) in deriuing vs from the *Troianes*, ſo as hee deriue the *Troianes* thẽſelues, from *Ashkenas* which will come to the ſame effect. Taking therefore the former opinion, or howſoeuer it be, the inhabitants of this Iſle being by all mens confeſsion, a moſt auncient nation of the poſteritie of *Iaphet*, and who (as *Gildas* ſeemeth to ſay) had at the firſt the knowledge of God; it ſtandeth with reaſon, & with beſt warrant of authoritie, to thinke they were gouerned by ſuch Lawes, and inſtitutions deriued from the Principles of the firſt age, that is from the Lawe of God written in nature, as moſt of the auncient nations did imbrace, & very

Beda. Li. 1.
Mel. Ch. 1.
Camden.
Polidor vir. Lib. 1.
Sir Iohn Prise.

Gildas cited by Polidor.

Britanniæ Legibus

veryе neere to thoſe which the Godly *Sem*, in whoſe tents God perſwadeth *Iaphet* to cõtinue, deliuered to his Children; of which I intend to perticulate ſome heerafter.

Cap. 5.

I Haue ſpoken of the Lawe in generall, and of the firſt inhabitants of this Land; and I haue to ſpeake ſomwhat in generall of the Lawes inſtituted by our Chriſtian King *Lucius* vpon receit of *Elutherius* Letters, meaning to deſcend in to perticularities, by eaſie paces and degrees.

But in ſetting down things of ſo ancient time, whereof remaine but fewe Hiſtoryes, through the rage of the *Romanes* and other ſauadge idolaters, the ſcourges of this kingdom, in her godly infancye; Leſt I ſhould ſeeme to ſpeake too much of mine owne braine; I would intreat euery prudent, ſober, & Chriſtian Politician, firſt to examine the contents, and ſentences of that godly Epiſtle, & ſecondly to conſider his owne minde, and to vnfolde his ſecret vnderſtanding, what he himſelfe would haue done, & what he would think fit to doe, if he had bene then King *Lucius*, or of counſell with him, hauing receiued ſuch a Letter as before is ſet downe?

D Touch-

De Antiquis

Touching the Epistle it selfe, it contayneth an answer to the demaund of King *Lucius*. The demaund was, to haue the Lawes of *Rome* and *Cæsar*. The answer consisteth of two partes; a Rejection, We may (saith he) alwaies reproue the Lawes of *Rome* & *Cæsar*, but not the Lawes of God. And an exhortatiō, to take a Lawe for his Kingdome, out of the Lawe of God. This he inforceth with diuers reasons and sentences of Scripture, which with an admirable consent, do euery one proue each other, and euery one the seuerall partes of the answer.

First you are Gods Vicar, therfore you must rule by Gods Law & not by *Cæsars*. The earth is the Lords, therfore it must be ruled by the lawes of the Lord, and not by *Cesars*. God hath annoynted you to be King, *Cesar* hath not annoynted you, therefore &c. O God, giue thy judgements to the King, therefore not *Cæsars*: what then would you doe, being a godly Christian, vpon the reading of such a Letter? Let our most Christian King St. *Edward* giue vs counsel; who in his Lawes, taking the words of this Letter for his ground-worke, saith thus: *Lāb. Arch.*

Rex autem, quia vicarius summi regis est, ad hoc est constitutus, vt regnum terrenum, & populum Domini,

Britanniæ Legibus.

Domini, & ſuper omnia ſanctã tueatur Eccleſiam eius, & regat, & ab iniurioſis defendat, & maleficos ab ea euellat. And a little after, he ſheweth how this may be done: *Debet vero Rex Deum timere ſuper omnia, & diligere, & mandata eius per totum Regnũ ſuum ſeruare. Debet etiam, ſanctam Eccleſiam regni ſui, cum omni integritate, & libertate iuxta conſtitutiones patrum, & predeceſſorum ſeruare, fouere, manutenere, regere, & contra inimicos defendere: ita vt Deus præ cæteris honoretur, & præ oculis ſemper habeatur. Debet etiam bonas eges, & conſuetu dines approbatas erigere, prauas autem delere omnes, & a regno deponere. Debet iudicium rectum in regno facere, & iuſtitiã per conſilium procerum regni ſui tenere.* Thus ſaith St. *Edward*, but if the counſell of ſo excellent a King doe not reſolue you, yet in the mouth of two witneſſes let euery word be confirmed, and peruſe the wordes of a moſt excellent Counſellor and Lawyer, I ſay *Bracton, lib.* 3. *cap.* 9. who there ſpeaketh to the ſame effect, grounding likewiſe vpõ the ſame golden foundation. *Rex eſt Dei Miniſter & Vicarius; Poteſtas itaque ſua iuris eſt non iniuriæ, Poteſtas autem iniuriæ Diaboli eſt, non Dei*, and ſo after to the like effect, as St. *Edward* had ſpoken.

Bracton.

D 2 I thinke

De Antiquis

I think therefore, there is no man but wil ſay that King *Lucius* did accordingly: namely, that according to the contents and directions receiued, he did call a Counſel or Parlament, a thing vſed in thoſe times, as I will ſhewe heer-after: He did ſuruay the State and Lawes of his Kingdome; that which was agreeable to Gods holy worde he did confirme, and that which wanted he did newly enact. Reaſons perſwading me to thinke, that King *Lucius* did ſo, are theſe: Firſt his Godly zeale, which would neuer haue written to *Rome* for Lawes, without a great deſire, to haue the beſt lawes to gouern his Kingdome; and to my vnderſtanding it is ſenceles and abſurd, to ſay that whē he had receiued an anſwer ſo good & agreeable to his deſire, that he would leaue it vnfollowed and vnperformed. It cannot be ſaid that he wanted will, ſeeing he ſent for Lawes, nor that he wanted time, opportunitye, power, or conſent of his Nobles or people, ſeeing all, or the moſt part, yea the *Druidæ* and *Flamnies* embraced Chriſtian religion together with him, as our Hiſtories teſtifie; and he ruled the *Britains* long time after in flouriſhing peace and tranquility. Againe, that he retayned ſome of the former Lawes; the common opinion of

Beda, ponticus virum. Polidor Monemuth

thoſe

Britannia Legibus.

those auncient Christians of the Primitiue age, perswadeth me, wherof I will speake more, whẽ I come to K. *Lucius* his lawes. Yet by the way one text will I cite, out of *Iunius*, who saith that as long as Heathen Emperors, & Kings held the raines of gouernment, the Christians gaue not their mindes to dispute the question of the vse and authoritie of *Moses* Lawes; but when the State changed, & Christian Emperors were aduanced, then those most sapient & orthodoxall Fathers, seeing it most expedient to turne about this world, without any greater noise, forbearing the troubles of secular affayres, left the authoritie, both of making lawes & giuing iudgements to the ordinarie Magistrates; but if any were instituted *Contra Rectã Rationem, quã in natura et scriptura explicauitus De*; against right & good reasõ, which God in nature & Scripture hath described, that either with gentle & calme admonitions they procured to be amended, or patiently suffred, if it were incurable, least the whole common good (which *Augustin* before called Peace) should be stirred in hope of some particular; For, that many times the importunitie of men bringeth to passe, whiles they seek to cure one euill, they shake and weaken the publike

Iun. in epist-ola, ad Poli-tiam Mos.

D 3

publike eſtate. In which wordes beſides the point in hand,is much to be obſerued,that nothing ought to bee in the Lawe againſt reaſon: which is the vniuerſall Maxim, the maine foundation,and as I may call it,the abridgement of all our common Lawe, which heere you ſee to be the rule of thoſe auncient fathers, and affirmed to haue been expreſſed by the Diuine wiſdome of God in nature and Scripture. This is it whereby all our queſtions, and controuerſies,all our arguments and iudgements, all our Statutes and cuſtomes,are ruled and ouerruled, enlarged and corrected.

But againe to our purpoſe,St. *Augustin* ſpeaketh much to the ſame effect. *Hæc ergo cæleſtis Ciuitas dum peregrinatur in terra &c.* This heauenly City whiles it is in Pilgrimage vpõ earth, calleth Citizens out of all nations; and in all tongues,aſſembleth a Pilgrime ſocietie; not regarding the manifold diuerſities of manners, Lawes and cuſtomes, not repealing or deſtroying any of thoſe thinges, whereby the terrene peace (ſo I reade) is eyther procured,or preſerued,but rather keeping and following that, which although it be diuerſe in diuerſe nations, yet ſtill is intended to one and the ſame end of

De Ciuit. Dei. lib.19 C.17.

Terrene

B itanniæ Legibus.

Terrene Peace, so long as it is no hindrance of the Religion, whereby the onely supreme and true God is taught to bee worshiped. To the same effect he speaketh againe in the nineteene Chapter of the same booke.

These authorities therfore leade me to beleeue, that King *Lucius* retayned such of the auncient institutions, as were not *Contra rectam rationem* (as *Iunius* saith) *quam in natura et scriptura explicauit Deus.* And that he did take some part of his Lawes, out of the Scriptures, is proued by the testimonies of our Chronicles, compared with the words of the most Godly & religious King *Alfred* in his Lawes. The Chronicles say that *Gildas* the auncient Godly *Brittaine* Priest who liued not much more, then 500. yeares after Christ, and not much aboue 300. after *Lucius*, translated the British Lawes into Latine, & afterward *Alfred* the Godly *Saxone* Prince, trãslated the same into *Saxon*; and so continued them to posteritie. *Alfred* in the entrãce to his Lawes, setting first the ten Commaundements, and many judiciall Lawes of *Moses*, and last the Apostolicall Epistle directed to the *Gentiles*, mencioned in the Actes, which hee concludeth with these wordes vsed in some translations.

Lamb. Arc. Higdẽ Pontic. virun: Galf. Mon.

Lamb. Ar.

Actes. 15.

That

De Antiquis

That you will not haue done your ſelues,do not vnto others; windeth vp all with this concluſion:By this one cõmaundement(ſaith he)it is euident inough, that Law and right is to bee giuen to all men equally.Neither ſhall we need of any other,whatſoeuer iudiciall booke, onely let this bee infixed in the minde of him that ſitteth as judge vpon others, that he giue no other ſentence of other men , then he wold haue to be giuen in his owne cauſe.

But in the propagatiõ of the goſpel(ſaith King *Alfred*) when many men beleeued in the word of God,then many *Synodes* were gathered; and alſo in England,the Biſhoppes & other the wiſeſt men aſſembled, who being taught by the mildenes of Chriſt, did ſet vpon euerie firſt offender a pecuniarie paine, the leuying whereof they cõmitted to the Magiſtrates. &c. And a little after. *These I Alfred the King haue gathered together and committed to writing.*

Lamb. Archaion.

Then ſpeaking alſo of the lawes of later time, he addeth that there were many thinges, alſo which he thought fit to be obſerued in the acts of *Ina*,*Offa* & *Ethelbert*: but the former words are plainely ſpoken of the Lawes heere eſtabliſhed vpon the firſt receiuing of the Goſpell by King

Britanniæ Legibus.

King *Lucius*,& doe fully prooue that the counsel of *Elutherius* was followed, but with the mercifulnes & mildehartenes of our Lord christ after the *Saxon* phrase, and the *Sinodes* which *Alfred* speaketh of in the first arriual of the Gospell, were the Parlaments of *Lucius*, whose course that it was such as I haue said, I pray you see also by that which followeth, wherein I wil first speake of the remnants of the Lawes of nature, secondly of the auncient Brittish Lawes made before and by *Lucius*, and lastlye of those that followed vntil the Norman.

Cap. 6.

IT is manifest in Histories, both sacred & prophane, that the moste auncient Nations had their Kings or Princes, their Priests, their Elders or Senators, and their Dukes or Captaines: and *Cic.3. Leg.* this seemeth to bee according to the Lawe of Gen. 18. God & Nature, & it is seene in the Histories of Iob. 12. Psa. 105.21 *Egipt*, *Iudæa*, *Madian*, *Arabia*, Greece, *Italy*. So *Cæsar* found in *Britaine*, *Reges*, *Druidas*, *Principes*, et *Nobiles Duces*. *Cæsar.* For it is to bee noted, that where hee nameth the foure Kinges of *Kent*, he sheweth withal, that they were all subiect to *Cassibellan*, and calleth *Cingetorix Nobilem*

E lem

lem ducem, which proueth that he ment by *Reges* (as commonly the *Romanes* vnderſtood) men of nobilitie, power & gouernemẽt, though it were but in one City, as he ſaith of *Immanuentius* in London, who perhaps might then be a
Preans. L. 2 Lieutenãt of the city, as the Lord Maior is now, and ſo dooth *Polidor* take it, ſaying that they were foure Princes, ſuch as wee now call Earles or Dukes.

It is prooued alſo amongſt Antiquaries, that the famous *Belinus* and *Brennus*, & it is not hard to be proued that *Mulmutius* and others were
Bed. Lib. 1. Kings of this Iland, and *Beda* the moſt faithfull Hiſtorian ſaith literally, that before the yere ſix hũdred after Chriſt in *Britaine, Seruabãt vtcunque Reges, Sacerdotes, priuati, et optimates ſuum quique ordinem.* But of the auncient Kings as likewiſe of their Elders or Nobles, I finde two ſorts, the one fatherly, and the other tirannical. the firſt hauing and maintaining the authority
Aug. de Ciuit. Dei Lib 15. et 19. of the firſt age, wherein *Patresfamilias regebant*, the Fathers of the greateſt families which con-
Ariſt. 1. Polit. tained others, were Kings, as *Adam* and *Sem* taken to be *Melchiſedec*, and *Aſſur* his Sonne: the
Gen. 17.29 Gen. 27. 29 et 49. 10. Fathers of inferior families, yet populous and great, were Elders, or Princes; as ***Abraham, Iſack,***

Britanniæ Legibus.

ſa⁻l, *Iacob*, and *Iob*. Such there were in *Britain*, as *Ceſar* & *Gildas* doe ſhew. The ſecond ſorte obtained their authoritie by warre, violence or Rebellion, as before the floud, *Cain* and afterwards *Nimrod*, *Eſau* and the like.

And of this ſort there was alſo in *Britaine* whoſe times *Gildas* calleth *vetuſtos immanium Tyrannos annos*. But as I take it the moſt ancient Nobilitie of *Britaine* had a name ſignifying as much as Elders or Senators, as they had in other Countries before mencioned. Of that ſignification there is a name in many auncient recordes to be found, a name of auncient nobilitie, which importeth in ſignification an Elder, which I take it was the name of that firſt & moſt auncient Britiſh Noble man. The name it ſelfe is Thane, and I finde this name vſed for a Noble man in this Iland in *Denmake* & in *Ireland*. It muſt needes be a name proceeding frō ſome of the nations that raygned in theſe Countries, but neither the *Romans*, nor *Saxons*, nor the *Danes*, nor the *Irish*, can giue a reaſon whereby to claime it as a woord of theirs: Onely the *Britaines* haue a word moſt neere, both in letter, ſignification & vſe. For where the *Danes* call a Lord or a Noble mā Thane, as the *Britains* did, *Gildas in Epiſtola.*

E 2 and

De Antiquis

and where the Irish call him Tane, which by reason of his Eldership is next to succeede in some Lordshippe: yet neither of them giue a reason for it: onely the *Britaines* vse the woord *Heane*, or *Hane*, to signifie an Elder; which answereth to the word *Thane*, as I said both in letter, signification & vse. And to verifie the saying that all thinges make an Harmonious consent to truth, The Historie testifieth, that the *Saxons* immediately after their comming into this Iland, called their Nobles by a name of the same signification *viz*. Earles or eldermen, a name of Nobilitie vnknowne in their owne Countrie; where (as I take it) they are called *Graues* or *Greues*, signifying a gouernor: which name also they brought hither, and it remaineth in some vse to this day: But the name of Elder they learned of the *Britaines*.

And heereunto agreeth the text extant amongst the Lawes of S^t. *Edward*. *Sicut modo vocantur* Greue, *qui super alios perfecturas habent, ita apud Anglos antiquitus vocabantur* Ealdermen, *quasi seniores, non propter senectutem, cum quidam adolescentes essent, sed propter sapientiã. Et similiter olim apud Britones temporibus Romanorũ in regno isto Britanniæ vocabantur Se-* *Lamb. Archaion*

natores,

Britanniæ Legibus.

natores; qui postea temporibus Saxonum vocabantur Aldermann. And to say that the *Britaines* vsed the name of *Senator*, or borrowed this name of the *Romanes*, is very publikely, for they liued in perpetuall hatred and hostility with them, as they shewed vpon all occasions, & followed not their lawes, nor institutions in any thing: but by constraint, seeing them to be Paganes, Idolaters, oppressors of their liberty, and persecutors of their Religion.

Neither doth *Beda* nor any other Historian speake of any Lawes made in *Britaine* by the *Romanes*, nor of any iudgements by them exercised: but of those (if they be to be called iudgements) whereby *Albanus* & other holy Martirs were moste cruelly put to death. Therefore I conclude that the *Britaines* tooke this name & other institutions, not of them, but either of the auncient statutes of nature, or of the latter restitution by the Gospell. These Nobles therefore together with the Priests & other selected commons, made the common Counsel of this Iland whereof *Cesar* speaketh, and which at this day is called the Parlament, and in the moste of our Histories called *consilium Sapientum*. In the Lawes of *Edward* before the conquest, & in the

E 3 Lawes

Lawes of King *Ina* made about the yeare 720. after our Lord Christ, there is mencion of theis Parlament consisting of theise degrees of men.

Bed. Lib. 2 An hundred yeares before that, we read that *Bertha* the Christian Queene of *Kent* procured judgements to be established *Cum consilio sapientum*, that is by the Parlament, where also the venerable Bede speaketh warily, saying that it was after the exāple of the *Romans*, but not saying it was after the *Romane* manner. An hundred yeares before that againe in the time of *Arthur* the warrior, we reade of Parlaments, and the moste learned King *Alfred* in his lawes saith plainely, that vpon the propagation of the *Lamb. Ar-* Gospell, *Nonnulli tam in Anglia quam in alijs regionibus Episcoporum aliorumque clarissimorum sapientum conuentus agebantur*, which could not bee after the *Romane* fashion: & whosoeuer obserueth the circumstances of the matter, he shal perceiue it euidently to bee spoken of the time of King *Lucius* (as I said before) for in his time being peaceable, the Gospell was first publikely receiued, and after his death, this Kingdome continually laboured with intestiue warres, in which it was almost impossible to gather counsels, and to establish Lawes and gouernment as he

Beda Galfrid. Monū. Polidor.

Britanniæ Legibus

he ſpeaketh. And as it was in this ſouth part of *Britaine*, ſo was it likewiſe in the north, as appereth by their Chronicles. They had Kinges, Prieſtes, Nobles, and Parlaments, agreeable to the forme of gouernment of the moſte auncient Kingdomes, and to the Lawes of God written in Nature & Scripture: & in this forme conſiſteth the eſtate of both the Kingdomes of great *Britaine* euen to this day. And thus much concerning the principall perſons, whereof the body of our ſtate did and doth conſiſt: the next thing to be conſidered is, of thinges according to the proceedings of the inſtitutes, but becauſe nothing can bee without a place, and wee ſhall haue better occaſion to ſpeake of the diuiſion, property and dominion of things heereafter, I will therefore vnder correction, intreate now ſomewhat of the auncient diuiſion of this Iland, the common place & ſubiect of our diſcourſe, and of the iudgements therein auncientiy vſed.

Cap. 7.

IT is thought by ſome, that this Iland before the comming of the *Romanes*, was rude and *Camden.* barbarous: & by other, that King *Alfred* was the diuider of this Iland into ſuch Shires and porcions

ons (for ſo the word importeth) as at this day we ſee. But theſe two opiniōs to be true in general, I cānot yeeld; for if I vnderſtād our ſtories, it wil eaſily appeare that this lād was aunciētly lōg, before *Alfreds* time, deuided almoſt into as many parts, & in like manner by the ſeueral families or nations of aūcient *Britaines*, which are thus reckoned by *Hooker* in his 2. Booke of the deſcription of *England*. Cap. 4. viz. *Nonantæ Selgouæ Dannonij, Gadeni, Ottadeni, Epdij, Cerones, Carmonacæ, Careni, Cornubij, Decantæ, Logi, Mertæ, Macomagi, Venicontes, Texati, Polij* or *Elgoui, Brigantes Pariſi, Ordouici, alias Ordoluci, Cattieuchlani, Coritani, Trinobantes, Demetę, Cangi, Silures, Dobuni, Atrebatij, Cantij, Regni, Belgæ, Durotriges, Giruij, Iceni, Tegenes, Cenimagni, Segontiaci, Deiri, Venedoti*, Bibr*oci*, with ſome other whome he and others name. And of theſe ſome (as Mr. *Camden* plainely ſheweth) poſſeſſed one, others two or three of theſe Shires which now are knowne, & theſe nations of *Britaines* are in part named by *Cæſar*, others by Mr. *Camden, Polidore* and others. So that King *Alfreds* diuiſion ſeemeth not altogether new, but rather a reuiuing and more exact deſcription of the old. And this is cōfirmed by the teſtimony

Camden Britann.

Britanniæ Legibus.

mony of *Polidore*, who in the lawes of *Mulnutius* maketh mention by name of Counties, or Shires. Of those Lawes more shall be said hereafter: In the meane time it appeareth that this land was deuided into porcions, or shares, euen by the *Britains*. There were also amongst those *Britains*, euen before *Lucius* & *Cæsars* times, diuers great Cityes, wherof 28. are named by our Chronicles, and some of thẽ by *Caesar*, besides Townes and Castles innumerable, as *Huntington* saith and as appeareth by the auncient *Iter Brittanniarum* described by the *Romans*, which are no signes of a barbarous people. For if ciuilitie take his name of a Citie, or Citizen; & Cities, & Citizens cãnot be ruled without good lawes, the Britaines were ciuill, and ruled with good Lawes which were Citizens of many great Cities. And the inconstancy of Cæsar and other *Romanists* is heere to bee noted, which call the Britaines barbarous, and yet confesse that they had many good Cities, Kinges, Nobles, Gouernors, discipline of warre, and peace, commerce, and traficke with forraine Nations, and al other parts of ciuilitie. And the question of *Polidore* is somewhat ridiculous, whẽ he asketh whether any man euer reade of *Canterbury*, *Bath*, *Carleil*,

Higden Polichron.
Huntingdõ.

Iter Britan
See the discription of England by Hooker.

F or

De Antiquis

or *Lecester*, in *Cæsar Tacitus*, *Strabo* or *Ptolomy*. No gentle Mr. *Polidore*; but in *Cæsar* wee reade of the City of *Trinobantes*, and of other Cities, and of the Citie of the *Brigantes*, *Londinium*, *Louentium* & *Maridunum*, in *Tacitus* and *Ptolomy*, & your selfe confesse in the same book that it was a Law among the *Britaines*, that the inner parts of the Iland should not be discouered to strangers. As for the fastnesse of *Cassibellan*, and the painting of their faces; if the storie be wel examined & circumstances compared, it will easily be prooued that such thinges were not originally in the gouernement, and maners of this our countrie, but were the wilde fruites of long continued ciuill warres, that raged amongst them, proceeding of tirranies in their Princes, superstition and Idolatry in their Priests; rebellion, sedition, murders, thefts, adulteries and disobedience in the Subiects, some of which thinges are to be gathered by the words of *Cæsar*, and al of them are laid to their charge
Ephes. 5. by *Gildas*, and other Histories. For such thinges procure the wrath of God to bee powred out vpon them (as saith the blessed Apostle,) as *Italy*, *France* and other Countries haue, by that meanes receiued some barbarous touches, and

Ireland

Britanniæ Legibus.

Ireland yet wasted and subiect to great calamities & desolation, is an eye witnesse of the same experience, which heeretofore was gouerned with peace ad ciuilitie, and now hath many examples extant of strange immannities. And as these are the iust plagues inflicted by the diuine Iustice vpon our Neighbour Iland for the contempt of the Gospel, and such offences as aforesaid: so were the same inflicted in those times vpon the *Britaines* for treading vnder foote the light of nature, and the knoweledge of God (which *Gildas* signifieth that the first inhabitāts had) & many excellent doctrines of Religion, & of iustice, which were but obscurelye, & in part preserued by the *Druidæ* and some fewe of the better sort.

But to returne where wee left, as in other thinges the *Britaines* maintained the manners of the auncients, so in that auncient diuision of this Land into seueral Nations and families, the most antique manner of great nations was obserued. For not onely amongst the *Hebrewes*, but amongst the *Persians*, *Athenians*, *Romans*, & in this Iland the *Scots* being freer from publike inuasions, had the like diuisions, being a poynt of ciuill gouernment, verie necessarie for many good

Diodor Sic.

Xenophon Liuy. et all.

F 2

De Antiquis

good and Politicke conſtitutions, and therefore vſed and preſerued amongſt all the primitiue Nations, as agreeable to reaſon and nature, and is to this day obſerued as moſt conſonāt to the word of God.

Cap. 8.

As in the diſtribution of perſons, and of the land, the *Britaines* were politick and ciuil: ſo in their proceedings of Lawe, in their iudgements, and in their Sciences, it appeareth that they were not ſo barbarous as hath been taken: for their varieties of excellent learning (to note that by the way) Sir *Iohn Priſe* in his booke to King Edward the ſixt, prooueth that all learned ſciences, were knowne and handled amongſt them. To his booke I ſend thoſe that are deſirous to be ſatisfied in that point. And although it may be ſtrongly inferred that a Nation giuen to the ſtuddies of all excellent learnings, muſt needes be poliſhed with good lawes: yet for the more cleere euidence heerof, I purpoſe to ſhew that their lawes in particular were moſt iuſt & good, as being deriued out of the lawe of God, written in nature, and in Scripture; and for that reaſon not altered, but tranſmitted to poſteri-

Sir Iohn Priſe. Hiſtoriæ Brit. Defenſio.

tye,

Britanniæ Legibus.

tye,and that they doe yet remaine amongst vs, as I said before. First of al vnder fauour I cannot agree,the opinion conceiued by *Gratian* that al thinges by the Lawe of nature, were common; but as I take it the distinction of properties was enacted by Almighty God in the beginning, & by him imprinted with other Lawes, in nature, by vertue of the wordes, Beare rule ouer the earth : which gaue to man, both dominion and propertie of all thinges. And to proue that it was so, & that it was so vnderstood, it appeareth by *Cain* and *Abel*, who in the verye beginning were seueral possessors of grounds, Lands, Sheep,fruites of the earth,and Cities inhabited, and in the Historyes of *Abraham*, *Iob*, and other the Patriarches, there is mencion made of buying and selling,and of diuers offences punished by Lawe. But by what Lawe, if not by the Law of nature? And if the Law of nature be the same which is contayned in the Lawe & the Gospell, as *Gratian* in the first entrance of his distinctions affirmeth ; If the tenne commaundements be an abridgement or exposition of the Law of nature,as he saith in an other place : And if distinction of propertyes be inacted, & the desire of other mens goods forbidden euery where in

Part.1.Dist.

Gen.1.verſ 28.29.

Gen.4.

F 3 the

De Antiquis

the Lawe; the Gofpell,and the tenne comm'an-dements; then is *Gratian* in this poynt, contra-ry vnto him felfe. But that it is fo forbidden, appeareth by the eight and tenth Commaun-dement, and in the firft to the *Romanes*, where
Rom. 1. Couetoufnes euen in an heathẽ man is accoun-ted for a fin,which could not be but by the lawe ofnature, as it is in that place vrged. For where there is no *L*awe, there is no tranfgresfion faith St· *Iohn*, & other lawe there is not to condemne a Pagan. Therefore, taking that for a point not hard to be proued,and which all lawes haue ta-ken as a principall, confeffed by vertue of that
Arift.Ethic lawe which is euery where the fame (how-foe-uer fome authorities haue fwayed to the con-trary) we finde partly by the wordes of Cæ*far* & *Dio*,that this Ifland had her owne lawes con-cerning the diuifion of groundes,inheritances, Iudges,& the diftinctiõ of properties,that there were certaine courfes of proceedings , and that there were punifhments for contempts and of-
Dio Lib.53 fences. Firft *Dio* faith that 20. yeares after the comming hither of *Cæfar*; *Britannia fuis Legi-bus vfa eft*; *Britain* vfed her owne Lawes. and what thefe owne Lawes of Br*itaine* were, *Cæfar* fheweth: his wordes be thefe: *Druidæ fere de*

omnibus

Brit.nniæ Legibus.

omnibus controuerſiis publicis priuatiſque conſtituunt, et ſi quod eſt admiſſum facinus, ſi cædes facta, ſi de Hereditate, de finibus controuerſia eſt, iidem diſcernunt, præmia pænaſque conſtituunt, ſi quis aut priuatus aut populus, eorum decreto non ſtetit, ſacrificijs interdicunt. The *Druidæ* ſaith *Cæſar* (whoſe diſcipline he affirmeth to be foūd out and moſt perfect in *Britaine*) doe iudge for the moſte part of all publike and priuate controuerſies. If any offence or Homicide be committed, or if the controuerſie bee for bounds or inheritance, they doe determine it, appointing punniſhments & rewardes, If any priuate man, or corporationſtand not to their decree, they forbid them their ſacrifices.&c. vnder the names of offences and Homicides, he comprehendeth all criminall cauſes; vnder controuerſies of lands or inheritance are contained all ciuil actions; by the words of coutrouerſie, iudgement, determination and decree, he ſheweth that they had a certaine forme of proceeding: by puniſhments and rewardes, he ſheweth that their ſentence was compulſiue.

So this teſtimony proueth that they had a ſetled forme of iudgements in thoſe three maine parts, whereof *Iuſtinian* hath compoſed his whole

De Antiquis

whole worke, I say *De personis rebus et actionibus.* To touch a few particulars, it must needes be inferred vpon *Caesars* words, that they had a certaine forme of conueyance and course of inheritāce in their lands; For else how could controuersies of inheritance and Lands arise to be decided in iudgement? Now if any man consider well of our auncient forme of conueyance by Feoffment and Liuerie, and the solemnitie thereof vsed, not onely after, but before the conquest, he shall finde it to bee a relike of the fatherly age, wherein the Law of nature was with great wisdome obserued. For if you compare it to the assurance of *Abraham*, you shall finde like precisenes of words: I giue thee (saith *Ephron* which is & euer was, our auncient word, *Do* or *Dedi.* Like descriptiō of things: The field of *Ephron* in *Machpelah* ouer against *Mamre*, the field and the Caue and al the trees &c, like assistance of witnesses; in the presence of my people; and that was also our manner, euen before the *Norman* conquest, and I can finde no beginning vnlesse I bring it to those auncient times. Our word of inheritance (heires) & that they by th'eldest Sonne shold inherite, is eyther taken from the same lawe of nature, and examples

Histor. Ely.

Gene. 23

Britanniæ Legibus.

ples of the Patriarkes, as *Sem* was heire of *Noah* and *Iaphet* was appointed to dwell in his tents. God ſaith to *Abrahã*, *Izhak* ſhalbe thine heire, & *Izhak* made *Iacob* his heire; Claime is made to ſome part of the Lãd of *Iſrael* in the name of *Iſraels* heires: Or elſe it was inſtituted by K. *Lucius* after the exãple of God himſelfe, who made Chriſt the Lord & heire of all things, and adopteth vs in parte onely to be heires with him. Laſtly, alſo the manner of our ſucceſsion by inheritãce, & how one heir is to take after an other, as they are in degrees of proximitie, is by the moſte exacte reporter of our Lawes Sr. *Edward Coke* (his maieſties Atturnie general) collected and declared, vpon the judgement of God, in the caſe of *Salphahads* daughters, cyted in *Ratcliffes* caſe; where he alſo obſerueth, that in this point, as almoſt in all others, the common lawe is founded vpon the Law of God. And this our maner of conueyance, and limitation of inheritance, I haue not read of in any other nation, neither can finde any other beginning for it. For other conueyances, I finde a patent of King *Arthur* the worthy, and another of one K. *Kenwalchius*, both recited in a Patent of King *Henry* the ſecond, made to the Monaſtery of *Glaſſenbury*,

Ierim. 49. 1

Hebr. 1. 2

Report. 3.

Numb. 27

G

Defensio Histor. Bri. bury as I learne of Sir *Iohn Pr.se*, who setteth downe words of King *Henries* Patent, as I wold King *Henrie* had done of the other. Also there are many other auncient Charters yet to bee seene of manors, landes and liberties, graunted to Abbeyes, Churches & other Religious houses long before the Conquest; as of King *Kenredus* to the Abbey of *Euesham*, of others to the Cathedrall Churches of *Landaffe* & St. *Dauies* &c. But of all other, moste excellent is the Patent procured by *Turketulus* Lord Chancellor, & Lord of threescore Manors, who surrendred them all to King *Eared*, and obtained sixe Manors, which are also named by *Ingulfus*, to bee graunted to the Abbye of *Croyland*, together with many auncient Customes and new liberties; by which may be vnderstood the vse of the Common lawe then and long before. Concerning also the Maner of suites in Law, & taking distresses or pledges, & that the defendāt shold finde sureties or mainpernors, a thing verie auncient, wherof we reade in the lawes of King *Lamb. Arc.* *Ina*, & yet continuing amongst vs; I finde some such matter noted by *Iob*, where hee speaketh *Iob. 17. 3. et 24. 3. et 9.* of taking pledges, and desireth that God would put in suretie to answere him.

Also

Britanniæ Legibus

Alſo the particular Lawes of diſtreſſes doe prooue that they are taken out of the word of God. For by the cõmon Law no man may diſtreine a Millſtone; a thing ſpecially prouided by God himſelfe. Our auncient kindes of punniſhments, as by impriſonments, Fetters, Stocks. &c are named likewiſe in ſeueral places by *Iob*. Capitall executions are deriued from the Law giuen to *Noah*; whoſoeuer ſheddeth mans blood, by man ſhall his blood bee ſhed. Laſtly our puniſhment by vtlary ſeemeth to be moſt auncient, & of the ſame beginning; for take *Bractons* deſcription of vtlary, and compare it with the words of *Cæſar*, and both with ſome paſſages of Scripture : and you ſhall finde them agree very neere together. *Bracton* thus deſcribeth the forfeiture of vtlary. *Forisfacit patriam et regnum, et exul efficitur, et talem vocant Angli vtlagh, et alio nomine vocari antiquitus ſolet, Friendleſman, et ſic videtur Forisfacere amicos; Si quis cum eo communicauerit aliquid, eadem pœna puniendus eſt; Caput gerit Lupinum*. And ſo foorth at large, which Mr. *Stanford* thus briefly comprehendeth. The out lawe forfeiteth his countrie, his friends, his peace, his law, his right, and his poſſeſsion: which is true euerie way, but

Deut. 24.

Gen. 9.6

Bracton.

Stanf. L. 3.

G 2 to

De Antiquis

to bee vnderſtood according to the ſeuerall natures of vtlaries that are amongſt vs. Now *Cæſar* of the *Druidae* ſaith thus: *Si quis eorum decreto non ſtetit, ſacrificijs interdicunt. Hæc pæna apud eos eſt grauiſsima. Quibus ita eſt interdictum, ij numero impiorum et ſceleratorum habentur, ab ijs omnes decedunt, aditum eorum ſermonemque diffugiunt, ne quid ex contagione incommodi accipiant. Neque ijs petentibus ius redditur neque honos vllus communicatur.* Conferre this with the ſentēce pronounced againſt *Cain*, Thou art curſed from the earth, when thou tilliſt the ground, it ſhall not yeeld her ſtrength to thee; a vagabond and a runnagate ſhalt thou be in the earth.

Cæſar.

Geneſ. 4.

Thus he forfeited his Countrie and his poſſeſſiōs, the profits of his labour, & of his groūd, his friendes and his peace. And this is the nature of our vtlary vſed to this day in capitall offences, but in leſſer contempts more eaſye and tollerable. Now of theſe thinges before deſcribed, haue conſequently followed all our proceedings, aſwell in Real as in perſonall actions; for the proces of diſtreſſe in the parſonall, was but the taking of pledges of the defendant, for apparance, and the proceſſe by Cape

in

Britanniæ Legibus.

in the Real, was but the ſeiſing of the Land, for a ſurety to the ſame prepoſe; from whence alſo many other ſecundarie concluſions of reaſon haue neceſſarilye enſued, as the returne and loſſe of Iſſues, defaults, contẽpts, forfeitures, &c. Further in our Chronicles wee reade of Lords & tennants in the daies of *Gorbonian* the good, and of fealtie ſworne to the Prince in the time of *Elidurus* the godly, which of neceſſitie were accompained with tenures, ſeruices, diſtr eſſes, and ſuch like: And thus much be ſpoken of the auncient viſible footeſteppes, of the lawe of nature, which were before *Lucius*; Of which you may reade alſo in the learned diſcourſe of the aboue named, Sir *Edward Corke* before the third Booke of his Reportes, where he citeth the ſentence of *Caeſar*: ſaying that the diſcipline of the *Druidæ* was found out in *Britannia*, and that we had ſome formes of proceeding from the *Greek*; which may well bee; but you ſee the grounds and beginnings are much more apparant to bee ſeene in the records of that firſt age deſcribed in the ſacred Hiſtory, & doe yet remaine amongſt vs.

Galfrid mõ.

Pontic. virũ.

Now followeth to ſpeake of the ordinances inſtituted by our auncient *Britain* Kings, agree-

G 3 able

able to the word of God, and to this day alſo remayning: and firſt of the Lawes of *Mulmutius* & others which were called the Marchen law.

Cap. 9.

ALthough concerning the Hiſtorie of *Brutus*, there may bee ſome reaſons to doubt which learned men haue gathered, yet, why there ſhould not be one Brit or *Brute* King of this Land, whoſe Pedegree Sir Iohn *Priſe* out of an auncient Chronicle deriueth from *Iaphet*: And if there were no ſuch *Brit*, yet why the whole Hiſtorie of Britaine Princes ſhould for the fabulous interpoſition of one or two men be reiected, as ſome haue done? I ſee no reaſon ſeeing the concurrẽt teſtimonies of diuers Britiſh monumẽts of great credit, which Sr *I. Priſe* citeth, & the concordance of the Scottiſh Hiſtory in many thinges, and that of ſome of thoſe Princes remains to this day, apparãt monumẽts of others credible Hiſtories, of others the moſte ineuitable teſtimony of auncient Lawes. The learned Mr. *Cambden* a iudicious examiner of theſe things, offereth to prooue that the famous *Brennus* that ouerranne *Italy*, was King of *Britain*, (a thing which the ſaid Sr. *Io. Priſe* hath al-

Cambden in Britannia

readie

Britanniæ Legibus.

readie most learnedly performed:) to me it is as well prooued that *Mulmutius* his Father was King likewise of this Land: neither doe I thinke the warres of the one so glorious, as the Lawes of the other. But if any be so wilfully ignorant, as to deny, not onely the Historie of Brit, but of his successors: Let them name if they can imagine, who built these auncient Monnuments, Ludgate, Bellingsgate, Caerebranke or the Citye of Yorke, *Carleil*, and *Caercoil* or Colchester and such like? and who made these auncient Lawes, called the *Mulmutian*, & Mercian Lawes, of which we haue to speake. Many writers which without questiō did see, or might see and reade the writinges of *Gildas* the wise Priest, and *Alfred* the excellent Prince, doe constātly avouch that *Mulmutius Dunwallo* Father of *Belinus* and *Brennus*, established those Lawes which were afterward called *Mulmutinæ*, which *Gildas* translated into Latin, as hee confesseth himselfe (say they) and afterwards King *Alfred* turned them into English. Out of which wordes I gather these obseruations, first that there was such a King and hee made these Lawes without question. Secondly that these Lawes were verie iust, for else such men as Gil-

Ponticus virun Lib. 2. *Higden. Cest lib. 1.* *Galfrid mō.* *Baleus.* *Hooker.* *Pol. virgil.*

das

das and *Alfred* would not haue tranſlated and preſerued them. Thirdly that they doe yet remaine amongſt our common Lawes, although hardly to be diſcerned which they bee: for the ſame writers teſtifie that they being mingled amongſt the lawes of *Alfred*, were by St. *Edward* reduced to one common Law, which the Norman yeelded vnto, and himſelfe and all his ſucceſſors are ſworne to obſerue them. And ſo ſay *Virũnius & Monemuthenſis. Leges Patris quæ Molmutinæ dicebantur inſtituit inter Britones quæ vſque ad hoc tempus celebrantur inter Anglos.* So alſo ſaith *Higden*: where ſpeaking firſt of the Marchen Lawe, containing both Lawes of *Mulmutius* and *Mertia*, and of the *Dane* Law, & weſt *Saxon* Law, *Ex his tribus Legibus* (ſaith he) *Sanctus Edwardus tertius vnam Legem communem edidit, que Leges Edwardi vſque hodie vocantur*: of theſe three lawes St. *Edward* the third made one common Law, which to this day are called the Lawes of *Edward*. Beholde therefore the Fathers, yea and the very name of our common Law. Beholde a full proofe of Sir *Iohn Forteſcues* teſtimonye concerning our Lawes. Some particulars wherof as they were in thoſe times, are alſo mencioned in Chronicles.

Pontic. virũ Monemuth.

Ceſtrencis. Pol. virgil.

For

Britanniæ Legibus.

For by *Polidore* it is thus recorded: *Mulmutius ius atque Leges nouas , et illas quidem salutares dedit, quas deinceps Mulmitianas Leges appellarunt. Templa deorum immortalum Loco asyli omnibus ad ea confugientibus esse constituit* ; & a little after, *Pondera ac mensuras rebus vendendis emendisque posuit, fures et noxium omne genus hominum seuerissime puniuit, fecit quamplures vias, decreuitque in quam Latitudinem fieri deberent, ac Lege sanxit earum ius ad Principem duntaxat pertinere: eiusque iuris violatoribus, atque ijs qui in illis maleficium aliquod facerent constituit pœnas: præterea vt ne terra vacaret, neue populus rei frumentariæ inopia frequenter premeretur, aut minueretur, si pecora sola occuparent agros, qui ab hominibus coli deberent, cõstituit quot quisque Comitatus aratra haberet*, and so foorth: where you see that he made lawes for Sanctuaries, for weights, for measures; against theft, robbery, and other offences : for high waies & Nusances, and for tillage and Husbandrie : and by the words you may easily gather, that they were the same, or much to the same effect, as they are now, either continuing in the common Law, or reuiued by Statutes: and that in those daies also the land was deuided into certaine parts, which *Pol Virgil.*

H are

De Antiquis

are now called Counties. *Brecus* and *Fergusius* likewise in Scotland, neere about the same time also made Lawes for diuision of their Land into Tribes, hundreds, and wapentakes saith the Chronicle, and for punishment of murder, theft and other offences.

Againe by *Higden* it is thus recorded *Anno mundi* 3529. *ante Christum* 445. *Mulmutius* King of the *Britaines* the 23, but the first Lawmaker, ordained that Churches, Plowes, Cities and High-waies, should inioy a Priuiledge or libertie. This *Higden* expoundeth to be a kinde of Sanctuarie, that if any offender did fly to any of these, he should no further be pursewed but suffered to escape, which interpretation cannot be made but onely of the Church, and therfore to be let passe, as made by a Monke ignorant of Law.

But our common Lawe giueth a sound and verie consonant exposition. For euen from the most auncient times to this day, there is a kinde of priuiledge in vse, that these foure should bee free from distresse. For no man ought to be distrayned by the beastes of his Plowe, nor in high waies, nor in Markets or Churches. This freedome from distresse then I take to be the priui-

ledge

Britanniæ Legibus.

ledge ordayned by *Mulmutius*,chiefly becauſe it is indifferently commõ to al the foure things aboue mencioned:& although diuers later ſta-tutes doe confirme & enlarge this priuiledge to ſome one or other of the foure,yet none of thẽ name altogether, as they were in *Mulmutius* Law,and by the likenes of the Priuiledge it ſee-meth they were ioyned at firſt, Alſo by the words of *Articuli Cleri* : it ſeemeth to bee more aũcient then the ſtatutes. For the Clergie there cõplained of diſtreſſes taken in their glebe as a wrong. Beſides ſome of the writs made vpon this priuiledge haue theſe words *Contra Legem et conſuetudinem Regn* ,which for the moſt part is intended to be the moſte auncient common Law: yet if this interpretation be not accepted: then take another collected vpon the auncient *Lawes* of the *Saxons* and the *Norman*. They ſaie that the Church hath a priuiledge which they call *Pacem*, and is vnderſtood the Sanctuarie. The foure waies haue a peace, which is,that all Nuſances in them ſhall bee a-mended (note the antiquitie of our Lawes, of Nuſanz.)But for markets and plowes, no other priuiledge can be heard of,but onely this wher-of I haue ſpoken,to be free from diſtreſſe,which

Marlebr. Cap.2.et 15 w.1.Cap.16 51. H. 3. Art. Cleri. Cap. 9. Fitz. N.B. 90.

H 2 is

is ſtill continued. And this *Polidor* ſeemeth to ſay,expounding the law of *Mulmutius* , to bee, that the beaſtes of the plow ought not to be led away for debt , ſo long as the debtor had other goods.Now if the Priuiledge from diſtreſſe was ſo auncient,it muſt needes follow that diſtreſſes were much more auncientiy in vſe as I noted alſo before. And from the vſe of diſtreſſes by ſecundary concluſions and deductions of reaſon,followed many Lawes amongſt vs, yet in cõmon practiſe; as of Attornments,Repleuies, Auouries, Tenures Seruices: *Quid Iuris clamat, quem redditũ reddit*.Per *quæ ſeruicia* & ſuch like, which by neceſſitie muſt be vnderſtood , where diſtreſſes are frequent ,and ſo much of the *Mulmutian* Lawe. Now followeth of King *Lucius*.

Cap. 10.

BY many ſteppes and degrees I am come to the Lucid ſtarre of Britaine, well deſeruing that name,for that in his time,religiõ,Iuſtice, & gouernmẽt, begã to ſhine more brightly in this kingdõ.And in the hiſtory of him,& his ſucceſſeors the Readers may obſerue three things : Firſt that this Nation aboue all Nations of the earth (except

Britanniæ Legibus.

(except the Hebrewes)hath had most vertuous, religious & Godly Princes. Secōdly that as our auncient lawes were moste righteous,being deriued from the lawes of God written in nature: So *Lucius* and his succeßiors established onely such good and iust Lawes, as were agreeable to Christianitie, and deriued out of the Scriptures. Thirdly that all calamities of this Land hath proceeded of publike & notorious crimes against God and his seruants,our good Princes, and against religion and religious lawes. Concerning *Lucius* himselfe, I cited before the testimony of King *Alfred*,a witnesse farre aboue all exception: who saith directly and expresly in his Lawes, that vpon the propagation of the Gospel, when many men receiued the faith of Christ as well in England as in other regions, certaine Synods,aswel of Bishoppes,as of other most noble wise men were gathered,which appointed punishments for offendors.And a little after, these Sanctions or Lawes,I *Alfred* King haue collected & cōmitted to writing,where he speaketh of certaine Sinodes,of Bishops & Noble & wise men;it must needes be meāt of Parlaments,as we shewed before.For wee reade of no generall counsell in Britaine,and of Prouin-

H 3 ciall

De Antiquis

ciall Sinodes,it cannot be intended; where hee ſaith that they were gathered vpon the propagation of the Goſpell, he ſignifieth the time of King *Lucius*, when the Goſpell was firſt publikely receaued in this Land, For it cannot bee vnderſtood of the Chriſtian *Saxons*, for of them he ſpeaketh by name afterwards, ſaying that he vſed choice and iudgement in refuſing ſome of their lawes, and taking others; whereof I inferre firſt that thoſe words before were meant of the firſt Chriſtian *Britaines*, (whom he nameth not becauſe they were enemies to the *Saxõs*) Secõdly that thoſe Britiſh lawes were more ſincere & agreeable to Godlynes then the *Saxon*. Thirdly that thoſe ſanctions by him collected, are ſome of the auncient common Lawes, which yet remaine, for that we finde no other collection of Lawes made by him: But this all Hiſtories teſtifie that he tranſlated into *Saxon* the ſame which *Gildas* turned into Latin, & that the ſame were gathered into our common Law by S^t. *Edward* and called Saint *Edwards* lawes.

Beda. L. 1.

Beſides it cannot be ſayd that theſe good lawes were made by any other, but onely by *Lucius*, for neither was any other of the Britaine Princes ſo Godly & religious, as he, neither had any of

Britanniæ Legibus.

of his ſucceſſors ſuch peaceable poſſeſſiō of the Land or conueniency to make lawes as he had. For immediately after his death, and continually till the Saxons time, the whole ſtate trauelled with forein and inteſtine enemies. Laſtly the teſtimony of *Polidore* confirmeth this, who giueth this moſte honorable teſtimonie of King *Lucius*: that he left his kingdome aſwell *Optimis inſtitutis prouectum* aduaunced or amended with the beſt inſtitutions or Lawes, as *diuina religione auctum*; ſo that without queſtion it is that he made ſome of our Lawes. *Pol. Virg.*

But particularly which of theſe lawes or inſtitutions now extant were enacted by *Lucius*, it is hard to ſay: yet to ſpeake my opinion, I think firſt our Lawes of fines and amercements was eſtabliſhed in his time. For ſo ſaith *Alfred*, that thoſe firſt Chriſtian Parlaments conſiſting of Biſhops & moſt noble wiſe men, being taught by the mercifulneſſe of Chriſt, did appoint for euerie firſt offender a pecuniary paine, where you ſee not onely the thing, but almoſt the verie name of *Miſericordia*, which is vſed to this day in amercenents, and is afterwards frequently vſed in the Saxon and Norman Lawes, and this was for ſmaller offences. But

for

for the greateſt,the words of *Alfred* goe further; ſaying of the ſame firſt Chriſtiās, *Proditori tantummodo ac Domini deſertori hanc mitiorem pœnam haud infligendam exiſtimarunt, quippe qui eiuſmodi viro minime parcendum cenſuerunt tum quod Deus contemptores ſui omni miſeratione indignos voluit,tum quod Chriſtus illorum qui ei mortem obtulerunt non eſt omnino miſertus.* Where you ſee that by the teſtimonie of *Alfred* they tooke the preſident of their Law againſt

Lamb.Arc. Treaſon,from the examples of Chriſt and of God. What was that Lawe?It followeth afterwards. *Qui capiti et ſaluti Regis perfidioſe inſi-*

In leg.Alf. Cap. 4 *diabitur vita et fortunis eius omnibus priuator.* that the Traytor ſhould forfeit, life, Lands,and

Actes. 1. goods.So was *Iudas* puniſhed and that puniſhment *Elfredus* felt being conuicted of treaſon in the daies of King *Athelſtane* as appeareth by the ſaid Kings Charter,recited by Mr. *Fox*:

Fox in mon. here alſo appeareth not onely the Eſchet which you ſee is expreſſely ſet downe in the words,but alſo trialls, for it would be iniurious & vaine to ſet downe a puniſhment for offences , and not ſet downe a courſe how the offender might be cleered or condemned:and it is moſte vnlikely, that King *Lucius* and thoſe firſt Chriſtians wold

immitate

Britanniæ Legibus.

imitate God and Chriſt in ſeueritie of puniſh-ment,and not much more ſtudie to imitate him in the Iuſtice & ſinceritie of their Trialles.

Therfore I think that the ſame *Lucius* ordey-ned our Tryals by twelue,& that according to the example of Chriſt. For , that it is agree-able to the Scriptures , the learned Sir *Iohn Forteſcue* hath fully prooued , and whoſoeuer ſhall conſider of it indifferently,ſhall finde that it is the moſte righteous and Godly courſe that euer was found out, and therefore moſte likely to proceede from the piety of that holy King. *Sir Iohn Forteſcue.*

Alſo in that pureſt age of Chriſtianity,it was held for a ground,that firſt the Scriptures ought to be ſearched , whether any rule might bee found for the action intended , or not ; if not, then *Mos populi dei et Sanctorum exempla* the manner of Gods people and the examples of holy men were to be followed. *Gra. Diſt. 11. et Diſt. 20.*

And if holy men ought to be imitated, then who if not our moſte holy Sauiour? as the A-poſtle ſaith: Be followers of God as deere Chil-dren :and be followers of mee as I am of Chriſt. *Epheſ. 5* *1.Cor.11.*

Quo eſt deteſtabilior iſtorum immanitas : So much the more is their crueltie to be abhorred, which labour to hide,not onely the words , but

I alſo

De Antiquis

alſo the exāples of Chriſt away from vs. Therefore I ſay *Lucius* did inſtitute the trial of al matters in fact, to be by twelue witneſſes, as our Sa-
Act. 1, 22. et 10 41. uiour Chriſt ordayned, & choſe twelue to beare
Iohn. 15. 27 witneſſe of his reſurrection; neither doe I finde any other law preſident or exāple from whence this manner of Trialls ſhould be taken. But I finde that the reuerēd *Elutherius*, from whom *Lucius* had much of his light, vſed the ſame rule & practiſe, for that good Biſhop *Iuxta or-*
Faſcic. Tēp. *dinationem Apoſtolorum* according to the Apoſtles ordinance, did decree that no meates vſuall for mankinde ſhould be refuſed of Chriſtians; And *Exemplo Chriſti* by the example of Chriſt, ordained that none ſhould be regraded before he were condemned.

Thus they tooke a rule or preſident for euerie thing out of the Scripture. And the authoritie of *Moſes* to the contrarie is not to be obiected; for although he ſaieth that at the mouth of two or three, an offender ſhall die; yet he addeth not the negatiue, that more ſhould not be vſed. Therefore the Apoſtolicall Canons before cired, and the example of our Sauiour in the affirmatiue was a better warrant. And it is moſt apparant that Iuries were vſed among the

Britanniæ Legibus.

the Chsiſtian *Britaines* and before the *Saxon* times; for proofe whereof, although in mine opinion, the teſtimony of the profoundly learned Sir *Iohn Forteſcue* ſhould bee ſufficient ſaying expreſſely that theſe lawes were vſed in the time of the *Britaines*, yet for the further ſatiſfaction of thoſe that leane to much to the opinion of *Polidor* and other Italians, I will adde more reaſons & authorities to the ſame point. Firſt the moſt learned Antiquary of our Nation Mr. *Camden*, ſheweth plainely that it was not inuented by the Conqueror, (as *Polidor* ſaith,) but it was in vſe in the daies of King *Etheldred* the *Saxon*; Secondly the moſt excellent profeſſor of our Lawes, Sir *Edward Cooke* before cited, prooueth by ſubſtantiall records, that this triall was before the Conqueſt. So there are three witneſſes euerie one of exceeding great learning againſt one Maiſter *Polidor*.

Sir. Iohn Forteſcue.

Camden Britannia.

Praef in L. 3.

Tantæ molis erat Romanam excindere gentem.

Such a labour it is to ouerthrowe theſe Italian opinions, of which our nation is too fondly credulous. But let vs goe forward, & although my ſimple diſcourſe can adde no weight vnto their moſt graue iudgements, eſpecially the laſt cited, which is grounded vpon records: yet vn-

I 2 der

der fauour, I will adioyne some other testimonies and proofes. In the time of King *Edward* the third, when by all mens consent our Iudges were most exactly learned (as in deede it was a time excelling, not onely in Martiall glorie, but in learning and wisdome) I finde Mr. *Belknap* a reuerend Iudge, concurring in opinon,
41. *E*.3.31. with these before named. The Law (saith hee) was founded in this, that euery Inquest sholdbe taken *Per duodecim liberos et legales homines et non per pauciores.* If it were a foundation of the common law, then without question it was one of the first Lawes; and we must needes confesse that no Law can be without tryalls, and it cannot be proued that euer any other triall was vsed, besides this in pleas of land or inheritance in this kingdome.

But to make it yet more plaine, the City of Lōdon is and was in the times of the *Britaines*, by the confession of many learned writers, namely *Cæsar Tacitus, Ptolomy, Ammianus Marcellinus, Gildas Galfridus &c.* a moste auncient City, a place of gouernmēt, & ruled by a gouernor, the sea of a Flamine or Bishop, not a fastenes of the woodes as some haue imagined vpon the generall and vncertaine words of authors, which ne-

uer

Britanniæ Legibus.

uer ſaw it,but frequented and celebrated with concourſe of Merchants & plēty of commerce as *Tacitus* affirmeth. Now I pray you beholde with the eyes of your minde,the forme of ſuch a Citie: and tell mee how you can imagine it to ſtand without a Court of Iuſtice, the bond of commerce,for the deciding of controuerſies? or how you can imagine that ſuch a Court ſhould be without a due forme of Trialls? But leaſt I may ſeeme to deale by immagination; for the firſt point that it had a Court; *Galfridus Monemuthenſis* and *Ponticus virunnius* out of the auncient Britiſh Hiſtorie, doe teſtifie in playne words; that in the daies of *Iulius Cæſar*, *Irelgas*, Nephew of *Caſsibellan*,being ſlaine by *Cuelinus*, Nephew to *Androgeus* Gouernor or Lieftenant of London,a commaundement was giuen to *Androgeus* to bring *Cuelinus* to the K.Court, there to receiue Iuſtice: his anſwere was *Seſe ſuam habere curiam,et in illa definiri debere quicquid alquis in homines ſuos clamaret, ſi ergo rectitudinem de Cuelino decreuiſſet appetere ipſam in vrbe Trinobantum ex veterum traditione fieri præciperet.* He alledgeth that hee hath his Court, wherin ought to be determined whatſoeuer any man laide to the charge of his men, & *Galf.Mon.* *Pontic. vir.*

I 3 that

that right ought to be done vnto them in the Citie of London according to the auncięt cust-ome. For the second point, if Mr. *Polidor* will not giue vs leaue to thinke that London had this iurisdiction in *Cæsars* time; yet without his leaue, I wil proue by many infallible records that the same City of Londō had this iurisdiction, and namely this tryal by twelue in the time of the *Britaines*, thus:

This City of London hath and had alwaies from time out of minde their Hustings, & the writ of right in London tryable by twelue; the Assise of Freshforce tryable by twelue; and the tryall of pleas of the Crowne by twelue; it must needes be that these Liberties were begun eyther by Parlament or prescription, eyther in the time of the Normās, of the Saxons, or of the Britaines. But in 14. *E*. 2. when they must needes haue knowne if there had bin any Patent or Acte of Parlament, either of the *Saxons* or *Normans* for it. *A quo warranto in Itinere in Turri London* being brought, for these and other Liberties: The cominaltie of that City make their claime to the rest by seueral Patęts, but to these by auncient custome and prescription confirmed by Charters in these words. *Quoad articu-*

lum

lum quod &c.proferunt cartam Henrici aui Regis nunc in qua continetur quod idem H.rex, 16. die Marcij Anno regni sui vndecimo concessit ciuibus predictis, quod Hustingum semel tantum in hebdomada teneatur secundum consuetudinem ciuitatis. Et proferunt aliam cartã eiusdem Domini H. Regis in qua continetur quod idem Dominus Henricus Rex 20. die Martij Anno regni sui 52. cõcessit ciuibus suis London quod de placitis ad coronam pertinentibus de his maxime quæ infra ciuitatem prædictam et eius suburbia fieri continget, se possunt dirationare secundum antiquam consuetudinem ciuitatis prædictę. By these Charters you see, that the pleas aforesaid are to be proceeded and tried according to the prescription or custome of the Citie, & so are the words of the Assise of Freshforce. By the way the reader is to vnderstand, that prescription or custome here, is not said to be the continuance of many yeres, as 50.60. or an hundred: But that in Law is said to be by prescription, the beginning whereof cannot be proued by any record, writing, or lawful testimony, & such a prescription is heere to be vnderstood.

Now that the custome & such a prescriptiõ of London is & was in the Conquerors time and

before,

before,that their trialls ſhould be by a Iurie of twelue,all their records teſtifie : The reuerend Iudge *Fitsherbert* teſtifieth and moſt euidently the Record of the *Quo warranto* aboue cited teſtifieth,for ſo it goeth forward, *Quoad articulum predictum quod ipſi de placitis ad coronam Regis pertinentibus ſe poſsint diſrationare ſecundum antiquam conſuetudinem ciuitatis; dictum eſt eis per iuſticiarios quod declarent Curiæ modum et formam huiuſmodi diſrationamenti et conſuetudinis. Qui dicunt quod Antiqua conſuetudo ciuitatis eſt quod ſiquis liber ciuitatis aliquod delictum fecerit per quod periculum vitæ incurrere debeat, et vſque Iter Iuſticiariorum manucaptus fuerit, et inde in Itinere poſtea, ſit ad Rationē poſitus, ſe diſrationare poteſt per duodecim Iuratores patrie ſecundum Legem communem vel per magnam Legem Ciuitatis, viz. per triginta ſex legales homines ciuitatis. &c.* Nothing can bee more plainely proued, then the point in queſtiō is by this record: viz.that the trial by twelue was vſed both by the common Law, and by the moſt auncient cuſtome of London, I ſay by cuſtome,whereof no beginning could be prooued. Wel then it was cleere in the times of *Edw. 2. Edward. 1.* and *Henry* the third,and ſo much

Fit.N.B.6.

is

Britanniæ Legibus.

is alſo proued not onely by this record, but by their great Charter, for they giue them no new liberties, but *Ciuitas London habeat omnes antiquas conſuetudines*, & this was within two hundred yeares after the Conqueror: if any Law or Patent had bene made of it in al that time; without queſtion, they would haue pleaded the patent or Law, and not preſcription. For a Satute or patent doth determine a preſcription. *Mag. Car.*

The Conqueror, dooth he make them any graunt or Patent heereof, or dooth *Edward* the Confeſſor one of the *Saxon* Princes, graunt any ſuch matter or make mention that any ſuch thing was graunted by patent vnto London? *Ne my*: Not a minim of any ſuch matter, It is written in their Lawes, *Debet etiam in London quæ caput eſt regni et Legum, ſemper curia Domini Regis ſingulis Septimanis die Lunæ Huſtingis ſedere et teneri.* Marke how it agreeth with the patent before pleaded. *In ea itaque ſuperſunt ardua compeꝛta et ambigua placita coronæ et curiæ domini regis totius Regni predicti quæ hæc vſque et cōſuetudines ſuas vna sēper inviolabilitate cōſeruat vbicūque ipſe rex fuerit ſiue in expedicione, ſiue alibi, propter fatigationem gentium et populorum regni iuxta veteres Conſuetudines bono-* *Lamb. Arc. in Leg. Edwardi. Liber Recordorum. London Dunthorne*

K rum

De Antiquis

See the Charter of K. William the conqueror in Hookers Chron.

rum patrum et predecessorũ et omniũ principum et procerũ et sapientũ seniorum totius regni predicti. Beholde then here is no new institution mencioned neither by the Conqueror nor by the Cõfessor, but still the auncient customes.

And if this had bene by patent or Parlament of any *Saxon* Prince; without all question these two Princes would haue knowne it. For all the *Saxon* gouernment in peace from the first King vnto the last was not aboue 300. yeeres, & both *Edward* and *VVilliam* were most diligent searchers and Registers of all the lawes, Liberties & Customes of their kingdome, as appeareth by the Domesday Booke, and by that which is recorded by *Houeden* and others.

Besides in the *Saxon* times, not a peece of lãd passed from the Crowne, and much lesse any liberties or Iurisdictiõs, which are parcel of the royal prerogatiue without Patent, as appeareth by the manifolde patents of manors. Landes, & Liberties made to Churches and Monasteries, whereof those that belonged to the Abby of Croyland, are faithfully recorded by *Ingulfus*, those of the house of *Ely* by another; and others are to be seene in the Churches that remaine.

Ingulfus Historia Eliensis.

The City of London therefore had this Libertie

Britanniæ Legibus.

bertie and Maner of trial in the *Normans* time, not by patent or new Law, but by prescription; they had it in the *Saxons* time not by patent or new Law: therefore by prescription, & it must needes bee true, that they had it from a time whereof no proofe could be made, that is, long before the *Saxons*. I say by prescription as it is pleaded euen from the Britaines. And this that I haue said of London, I may say of all auncient Cities where they haue like customes and Liberties; yea the auncient hundred, Courts, Shiermotes, Wardmotes, Swainmotes, Leets, and Wapentakes, which are often mencioned in the *Saxons* Lawes as thinges in vse. Let any man shew me, what other kinde of triall or inquisicion, they had then this, and *Quo warranto* by what law they had this, but by like prescription. If you bring foorth the triall by fire and water called *Ordell*, it was by al likelyhood but a superstitious inuentiõ, in the *Saxon* times, & was vsed onely in criminall causes where the truth could not otherwise be known as appeareth by the Law of *Canutus*. And although the Conqueror in his absolute commaund did something of his owne head, yet it appereth plainely that when by the earnest

In Legibus Canuti de Foresta.

Houeden Lamb.

K 2 intreaty

intreaty of his Nobles, he was perswaded to establish the former lawes; he then by the counsell of his Nobles, and according to the course and common Lawes of the Realme, impanelled twelue men of euerie Shire, to inquire & make a true presentment of the said auncient Lawes and customes, for so be the words: *Electi de singulis totius patriæ comitatibus duodecim viri, iureiurando Coram Rege primum confirmauerunt, vt quoad possent recto tramite incedentes, nec ad dextrā nec ad sinistrā diuertentes, legum suarum, et consuetudinum, sancita patefacerent &c.* And amongst the rest, they make menciō of the customes of London, which I cited before. I say nothing here, that the footesteps of this triall, are found in the lawes of *Etheldred* made at wantage, which is cited by Maister *Camden*; nor of the ordinance, made for the mountainers of Wales: nor of the law of *Kennethus*, the famous Scottish King about the yere of our Sauiour Christ, 840. mentioning some such matter; nor of the learned & diligent Historians, that liued neere about the conquest: & might easily haue tolde vs if any such thing had been begun by the Saxons; nor of the Historie of *Ely*, written before the conquest: and *Ingulfus* soone after, plainly

Lamb. Arc. *Houeden.*

Malmesbury. *Huntingdō.* *Ethelwardus.* *Historia Ely remaining with Sr. Robert Cotton.* *Ingulfus.*

plainly ſpeaking of Mannors, Feoffements, Shiriffes, Coũty Courts, Tearmes at Londõ, recoueries in an aſſiſe or writ of right, as of thinges thẽ common and vſuall.

We read alſo of Parlaments, wapentakes, homages, fealties, diſcents from the Grandfather to the Nephew, *Eſchets* to the King for want of heires, in the daies of *Aurelius Ambroſius*, and of *Arthur* the worthy, & ſtreight way after, *Gildas* maketh mencion of Courts, Iudges, Freſhſuit after thieues, & Iudgements which could not be without trialls. By all which I thinke it is manifeſt that theſe points of common law, & namely theſe trialls by twelue, are of moſt aunciẽt antiquitie, according to the commõ law, and vſed amongſt other cuſtomes of the citie of London before the times of the *Saxon* and *Norman* Princes, of whome no ſuch Libertie or courſe of proceeding could be gotten without patent, and no other forme of auncient tryalls doth appeare: vpon which I conclude, as before, that they had it in the times of the *Britaines*. *Leland. Hooker. Galf. Mon. Gildas.*

The ſame is prooued by al the auncient and new records of Aſſiſes, of Freſhforce, of writs of right, and other tryalles in London, which muſt bee all falſified and many thouſands

K 3 of

De Antiquis

of records besides, if wee ouerthrowe this prescription. And this being so consonant to the iudgments of those excellent men before cited, Cāden, *Belknap*, Sr. *Io. Fortescue*, & Sr. *Ed. Cook*, Let vs now leaue Maister *Polidor* & his followers which either neuer saw or did not vnderstand, our auncient Histories and Records; let vs leaue them (I say) to their owne imaginations, with this admonition to all discreet Antiquaries, that they be not ouer-hasty to beleeue either the *Roman* or other Authors, speaking of the Br*itaines* thire enemies, but holding them suspect for partialitie or ignorance, which may easily appeare to euerie iudiciall Reader, let vs followe the true groundes confirmed by these faithfull Monuments of our Lawes, and the Histories thereunto agreeing. And this being ascertained, it is easie now to beholde, from whence all our Assises of nouel diseisin of Mordancester, of darrain presentment, our great Assises, Iuries, Challenges & the rest, of which Mr. *Bracton* at large discourseth, are lineally descēded, being as I take it the greatest part of our common Lawes, and it appereth by that which is before spoken, that these also are most agreeable to the Scripture of God; whereupon I conclude

Britanniæ Legibus.

clude fully, that all our common Lawes was in vſe in the *Britaines* time long before the *Saxons*, howſoeuer ſuppreſſed & the bookes thereof defaced by forreine inuaſions, and inteſtine diſſentions. And thus much of *Lucius* and the *Britaines*. Now of the *Saxon* Princes.

Cap. 11.

IT hath bene a worke of the ſpecial prouidẽce of Almightie God, & of his infinite mercie to this Iland, in the middes of Poetical fables wherwith the Britiſh Hiſtories haue bene mixed, and of thoſe Barbarous inuaſiõs, which haue waſted and ſpoyled them, to leaue vs yet certaine remnants and monuments, whereby to iudge of thoſe long paſt Antiquities; in iudging wherof, men by taking contrarie courſes, haue made the controuerſie more difficult, that the truth foũd out might be the better confirmed. For ſome haue giuẽ thẽſelues to fauour the *Romane* Hiſtorie ſo much, as to abrogate all faith and credit from the Britiſh, as if the ambitious Romanes & *Cæſar* would ſay nothing for their owne aduantage, who of all others moſt couetous of glorie is iuſtly noted by *Suetonius*, *Lucian*,

De Antiquis

cian,and *Asinius Pollio* to haue written his commētaries,as much as he might,to saue his owne Honour, especiallye of his Actions in these remote places.

Others haue gone so farre to the bowehand, as to fauour all the vanities of the Poeticall Bardes, as if nothing could bee denied, which they had once turned into Rythme. But that God which came into the world to beare witnesse of the truth(so much doth he loue it)hath left vs rules and directions to trie out the verity of auncięt times. By the mouth of two or three witnesses,euerie word shall be confirmed sayth *Moses*,and(as it is moste certaine)truth cannot be so much oppressed as to be vtterly destitute of proofes. Let therefore the proofe rest vpon witnesses and comparison of circumstances, & it will appreare as Sir *Iohn Prise* truely auerreth and learnedly prooueth, that the British Story is in many things more to be credited then *Caesar*,and *Polidore*,and other *Italians*. Besides the Scottish Historie agreeing in many things with vs,manifestly conuinceth the *Romanes* of their Arrogancie and vanitie,and with all ministreth further groundes, not onely to proue the antiquitie and sincerity of our common Lawes,but that

Britanniæ Legibus.

that the ſame or others much like obtained in Scotland alſo, as well as heere, which may bee ſeene by the Lawes of *Brechus* & *Fergusius* anſwering in time to *Mulmutius* and *Mercia*, and by the Lawes of *Kennethus*, not much diſtant from *Alfred*, and laſt of all by their Bookes of Regiam *Maieſtatem* a principal booke of Common Law amongſt thẽ, agreeing in effect with our *Glanuill*. And to ſay truth there was litle difference in Lawes and Religion, betwixt theſe two Nations, vntill the bloody warres, that began after the time of our King *Henry* the third, before whoſe daies *Glanuill* did write. Againe the moſt auncient of the *Saxon* Princes, & lawmakers, doe make mencion of many thinges in our common Law, which we are forced to beleeue, that they receiued from the *Britaines*; for that, they ſpeake of them, as of things vſual and common, *Ina*, *Alfred*, *Edgar* & other the *Saxon* *Lamb. Arc.* law makers, ſpeake of the Parlament, of Iudgemẽts, of Treaſon, of Sanctuaries, of Purgatiõ, of execution by hanging, for theft, of freſhſute after theiues & homicides, of eſcapes, of Tearmes kept at London, of Recoueries, of Exchanges, of *Hiſtoria* Feoffements, of intales, of Cõmons, incloſures, *Elienſis.* and the Law of *Curia Claudenda*, of the lawe of

L diſceit

discеit,it in ſelling thinges corrupt or vitious;of dowers,Leaſes,Rents,Farmes,ſeruices &c. And many other,as things thẽ in vſe, which were allowed as agreeable to Gods word, by thoſe *Saxon* Chriſtiãs being vtter enemies to the *Britaines*,and yet moſt deuout in Religion,and ſincere in Iuſtice,as their Lawes doe teſtifie. For which cauſe I will touch certaine of the notable *Saxon* lawes, onely to ſhew the Godlineſſe of thoſe auncient *Saxons* and Scottiſh Kings, and how in that time the matters of our common Lawes were vſuall and common.

Inas about the yeare of our Lord 720. beginneth his lawes thus: *Inas* by the grace of God, weſt *Saxon* King , by the perſwaſion and inſtruction of *Cenred* my Father , and of *Hedda* and *Erkenwald* my Biſhops,and with al my Aldermen,& the eldeſt wiſemen of my people, & in a great ſummons of Gods Seruants,for the health of our ſoule & conſeruation of our kingdome, (I haue enacted) that right Lawes and Iudgemẽts be confirmed throughout our kingdome. Cap. 1. That the miniſters of God obſerue the appointed rules and maners of liuing: Then followeth Lawes for obſeruation of the Sabaoth,againſt theft,robbery,murder, & many

Britanniæ Legibus.

ny other offences; and therein, is mencion alſo made of Land-lords, of Tennants, of Rents, and ſeruices. *Kennethus* the moſt worthy Scottiſh King, ſoone after the ſame time, maketh verye iuſt and good Lawes, wherof this was one. In euery Shire (this was before *Alfred*) Let skilfull men in the Lawes bee appointed to reſide, hee that blaſphemeth the name of God, of the Saints, of his Prince, or of the Captaine of his tribe, let his tongue bee cut out. The moſt religious K. *Alfred* about the yeare 880. beginneth his lawes thus: The Lord ſpake vnto *Moſes* theſe words, ſaying: *I am the Lord thy God which brought thee out of the land of Egipt, out of the houſe of Bondage, thou shalt haue none other Gods beſides mee.* And ſo foorth as in the decalog and other Iudicialles of *Moſes*. Then follow certaine lawes againſt periury, concerning Intayles, againſt Sacriledge, Treaſon, Quarrelling, Fighting, Fornication, yea & againſt immodeſt touching of a womã; with other lawes of greate ſinceritie, a maniſeſt and approued Vicar and Lieuſtenant of God, a ſecond *Dauid*, whoſe delight is in the Lawe of the Lord, which to confirme, the ſame King tranſlated the new Teſtament out of Latin into the Vulgar Saxõ, for the

L 2 vſe

vſe of his ſubiects, ſome Copies whereof (as it is ſaid) are yet remaining amongſt vs. So farre did the learning of thoſe daies differ from the ignorance of theſe *Romane* innouators. *Edward Anno Dom.* 920. Thus beginneth: I *Edward* K. commaund all *Greeues* that they giue right iudgements to all according to their iudgement Bo oke. *Alfred* and *Guthrun* thus made their league by act of Parlament *Ante omnia Deum vnum &c.* before al things that one God is to be loued & Worſhipped. Secondly that humane Lawes are to be proclaimed as common to Chriſt and the King. Then followe Lawes for payment of Tithes, for obſeruation of the Sabaothes. &c. And by this league *Guthrunus* which ſome call *Gurmundus*, & was in Baptiſme named *Ethelſtane*, obteyned *Suffolke*, *Norfolke*, & *Northumberland*, to be giuen to him to holde by Fealty of the King. *Edmund* ſets this preface to his Lawes: I *Edmund* King to al my Subiects doe plainely ſignifie, that in a ſolemne aſſembly both of the Clergie and Laity, I haue ſtudiouſly inquired of the wiſeſt of my kingdome, by what meanes the Chriſtiã faith might be moſt aduanced. And to vs all it ſeemed moſt comodious that loue and mutual kindnes ſhould be main-

Ioh. Picus cited by Mr Lamb. Arc.

tayned

Britanniæ Legibus.

tayned amongst all men throughout our Kingdome. *Etenim tædet nos harum quotidianarum pugnarum*, For we are tired with these quotidian fightings and contentions. O godly Prince! O true Vicar of the God of Peace! *Edgar* enacteth Lawes for the obseruation of the Sunday, and of publike feasts and fasts vnder the paines contained in the iudiciall booke. And that euery man shall freely enioy the benefit of the common Law. Note the common lawe euen then named, before St. *Edward* & the Conqueror. *Canutus* the Dane thus: First let all men most deuoutly & religiously worship one God. Al men obserue one rule of Christian Religion. Al men obey *Canutus* the King with due fidelity and obseruance. All defend and keepe the church of Christ with holy & euerlasting peace, & continually frequẽt the same &c, with many other most Godly and Christian lawes, & after many Footesteps of auncient Lawes, which yet remaine in vse, he concludeth with a moste ardent exhortation to all men to turne vnto God and to obey his commaundements, another Lieftenant or vicegerent of Christ. *Edgar* the peaceable confirmeth the Liberties & rights of the Church, & amongst other things, enacteth

L 3 eth

De Antiquis

eth that euerie man ſhall enioy the benefit of the common Lawe. Like matters are found in the Lawes of *Ethelſtane*, *Etheldred*, S^t^. *Edward* and *VVilliam* the Conqueror, who confirmeth the ſame with ſome ſmall addition, and hath left them to vs conſecrated by his owne othe, and the othe of all his ſucceſſors. You ſee then the ſacred Maieſtie of our Imperaill Princes, whō God hath vouchſafed not onely by the cō-feſſion of ſtrangers & enemies, but by theſe their Lawes to be his Vicars & defenders of his faith. And by theſe things that haue been ſaid, it may fully appeare, firſt how ſincerely and deuoutlye thoſe excellent Princes followed the counſell of *Elutherius* giuen to *Lucius*, in taking lawes for their kingdome out of the word of God, and how true it is that we affirme that our auncient common lawes were begun in the times of the firſt *Britains*, grounded vpon the lawes of God, printed in Nature and Scripture, continued by the *Saxons* in their iudgement bookes, & tranſ-mitted to vs by Saint *Edward* and the Conque-ror. And conſequently the ground of Sir *Iohn Forteſcues* teſtimony, that this land hath bene poſſeſſed by *Britaines*, *Romanes*, *Saxons*, *Danes* and *Normans*: And in all the times of theſe ſe-

uerall

Britanniæ Legibus

uerall Nations,and of their Kings, this Realme was still ruled with the selfe same lawes and customes,which if they had not bene right good, some of those Kings mooued eyther with Iustice or with reason,or affection,wold haue chāged or abolished them, speciallye the *Romanes*, who did iudge all the world by their owne Lawes. Thirdly what direction and Presidents our Princes and Parlaments haue had to follow in making Lawes, and what Lawes the whole Kingdome is bound to obserue, by that solemn othe that is taken for the obseruation of St. *Edwards* lawes and the Lawes of the Realme, as partly also is noted vnto vs in the preface of that famous Statute,made against Prouisors in the 25. yeare of King *Edward* the third. And lastly what reason may be giuē of the manifold calamities,sent by Almighty God,the most iust & seuere judge at sūdry times vpō this Realm, namely the suppressing, and consequentlye the violation of this his Couenant, of these our auncient lawes, and of the law of God, whereupon they are founded,by the predominant violēce of Idolatry,superstitiō, iniustice,vncleannesse,Breach of faith, and loialtye,both before the *Norman* and sithence. If it be not so, peruse

use the Particulars that the holy *Gildas*, and after him, the learned Sir *Iohn Prise* obiecteth against the first *Britains*; that the reuerend *Bede* and *Geffery* of *Monmouth* vrge against the second age; that Maister *Camden* & other Chronicles, but specially Maister *Fox* collecteth against the *Saxons*; that are at large described in the times of King *Iohn* & King *Henry* the sixth, who suffered themselues and these lawes to bee ouerswaied by the supreheminence of *Rome*, & of the cōtrary side, if we cōsider the best meanes to establish the perpetuall vnitie and felicity of these two mightie nations, now againe reunited, we shall finde it to consist principally in conforming them, both as much as may bee to the lawes, of that God of vnitie which ordeyned the auncient Lawes of both kingdomes to be very like, & almost the same, as I haue shewed. For what Kings haue reigned in more magnificence and glory then the Britaine Princes instiled by *Elutherius*, the Vicars of God in their kingdome, then the *Saxon* Princes indowed by *Beda*, with the Title of *Christianissimi*, thē the *Normans* which haue moste mainteyned these Lawes, & most opposed themselues against the vsurping power of the forraine Prelate, namely

Edward

Britanniæ Legibus.

Edward the 1. the 3. and the 6. *Henry* the 7. and the eight, acknowledged by the enemie of our faith to bee defender of the faith,& the late moſt of all excellent, *Elizabeth*, which was bleſſed with a kingdõe,longer then the raignes of ten that curſed her. And now the no leſſe excellent Maieſty of K. *Iames*,the true heyre aſwell of the goodneſſe as of the greatneſſe of his Predeceſſors. And who haue fallen into greater miſeries then thoſe that beeing inueſted with ſuch magnificent Titles by right, haue ſuffered others to take their Titles & authoritie by vſurpation; of whoſe Calamities becauſe my heart doth tremble to thinke, I will forbeare my pen to write. Yet by this we ſee how God hath fed and directed vs with the ſtaffe of Beautie, and with the ſtaffe of Bandes,but now hee will breake his ſtaffe of beautie, to diſanull his couenant, made with all people, and hee will breake his ſtaffe of bãdes, to diſſolue the Brotherhood between *Iuda* & *Iſraell* except we repẽt of our manifold ſinnes. I will therefore conclude with the Godly words of one of our famous and learned Iudges *Bracton*,and one of our vertuous and Heroical Kings *Canutus*, The firſt taking his ground out of the many times remembred, and neuer to bee forgotten, Epiſtle of *Elutherius*,ſaith thus: *Rex non debet eſſe ſub homine,ſed ſub deo et Lege, ad ſimilitudinem Ieſu Chriſti,*

Zach. 11.

Bractõ.L. 1

M *cuius*

cuius vices gerit. And againe Iudges doe ſit in the ſeate of the K. himſelf, as in the throane of God, inſteed of the K. as inſteed of Ieſus Chriſt. For the K. is the Vicar & Lieftenant of God, & iudgemēts are not the iudgements of men, but of God; and therefore it is ſaid that the heart of the King is in the hād of God. And a little after, into the ſeate therefore of judgement, which is as the Throne of the Diuine Maieſtie, let no man vnwiſe or vnlearned, preſume to aſcend, leaſt hee turne light into darkeneſſe, and darkeneſſe into light, and leaſt with an ignorant hād like a mad mā, he ſtrike the innocent & ſpare the offender, and leaſt he fall from aboue as from the Tribunall of God, by attempting to flye without winges to ſupport him. And when any mā is to judge, or to be made a judge, let him take heed, leſt by iudging peruerſly and againſt the Lawes, for requeſt or reward, or a litle temporall comoditie, He purchaſe to himſelfe ſorrow & griefe eternall: and leaſt in the daie of Gods wrath, he feele him to be a iuſt reuenger, who hath ſaid. To me vengeance & I wil recompence, when the Kings & Princes of the earth ſhal weepe & lamēt at the ſight of the Sonne of man, for the terror of his iudgemēts, from which neither gold nor ſiluer can deliuer them. Who will not be affraid of that feareful trial, where the Lord himſelfe ſhall be accuſer, aduocate and iudge? from

Bracto li.1.

whoſe

whoſe ſentẽce none cã appeale.For the Father hath giuẽ al iudgemẽt to the ſon,who ſhutteth& no mã openeth,& openeth & no man ſhutteth.O ſtrict & ſeuere iudgment wherin mẽ ſhal giue account not onely of their actions ; but of euery idle word that they haue ſpoken ! who ſhall eſcape from that anger to come ? When the Sonne of man ſhal ſend his Angels,which ſhal gather out of Gods kingdom euerie ſcandal,& thoſe that doe iniquitie,& of them ſhall make faggots to burne and caſt them into the furnace of fire, where there ſhall be weeping and gnaſhing of teeth. Without queſtion God is a Iealous God,and whoſoeuer taketh his Couenant, his oathe ,his name in vaine,hee ſhall ſmart, for it he ſhall ſmart. Now therefore ſaith *Canutus* in the conclufion of his Lawes; I beſeech all men in generall , and commaund euerie man in particular in the name of the immortall God that ſincerely,& withall their hearts they turne to God, and withall care and diligence, ſearch what is to be done,and what it is to bee auoided (as it is a thing moſt conueniẽt for our ſaluation)that we loue God & keepe his commaundements, & giue diligent heed to the words of his meſſengers For they ſhall produce vs before his ſight in the day, wherein the Lord ſhall come to iudge euery man according to his workes. Then happie ſhall that keeper bee,that ſhall bring *Lamb.Arc.*

M 2 the

De Antiquis

the flocke committed vnto him into the ioyes of heauen,by the paines that he hath takẽ vpon earth, And blessed shall bee the flocke that followed such a shephard which hath pulled thẽ from the pawes of the Deuill,and commended them as a purchase vnto God. Therefore let vs all in concord and vnitie studdie to please God, and fly from the fearefull torments of his wrath,& iudgement. Let the Preachers: and Ministers of Gods word (as it is their charge and needefull to all mens saluation) oftentimes preach the glory & ioyes of Gods kingdome, and let all men with diligent,serious, and attentiue eares and mindes,heare and obserue them : yea let them beare the commaundements of God alwaies imprinted and infixed in their hearts. To conclude euerie man for the greater aduauncement of the diuine glorie, both in word and deed, Godly and cheerefully apply himselfe to doe well, by what meanes soeuer they may. So at length in the end we all aboundantly shall obtaine his gracious mercy.Blessed be the name of the Lord,& to him bee honor,praise,and glorie,from this time foorth for euermore.

Deus non deseret.

BIBLIOGRAPHY

Primary Sources

WILLIAM ADAMS, CHRONICLE OF BRISTOL (Francis F. Fox ed., Bristol, 1910) (ca. 1623–1648).

ROGER ACHERLEY, THE BRITANNIC CONSTITUTION: OR, THE FUNDAMENTAL FORM OF GOVERNMENT IN BRITAIN. DEMONSTRATING, THE ORIGINAL CONTRACT ENTERED INTO BY KING AND PEOPLE, ACCORDING TO THE PRIMARY INSTITUTIONS THEREOF, IN THIS NATION. WHEREIN IS PROVED, THAT THE PLACING ON THE THRONE KING WILLIAM III. WAS THE NATURAL FRUIT AND EFFECT OF THE ORIGINAL CONSTITUTION. AND, THAT THE SUCCESSION TO THIS CROWN, ESTABLISH'D IN THE PRESENT PROTESTANT HEIRS, IS DE JURE, AND JUSTIFY'D, BY THE FUNDAMENTAL LAWS OF GREAT BRITAIN. AND MANY IMPORTANT ORIGINAL POWERS AND PRIVILEGES, OF BOTH HOUSES OF PARLIAMENT, ARE EXHIBITED (London, 1727).

[ANONYMOUS], THE BOOK OF OATHS, AND THE SEVERAL FORMS THEREOF, BOTH ANCIENT AND MODERN, FAITHFULLY COLLECTED OUT OF SUNDRY AUTHENTICK BOOKS OF RECORDS (London, 1715).

[ANONYMOUS], COLLECTION OF COPIES OF DOCUMENTS RELATING LARGELY TO CONSTITUTIONAL AND LEGAL CONTROVERSIES OF 1610-CA. 1621, COMPILED CA. 1625. Folger Shakespeare Library mss. V.a.121.

[ANONYMOUS], GLASTONBURY ABBEY, PAST AND PRESENT. THE RISE AND INFLUENCE OF ENGLISH MONACHISM, 66 DUBLIN UNIVERSITY MAGAZINE 631, 640 (Dublin, 1865).

FRANCIS BACON, THREE SPEECHES OF THE RIGHT HONORABLE, SIR FRANCIS BACON KNIGHT, THEN HIS MAJESTIES SOLLICITOR GENERALL, AFTER LORD VERULAM, VISCOUNT SAINT ALBAN. CONCERNING THE POST-NATI,

NATURALIZATION OF THE SCOTCH IN ENGLAND, UNION OF THE LAWES OF THE KINGDOMES OF ENGLAND AND SCOTLAND. PUBLISHED BY THE AUTHORS COPY, AND LICENSED BY AUTHORITY. (London, 1641).

WILLIAM BLACKSTONE, COMMENTARIES ON THE LAWS OF ENGLAND (London, 1765–1769). 4 vols.

HENRICI DE BRACTON. DE LEGIBUS ET CONSUETUDINIBUS ANGLIÆ. LIBRI QUINQUE IN VARIOS TRACTATUS DISTINCTI. AD DIVERSORUM ET VETUSTISSIMORUM CODICUM COLLATIONEM TYPIS VULGAT [THE LAWS AND CUSTOMES OF ENGLAND] (Sir Travers Twiss ed. & trans., London, 1878–1883) (ca. 1230). 6 vols.

EDWARD BROOKE, BIBLIOTHECA LEGUM ANGLIÆ, PART II. CONTAINING A GENERAL ACCOUNT OF THE LAWS AND LAW-WRITERS OF ENGLAND, FROM THE EARLIEST TIMES TO THE REIGN OF EDW. III. AS ALSO OF THE PUBLIC RECORDS, AND OTHER AUTHENTIC LAW MSS. THE STATUTES, AND THE SEVERAL COLLECTIONS AND EDITIONS THEREOF; THE REPORTS, OR COLLECTIONS OF ADJUDGED CASES IN THE COURTS OF LAW AND EQUITY; TOGETHER WITH AN ACCOUNT OF THE PRINCIPAL WORKS UPON THE LAW AND CONSTITUTION, PUBLISHED DURING THE PRESENT REIGN (London, 1788).

ALEXANDER BRUCE, PRINCIPIA JURIS FEUDALIS (Edinburgh, 1713).

Calvin's Case, 77 ENGLISH REPORTS 377; 7 COKE'S REPORTS 1a (1609).

WILLIAM CAMDEN, BRITAIN, OR A CHOROGRAPHICALL DESCRIPTION OF THE MOST FLOURISHING KINGDOMES, ENGLAND, SCOTLAND, AND IRELAND, AND THE ISLANDS ADJOYNING, OUT OF THE DEPTHS OF ANTIQUITIE (Philemon Holland trans., London, 1637).

Le Case del Union, del Realm, D'Escose, ove Angleterre, 72 ENGLISH REPORTS 908 (n.d.), 2 STATE TRIALS 561.

WILLIAM CAXTON, CHRONICLES OF ENGLAND (Westminster, 1480).

THOMAS CRAIG, DE UNIONE REGNORUM BRITANNIÆ TRACTATUS [A TREATISE ON THE UNION OF THE BRITISH REALMS] (C. Sanford Terry trans., Edinburgh, 1909) (1605).

______. THE RIGHT OF SUCCESSION TO THE KINGDOM OF ENGLAND. IN TWO BOOKS; AGAINST THE SOPHISMS OF

PARSONS THE JESUITE, WHO ASSUM'D THE COUNTERFEIT NAME OF DOLEMAN: BY WHICH HE ENDEAVOURS TO OVERTHROW NOT ONLY THE RIGHTS OF SUCCESSION IN KINGDOMS BUT ALSO THE SACRED AUTHORITY OF KINGS THEMSELVES. WRITTEN ORIGINALLY IN LATIN ABOVE 100 YEARS SINCE BY THE EMINENTLY LEARNED AND JUDICIOUS SIR THOMAS CRAIG OF RICCARTOUN, THE CELEBRATED AUTHOR OF THE JUS FEUDALE, AND NOW FAITHFULLY TRANSLATED INTO ENGLISH, WITH A LARGE INDEX OF THE CONTENTS, AND A PREFACE BY THE TRANSLATOR, GIVING AN ACCOUNT OF THE AUTHOR AND OF HIS ADVERSARY (London, 1703).

SIR EDWARD COKE, THE REPORTS (Jos. Butterworth & Sons, London, 1826) (1600-16). 13 pts.

______. INSTITUTES OF THE LAWES OF ENGLAND (Garland ed. 1979) (1628-1644). 4 vols.

JOHN DEE, THE LIMITS OF THE BRITISH EMPIRE (Ken MacMillan ed., Praeger 2004).

THOMAS EGERTON, BARON ELLESMERE, THE SPEECH OF THE LORD CHANCELLOR OF ENGLAND, TOUCHING THE POST-NATI (London, 1609).

SIR ROBERT FILMER, PATRIARCHA, OR, THE NATURAL POWER OF KINGS (London, 1680).

SIR JOHN FORTESCUE, DE LAUDIBUS LEGUM ANGLIAE [IN PRAISE OF THE LAWS OF ENGLAND] (S.B. Chrimes ed. and trans., Cambridge, 1942) (ca. 1470)).

______. THE GOVERNANCE OF ENGLAND: OTHERWISE CALLED THE DIFFERENCE BETWEEN AN ABSOLUTE AND A LIMITED MONARCHY (Charles Plummer ed., 1885) (ca. 1471))

GEOFFREY OF MONMOUTH, THE HISTORY OF THE KINGS OF BRITAIN (Lewis Thorpe, ed., Penguin 1966) (circa 1136).

SIR MATHEW HALE, HISTORY AND ANALYSIS OF THE COMMON LAW OF ENGLAND (London, 1713) (ca. 1670).

WILLIAM WALLER HENING, 1 THE STATUTES AT LARGE: BEING A COLLECTION OF ALL THE LAWS OF VIRGINIA, FROM THE FIRST SESSION OF THE LEGISLATURE, IN THE YEAR 1619: PUBLISHED PURSUANT TO AN ACT OF THE GENERAL ASSEMBLY OF VIRGINIA, PASSED ON THE FIFTH DAY OF FEBRUARY ONE THOUSAND EIGHT HUNDRED AND EIGHT (New York, 1823).

RANULF HIGDEN, POLYCHRONICON (SIVE HISTORIA POLY-CRATICA) (London, 1480) (ca. 1350.)

THOMAS HOBBES, LEVIATHAN: OR THE MATTER, FORME, AND POWER OF A COMMONWEALTH ECCLESIASTICAL AND CIVIL (London, 1651).

HUMPHRY HODY, A HISTORY OF ENGLISH COUNCILS AND CONVOCATIONS (London, 1701).

RICHARD HOOKER, OF THE LAWS OF ECCLESIASTICAL POLITY (Via Media reprint 1994) (1887 7th ed.) (1594)). 3 vols.

ANDREW HORNE, THE MIRROR OF JUSTICES (Selden Soc. ed. 1895) (ca.1290).

EDMUND HOWES, ANNALES, OR, A GENERALL CHRONICLE OF ENGLAND. BEGUN BY IOHN STOW: CONTINUED AND AUGMENTED WITH MATTERS FORRAIGNE AND DOMESTIQUE, ANCIENT AND MODERNE, VNTO THE END OF THIS PRESENT YEERE, 1631 (London, 1632).

WILLIAM HUGHES, THE GRAND ABRIDGMENT OF THE LAW OR, A COLLECTION OF THE PRINCIPAL CASES AND POINTS OF THE COMMON-LAW OF ENGLAND, CONTAINED IN ALL THE REPORTS EXTANT, FROM THE FIRST OF ELIZABETH, TO THIS PRESENT TIME, BY WAY OF COMMON-PLACE. A WORK VERY USEFULL FOR ALL STUDENTS AND PRACTITIONERS IN THE LAW. WITH TWO TABLES, THE ONE CONTAINING THE NAMES OF THE CASES: THE OTHER, OF THE MATTER OF EVERY OF THE SAID CASES (London, 1660-62). 3 vols.

ARTHUR ROBERT INGPEN, THE MIDDLE TEMPLE BENCH BOOK: BEING A REGISTER OF BENCHERS OF THE MIDDLE TEMPLE FROM THE EARLIEST RECORDS TO THE PRESENT TIME, WITH HISTORICAL INTRODUCTION (J. Bruce Williamson ed., Middle Temple 2nd ed. 1937).

GILES JACOB, THE LAW-DICTIONARY: EXPLAINING THE RISE, PROGRESS, AND PRESENT STATE OF THE ENGLISH LAW, IN THEORY AND PRACTICE; DEFINING AND INTERPRETING THE TERMS OR WORDS OF ART; AND COMPRISING COPIOUS INFORMATION, HISTORICAL, POLITICAL, AND COMMERCIAL, ON THE SUBJECTS OF OUR LAW, TRADE, AND GOVERNMENT (T. E. Tomlin ed., London, 1797). 2 vols.

THE JACOBEAN UNION: SIX TRACTS OF 1604 (Bruce R. Galloway and Brian P. Levack eds., Scottish History Society, 1985).

THOMAS JEFFERSON, THE WRITINGS OF THOMAS JEFFERSON (Washington, D.C., 1853). 9 vols.

______. MEMOIR, CORRESPONDENCE, AND MISCELLANIES, FROM THE PAPERS OF THOMAS JEFFERSON (Thomas Jefferson Randolph ed., Boston 2nd ed. 1830). 4 vols.

______. *A Summary View of the Rights of British-Americans, in* THOMAS JEFFERSON, WRITINGS 105 (Literary Classics, 1984) (1774).

WILLIAM LAMBARDE, APXAIONOMIA [ARCHAIONOMIA] : SIVE DE PRISCIS ANGLORUM LEGIBUS LIBRI, SERMONE ANGLICO, VETUSTATE ANTIQUISSIMO, ALIQUOT AB HINC SECULIS CONSCRIPTI, NUNC DEMUM, MAGNO JURISPERITORUM, & AMANTIUM ANTIQUITATIS OMNIUM COMMODO, ÈTENEBRIS IN LUCEM VOCATI. GULIELMO LAMBARDO INTERPRETE. SEXCENTIS I LOCIS À LIBRO IPSIUS CASTIGATA, QUO PRO EXEMPLARI UTIMUR; CUM MULTIS ALIIS ADDITIONIBUS. ACCESSERE IN HAC NOSTRA ULTIMA EDITIONE LEGES HENRICI PRIMI NUNC PRIMÙM EDITÆ, EX MANUSCRIPTO IN FISCO REGIS HABITO: UNÀ CUM GLOSSARIO EARUM ANTIQUO EX MANUSCRIPTO CODICE OLIM S. AUGUSTINI DOROBORNIENSIS. REGU QUI HAS LEGES SCRIPSERUNT NOMENCLATIONEM, & QUID PRÆTEREA TUM PRIMÙM AB ILLO, & NUNC DENUO À NOBIS ACCESSERIT, SUBSEQUENS MONSTRABIT PAGINA (Cambridge & London, 1644) (1568).

JOHN LOCKE, TWO TREATISES OF GOVERNMENT: IN THE FORMER, THE FALSE PRINCIPLES AND FOUNDATION OF SIR ROBERT FILMER, AND HIS FOLLOWERS, ARE DETECTED AND OVERTHROWN. THE LATTER IS AN ESSAY CONCERNING THE TRUE ORIGINAL, EXTENT, AND END OF CIVIL-GOVERNMENT (London, 1698) (ca. 1680).

SIR GEORGE MACKENZIE, JUS REGIUM, OR, THE JUST AND SOLID FOUNDATIONS OF MONARCHY (Edinburgh, 1684).

MIDDLE TEMPLE RECORDS (Charles Henry Hopwood ed., Butterworth 1904). 3 vols.

MUNIMENTA GILDHALLAE LONDONIENSIS: LIBER ALBUS, LIBER CUSTOMARUM ET LIBER HORN (Henry Thomas Riley ed., London, 1860). 3 vols. in 4.

The Law Journal for Hilary and Easter Terms, 1803 (John Morgan and Thomas Walter Williams, eds. London, 1803).

John Pettingal, An Inquiry into the Use and Practice of Juries among the Greeks and Romans, from whence the Origin of the English Jury May Probably be Deduced (London, 1769).

Edmund Plowden, The Commentaries or Reports (London, 1779) (1548).

The Political Works of James I (Oxford 1918).

Robert Powell, A Treatise of the Antiquity, Authority, Uses and Jurisdiction of the Ancient Courts of Leet, or View of Frank-Pledge, and of Subordination of Government Derived from the Institution of Moses, the First Legislator: and the First Imitation of Him in this Island of Great Britaine, by King Alfred and Continued Ever Since (London, 1641).

John Prise. Historiae Brittanicae Defensio / A Defence of the British History: Studies and Texts (Ceri Davies ed. and trans., Oxford, The Bodleian Library, 2015).

Proceedings in Parliament in 1610 (Elizabeth Read Foster ed., Yale University Press 1966)). 2 vols.

T.H.B Oldfield, The Representative History of Great Britain and Ireland: Being a History of the House of Commons, and of the Counties, Cities, and Boroughs of the United Kingdom, from the Earliest Period (London, 1816).

Ratcliffe's Case, 76 English Reports 713; 3 Coke's Reports 37a (1592).

Les Reports del Cases en Ley: que furent argues à quadragesimo ad quinquagesimum annum de tres haut & puissant Prince Roy Edward le Tierce (London, 1679).

George Saltern, Of the Antient Lawes of Great Britaine (London, 1605).

______. Sacrae Heptades, or Seaven Problems concerning Antichrist. 1. Of his Place. 2. Of his State. 3. Of his Names. 4. Of his Rising. 5. Of his Raigne. 6. Of his words and actions. 7. Of his times. Necessarie to be

READ AND KNOWNE OF ALL MEN, WHO PROFESSE CHRIST IESUS, AND HOPE TO BE SAVED BY NO OTHER NAME. (London, 1625).

______. A TREATISE AGAINST IMAGES AND PICTURES IN CHURCHES. AND AN ANSWER TO THOSE WHO OBJECT THAT THE TIMES ARE CHANGED. (London, 1641).

WILLIAM SAMPSON, SAMPSON'S DISCOURSE, AND CORRESPONDENCE WITH VARIOUS LEARNED JURISTS, UPON THE HISTORY OF THE LAW, WITH THE ADDITION OF SEVERAL ESSAYS, TRACTS, AND DOCUMENTS, RELATING TO THE SUBJECT (Pishey Thompson compiler & publisher, Washington City, 1826).

SIR HENRY SAVILLE, RERUM ANGLICARUM SCRIPTORES POST BEDAM PRAECIPUI, EX VETUSTISSIMIS CODICIBUS MANUSCRIPTIS NUNC PRIMUM IN LUCEM EDITI. WILLIELMI MONACHI MALMESBURIENSIS DE GESTIS REGUM ANGLORUM LIB. V. EIUSDEM HISTORIAE NOUELLAE LIB. II. EIUSDEM DE GESTIS PONTIFICUM ANGL. LIB. IIII. HENRICI ARCHIDIACONI HUNTINDONIENSIS HISTORIARUM LIB. VIII. ROGERI HOUEDENI ANNALIUM PARS PRIOR & POSTERIOR. CHRONICORUM ETHELWERDI LIB. IIII. INGULPHI ABBATIS CROYLANDENSIS HISTORIARUM LIB. I. ADIECTA AD FINEM CHRONOLOGIA. (London, 1596)

JOHN SELDEN, JANI ANGLORUM FACIES ALTERA, RENDERED INTO ENGLISH, WITH LARGE NOTES THEREUPON, BY REDMAN WESTCOT, GENT., IN TRACTS WRITTEN BY JOHN SELDEN OF THE INNER-TEMPLE, ESQUIRE (London, 1673) (1610).

______. ENGLAND'S EPINOMIS, IN TRACTS WRITTEN BY JOHN SELDEN OF THE INNER-TEMPLE, ESQUIRE (London, 1673) (ca. 1609).

SIR HENRY SPELMAN, HENRICI SPELMANNI EQUIT. ANGLO-BRIT. ARCHAEOLOGUS IN MODUM GLOSSARII AD REM ANTIQUAM POSTERIOREM: CONTINENTIS. LATINO-BARBARA, PEREGRINA, OBSOLETA, ET NOUATAE SIGNIFICATIONIS VOCABULA, QUAE POST LABEFACTATAS À GOTHIS VANDALISQ[UE] RES EUROPAEAS, IN ECCLESIASTICIS PROFANISQ[UE] SCRIPTORIBUS; VARIARUM ITEM GENTIUM LEGIBUS ANTIQUIS, CHARTIS ET FORMULIS OCCURRUNT. SCHOLIIS ET COMMENTARIIS ILLUSTRATA, IN QUIBUS PRISCI

RITUS QUÁM PLURIMI, MAGISTRATUS, DIGNITATES, MUNERA, OFFICIA, MORES, LEGES, ET CONSUETUDINES ENRRANTUR [sic] (London, 1626).

______. GLOSSARIUM ARCHAIOLOGICUM. CONTINENS LATINO-BARBARA, PEREGRINA, OBSOLETA, & NOVATAE SIGNIFICATIONIS VOCABULA. QUAE POST LABEFACTATAS A GOTHIS, VANDALISQUE RES EUROPAEAS, IN ECCLESIASTICIS, PROFANISQUE SCRIPTORIBUS, VARIARUM ITEM GENTIUM LEGIBUS ANTIQUIS MUNICIPALIBUS, CHARTIS, & FORMULIS OCCURRUNT. SCHOLIIS & COMMENTARIIS ILLUSTRATA. IN QUIBUS PRISCI RITUS QUAM-PLURIMI, MAGISTRATUS, DIGNITATES, MUNERA, OFFICIA, MORES, LEGES IPSAE, & CONSUETUDINES ENARRANTUR. AUTHORE HENRICO SPELMANNO, EQUITE, ANGLO-BRITANNO (London, 3rd ed. 1687).

ROYAL PROCLAMATIONS OF KING JAMES I 1603–1625 (James F. Larkin & Paul L Hughes eds., Oxford Clarendon Press 1973).

POLYDORE VERGIL, ANGLICA HISTORIA (Basel: 1555), hypertext edition with English translation by Dana F. Sutton available at http://www.philological.bham.ac.uk/polverg.

JAMES WILSON, THE COLLECTED WORKS OF JAMES WILSON (Kermit L. Hall & Mark David Hall eds., Liberty Fund 2005).

______. THE WORKS OF THE HONOURABLE JAMES WILSON, L.L.D. LATE ONE OF THE ASSOCIATE JUSTICES OF THE SUPREME COURT OF THE UNITED STATES, AND PROFESSOR OF LAW IN THE COLLEGE OF PHILADELPHIA (Bird Wilson ed., Philadelphia, 1804).

Witrong *v.* Blaney, 84 ENGLISH REPORTS 789; 3 KEBLE'S REPORTS 401 (1675).

Secondary Sources

JACK M. BALKIN, LIVING ORIGINALISM (Harvard University Press 2011).

REID BARBOUR, JOHN SELDEN: MEASURES OF THE HOLY COMMONWEALTH IN SEVENTEENTH-CENTURY ENGLAND (University of Toronto Press 2003).

RANDY BARNETT, RESTORING THE LOST CONSTITUTION (Princeton University Press 2004).

SUSAN J. BLACKMORE, THE MEME MACHINE (Oxford University Press 1999).

______. *Dangerous Memes; or, What the Pandorans Let Loose, in* COSMOS AND CULTURE: CULTURAL EVOLUTION IN A COSMIC CONTEXT 297 (Steven J. Dick & Mark L. Lupisella eds., NASA 2009).

BLACKSTONE'S COMMENTARIES ON THE LAWS OF ENGLAND (Wayne Morrison ed., Cavendish Publishing 2001). 4 vols.

Christopher W. Brooks, *The Place of Magna Carta and the Ancient Constitution in Sixteenth-Century Legal Thought, in* THE ROOTS OF LIBERTY: MAGNA CARTA, ANCIENT CONSTITUTION, AND THE ANGLO-AMERICAN TRADITION OF THE RULE OF LAW 57 (Ellis Sandoz ed., University of Missouri Press 1993).

JOHN CARTWRIGHT, EVOLUTION AND HUMAN BEHAVIOR: DARWINIAN PERSPECTIVES ON HUMAN NATURE (MIT Press 2008).

T. M. CHARLES-EDWARDS, WALES AND THE BRITONS 350–1064 (Oxford University Press 2013).

Paul Christianson, *Royal and Parliamentary Voices on the Ancient Constitution, c. 1604-1621, in* THE MENTAL WORLD OF THE JACOBEAN COURT 71 (Linda Levy Peck ed., Cambridge University Press 1991).

______. *Young John Selden and the Ancient Constitution,* 128 PROCEEDINGS OF THE AMERICAN PHILOSOPHICAL SOCIETY 271 (1984).

ANTON-HERMANN CHROUST, THE RISE OF THE LEGAL PROFESSION IN AMERICA (University of Oklahoma Press 1965). 2 vols.

Morris L. Cohen, *Legal Literature in Colonial Massachusetts, in* LAW IN COLONIAL MASSACHUSETTS 243 (University of Virginia Press 1984).

COSMOS AND CULTURE: CULTURAL EVOLUTION IN A COSMIC CONTEXT (Steven J. Dick & Mark L. Lupisella eds., NASA 2009).

Robert Cover, *The Supreme Court 1982 Term – Foreword: Nomos and Narrative*, 97 HARVARD LAW REVIEW 4 (1982).

PAULINE CROFT, KING JAMES (Palgrave 2003).

JOHN E. CURRAN, JR., ROMAN INVASIONS: THE BRITISH HISTORY, PROTESTANT ANTI-ROMANISM, AND THE HISTORICAL IMAGINATION IN ENGLAND, 1530–1660 (University of Delware Press 2002).

James Daly, *Cosmic Harmony and Political Thinking in Early Stuart England*, 69 TRANSACTIONS OF THE AMERICAN PHILOSOPHICAL SOCIETY 1 (1979).

NORMAN DAVIES, THE ISLES: A HISTORY (Oxford University Press 1999).

RICHARD DAWKINS, THE SELFISH GENE (Oxford University Press 1976).

Paul R. Dean, *G.U. "Unbeguiled By The Trumpet Of The False Progressive"*, 2 GEORGETOWN LAW WEEKLY 3 (Apr. 29, 1969).

Daniel C. Dennett, *The Evolution of Culture, in* COSMOS AND CULTURE: CULTURAL EVOLUTION IN A COSMIC CONTEXT 125 (Steven J. Dick & Mark L. Lupisella eds., NASA 2009).

ELIZABETH EVENDEN AND THOMAS S. FREEMAN, RELIGION AND THE BOOK IN EARLY MODERN ENGLAND: THE MAKING OF FOXE'S BOOK OF MARTYRS (Cambridge University Press 2010).

EDWARD FOSS, THE JUDGES OF ENGLAND: WITH SKETCHES OF THEIR LIVES, AND MISCELLANEOUS NOTICES CONNECTED WITH THE COURTS AT WESTMINSTER, FROM THE TIME OF THE CONQUEST (London, 1857). 9 vols.

JOHN FOXE AND THE ENGLISH REFORMATION (David Loades ed., Scholar Press 1997).

Michael S. Fried, *The Evolution of Legal Concepts: The Memetic Perspective*, 39 JURIMETRICS 298 (1999).

LAWRENCE FRIEDMAN, A HISTORY OF AMERICAN LAW (Simon & Schuster 1973).

HERBERT JOHNSON, IMPORTED EIGHTEENTH CENTURY LAW TREATISES IN AMERICAN LIBRARIES, 1700–1799 (University of Tennessee Press 1978).

BRUCE GALLOWAY, THE UNION OF ENGLAND AND SCOTLAND, 1603–1608 (John Donald Publishers 1986).

DENNIS J. GOLDFORD, THE AMERICAN CONSTITUTION AND THE DEBATE OVER ORIGINALISM (Cambridge University Press 2005).

A. WIGFALL GREEN, THE INNS OF COURT AND EARLY ENGLISH DRAMA (Yale University Press 1931).

JANELLE GREENBERG, THE RADICAL FACE OF THE ANCIENT CONSTITUTION: ST. EDWARD'S "LAWS" IN EARLY MODERN POLITICAL THOUGHT (Cambridge University Press 2001).

Kermit L. Hall, *Introduction to* THE COLLECTED WORKS OF JAMES WILSON xiii (Kermit L. Hall & Mark David Hall eds., Liberty Fund 2005).

Mark David Hall, *Bibliographic Essay History of James Wilson's Law Lectures, in* THE COLLECTED WORKS OF JAMES WILSON 401 (Kermit L. Hall & Mark David Hall eds., Liberty Fund 2005).

DENYS HAY, POLYDORE VERGIL: RENAISSANCE HISTORIAN AND MAN OF LETTERS (Oxford University Press 1952).

HISTORY OF PARLIAMENT ONLINE, available at http://www.historyofparliamentonline.org.

SIR WILLIAM HOLDSWORTH, A HISTORY OF ENGLISH LAW (Sweet & Maxwell 1982) (1903-36). 17 vols.

DANIEL J. HULSEBOSCH, CONSTITUTING EMPIRE: NEW YORK AND THE TRANSFORMATION OF CONSTITUTIONALISM IN THE ATLANTIC WORLD, 1664–1830 (University of North Carolina Press 2005).

DAVID IBBETSON, COMMON LAW AND IUS COMMUNE (Selden Society 2001).

Francis Ingledew, *The Book of Troy and the Genealogical Construction of History: The Case of Geoffrey of Monmouth's Historia Regum Britanniae*, 69 SPECULUM 665 (1994).

DAFYDD JENKINS, THE LAW OF HYWEL DDA: LAW TEXTS FROM MEDIEVAL WALES TRANSLATED AND EDITED (Gomer Press 1986).

DAVID MARTIN JONES, CONSCIENCE AND ALLEGIANCE IN SEVENTEENTH CENTURY ENGLAND: THE POLITICAL SIGNIFICANCE OF OATHS AND ENGAGEMENTS (University of Rochester Press 1999).

ERNST H. KANTOROWICZ, THE KING'S TWO BODIES: A STUDY IN MEDIAEVAL POLITICAL THEOLOGY (Princeton University Press 1957).

DONALD R. KELLEY, HISTORY AND THE DISCIPLINES: THE RECLASSIFICATION OF KNOWLEDGE IN EARLY MODERN EUROPE (University of Rochester Press 1997).

______. THE WRITING OF HISTORY OF AND THE STUDY OF LAW (Variorum 1997).

COLIN KIDD, BRITISH IDENTITIES BEFORE NATIONALISM: ETHNICITY AND NATIONHOOD IN THE ATLANTIC WORLD, 1600–1800 (Cambridge University Press 1999).

______. SUBVERTING SCOTLAND'S PAST: SCOTTISH WHIG HISTORIANS AND THE CREATION OF AN ANGLO-BRITISH IDENTITY, 1689–C.1830 (Cambridge University Press 1993).

KING ARTHUR IN LEGEND AND HISTORY (Richard White ed., Routledge 1997).

William Klein, *The ancient constitution revisited, in* POLITICAL DISCOURSE IN EARLY MODERN BRITAIN 41 (Nicholas Phillipson & Quentin Skinner eds., Cambridge University Press 1993).

L.H. LARUE, CONSTITUTIONAL LAW AS FICTION: NARRATIVE IN THE RHETORIC OF AUTHORITY (Pennsylvania State University Press 1995).

John L. Leland, *'Bealknap, Sir Robert (d. 1401)', in* OXFORD DICTIONARY OF NATIONAL BIOGRAPHY 528 (Oxford University Press 2004).

BRIAN P. LEVACK, THE FORMATION OF THE BRITISH STATE: ENGLAND, SCOTLAND, AND THE UNION 1603–1707 (Oxford University Press 1986).

Gavin Loughton, *Calvin's Case and the Origins of the Rule Governing 'Conquest' in English Law*, 8 AUSTRALIAN JOURNAL OF LEGAL HISTORY 143 (2004).

HASTINGS LYON & HERMAN BLOCK, EDWARD COKE: ORACLE OF LAW (Houghton Mifflin 1929).

FORREST MCDONALD, NOVUS ORDO SECLORUM: THE INTELLECTUAL ORIGINS OF THE CONSTITUTION (University Press Kansas 1985).

KEN MACMILLAN, SOVEREIGNTY AND POSSESSION IN THE ENGLISH NEW WORLD: THE LEGAL FOUNDATIONS OF EMPIRE, 1576–1640 (Cambridge University Press 2006).

______. THE ATLANTIC IMPERIAL CONSTITUTION: CENTER AND PERIPHERY IN THE ENGLISH NEW WORLD (Palgrave MacMillan 2011).

Hector L. MacQueen, *Regiam Majestatem, Scots Law, and National Identity*, 74 SCOTTISH HISTORICAL REVIEW 1 (1995).

Arnaldo Momigliano, *Ancient History and the Antiquarian, in* CONTRIBUTO ALLA STORIA DEGLI STUDI CLASSICI 67 (Ristampa Anastatica 1979).

A. L. MORTON, THE MATTER OF BRITAIN: ESSAYS IN A LIVING CULTURE (Lawrence & Wishart 1966).

Bruce R. O'Brien, *Forgers of Law and Their Readers: The Crafting of English Political Identities between the Norman Conquest and the Magna Carta*, 43 POLITICAL SCIENCE AND POLITICS 467 (2010).

JOHNATHAN O'NIELL, ORIGINALISM IN AMERICAN LAW AND POLITICS: A CONSTITUTIONAL HISTORY (John Hopkins University Press 2005).

ORIGINALISM: A QUARTER-CENTURY OF DEBATE (Steven G. Calabresi ed., Regneri Publishing 2007).

CLIVE PARRY, BRITISH NATIONALITY: INCLUDING CITIZENSHIP OF THE UNITED KINGDOM & COLONIES AND THE STATUS OF ALIENS (Stevens & Sons 1951).

Polly J. Price, *Natural Law and Birthright Citizenship in Calvin's Case (1608)*, 9 YALE JOURNAL OF LAW AND HUMANITIES 73 (1997).

STUART PIGGOT, ANCIENT BRITONS AND THE ANTIQUARIAN IMAGINATION: IDEAS FROM THE RENAISSANCE TO THE REGENCY (Thames & Hudson 1989).

J.G.A. POCOCK, THE ANCIENT CONSTITUTION AND THE FEUDAL LAW: A STUDY OF ENGLISH HISTORICAL THOUGHT IN THE SEVENTEENTH CENTURY (Cambridge University Press rev. ed. 1987) (1957).

______. *Time, Institutions and Action: An Essay on Traditions and Their Understanding, in* POLITICS, LANGUAGE AND TIME: ESSAYS ON POLITICAL THOUGHT AND HISTORY 233 (Methuen 1973).

______. THE MACHIAVELLIAN MOMENT: FLORENTINE POLITICAL THOUGHT AND THE ATLANTIC REPUBLICAN TRADITION (Princeton University Press 1975).

WILFRID R, PREST, THE INNS OF COURT UNDER ELIZABETH I AND THE EARLY STUARTS: 1590–1640 (Rowman & Littlefield 1972).

JOHN PHILLIP REID, THE ANCIENT CONSTITUTION AND THE ORIGINS OF ANGLO-AMERICAN LIBERTY (Northern Illinois University Press 2005).

M. A. Rogers, *Sacrae Heptades (1625)*, 20 NOTES & QUERIES 164 (May 1973).

ANTONIN SCALIA, A MATTER OF INTERPRETATION: FEDERAL COURTS AND THE LAW (Princeton University Press 1997).

Daniel Scavone, *Edessan Sources for the Legend of the Holy Grail*, PROCEEDINGS OF THE INTERNATIONAL WORKSHOP ON THE SCIENTIFIC APPROACH TO ACHEIROPOIETOS IMAGES (2010), available at http://www.acheiropoietos.info/proceedings/ScavoneGrailWeb.pdf.

______. *Joseph of Arimathea, the Holy Grail, and the Edessa Icon*, 9 ARTHURIANA 1 (1999).

David J. Seipp, *The Law's Many Bodies, and the Manuscript Tradition in English Legal History*, 25 JOURNAL OF LEGAL HISTORY 74 (2004) (reviewing J. H. BAKER, THE LAW'S TWO BODIES: SOME EVIDENTIAL PROBLEMS IN ENGLISH LEGAL HISTORY (Oxford University Press 2001)).

______. *The Mirror of Justices, in* LEARNING THE LAW: TEACHING AND THE TRANSMISSION OF LAW IN ENGLAND 1150-1900 85 (Jonathan A. Bush & Alain Wijffels eds., Hambledon Press 1999).

Ian Shapiro, *Introduction: Reading Locke Today, in* JOHN LOCKE, TWO TREATISES OF GOVERNMENT AND A LETTER CONCERNING TOLERATION (Ian Shapiro ed., Yale University Press 2003).

Alan Smith, *Lucius of Britain: Alleged King and Church Founder*, 90 FOLKLORE 29 (1979).

ARTHUR E. SUTHERLAND, THE LAW AT HARVARD: A HISTORY OF IDEAS AND MEN, 1817–1967 (Harvard University Press 1967).

ROBIN CHAPMAN STACEY, DARK SPEECH: THE PERFORMANCE OF LAW IN EARLY IRELAND (University of Pennsylvania Press 2007).

Winnifred Fallers Sullivan, *Finding a True Story of American Religion*, 53 WASHINGTON AND LEE LAW REVIEW 981 (1996).

RICHARD S. TOMPSON, ISLANDS OF LAW: A LEGAL HISTORY OF THE BRITISH ISLES (Peter Lang 2000).

______. THE ATLANTIC ARCHIPELAGO: A POLITICAL HISTORY OF THE BRITISH ISLES (E. Mellen Press 1986).

DAVID M. WALKER, 2 A LEGAL HISTORY OF SCOTLAND: THE LATER MIDDLE AGES (W. Green 1990).

______. 3 A LEGAL HISTORY OF SCOTLAND: THE SIXTEENTH CENTURY (W. Green 1995).

______. 4 A LEGAL HISTORY OF SCOTLAND: THE SEVENTEENTH CENTURY (W. Green 1996).

THOMAS GLYN WATKINS, THE LEGAL HISTORY OF WALES (University of Wales Press 2007).

Robin West, *The Literary Lawyer*, 27 PACIFIC LAW REVIEW 1187 (1996).

______. *Constitutional Fictions and Meritocratic Success Stories*, 53 WASHINGTON AND LEE LAW REVIEW 996 (1996).

Alain Wijffels, *A British ius commune? A Debate on the Union of the Laws of Scotland and England during the First Years of James VI/I's English Reign*, 6 EDINBURGH LAW REVIEW 315 (2002).

IAN DOUGLAS WILLOCK, THE ORIGINS AND DEVELOPMENT OF THE JURY IN SCOTLAND (Stair Society 1966).

DANIEL R. WOOLF, THE IDEA OF HISTORY IN EARLY STUART ENGLAND: ERUDITION, IDEOLOGY, AND THE 'LIGHT OF TRUTH' FROM THE ACCESSION OF JAMES I TO THE CIVIL WAR (University of Toronto Press 1990).

______. READING HISTORY IN EARLY MODERN ENGLAND (Cambridge University Press 2000).

JOHN YOO, CRISIS AND COMMAND: THE HISTORY OF EXECUTIVE POWER FROM GEORGE WASHINGTON TO GEORGE W. BUSH (Kaplan Publishing 2009).

INDEX

Note: Pages from *Of the Antient Lawes* are indicated by brackets (ex. [4]–[6]) following the bracketed pagination added to the facsimile of Saltern's original non-paginated text provided in Appendix III.

www.ingramcontent.com/pod-product-compliance
Ingram Content Group UK Ltd.
Pitfield, Milton Keynes, MK11 3LW, UK
UKHW041449071026
15587UKWH00010B/707

9 781616 195397